INSIDE the ROOM

INSIDE

the

ROOM

WRITING TV with the PROS at
UCLA EXTENSION WRITERS' PROGRAM

Edited by Linda Venis, Director, UCLA Extension
Department of the Arts and Writers' Program

GOTHAM BOOKS

GOTHAM BOOKS
Published by the Penguin Group
Penguin Group (USA) Inc., 375 Hudson Street,
New York, New York 10014, USA

USA | Canada | UK | Ireland | Australia | New Zealand | India | South Africa | China
Penguin Books Ltd, Registered Offices: 80 Strand, London WC2R 0RL, England
For more information about the Penguin Group visit penguin.com.

LIBRARY OF CONGRESS CATALOGING-IN-PUBLICATION DATA

Inside the room : writing TV with the pros at UCLA Extension Writers' Program / edited by Linda Venis, Director, UCLA Extension Department of the Arts and Writers' Program.
        pages cm
      Includes index.
    ISBN 978-1-592-40811-5
  1. Television authorship—Vocational guidance.   I. Venis, Linda editor of compilation.
      II. UCLA Extension Writers' Program.
          PN1992.7.I525   2013
    808.2'25—dc23   2013004221

Printed in the United States of America
1   3   5   7   9   10   8   6   4   2

Set in Adobe Garamond Pro
Designed by Spring Hoteling

ALWAYS LEARNING   PEARSON

CONTENTS

Contents

SECTION II
Writing Your Half-Hour Television Comedy Specs and Pilots

SECTION III
Being a Professional in the Television Business

To Laura

ACKNOWLEDGMENTS

Inside the Room: Writing TV with the Pros at UCLA Extension Writers' Program and its "companion" book, *Cut to the Chase: Writing Feature Films with the Pros at UCLA Extension Writers' Program,* grew out of creating and refining Writers' Program's film and television writing curriculum, in close collaboration with its instructors and staff, for more than two decades. My sincere hope is that these books appropriately thank and honor the expertise, generosity, and contributions of all of the Program's screenwriting and creative-writing teachers and staff members—past, present, and future. I have assigned all royalties over to UCLA Extension Writers' Program.

Foremost gratitude goes to Cindy Lieberman, Program Manager of the Writers' Program, my right-hand person, colleague, and friend who has been *Inside the Room*'s and *Cut to the Chase*'s most meticulous and dedicated reader. Special appreciation goes to Program Representative in Screenwriting Chae Ko for his helpful comments on every chapter; to Assistant to the Director Carla Janas for her abiding support; and to UCLA Extension Interim Dean Michelle Stiles, whose work on the highest administrative level of this project helped bring it to fruition.

I am indebted to and in awe of four screenwriters whom I call, for lack of a more elegant term, the books' "core authors": Writers' Program instructors Cindy Davis, David Isaacs (now at USC), Steve Mazur, and Billy Mernit. This dream team provided invaluable feedback on the books' content and organization, contributed spectacular sample chapters, and maintained a steadfast commitment to this project that is humbling. My gratitude also goes to the Editorial Board, whose constructive advice and insights, generously rendered, made every chapter better.

Thank you to my agent, Betsy Amster (Betsy Amster Literary Enterprises); Gotham Books/Penguin Group (USA) Executive Editor Lauren Marino; and Emily D. Wunderlich, Susan M. Barnes, and Aja Pollock of Penguin Group for their belief in and support of *Inside the Room* and *Cut to the Chase*. That my name would appear on the same page as the Penguin logo is amazing to me.

To my precious late parents, Grace Bullock Miller and Ashton and Dona Venis; to my "I'm so lucky I married into it" family Leona Berg Town, Alec Berg, and Maggie Trinh; to my dear friends David Bushnell and Karla Klarin; to my incomparable husband, Gary Berg; and last but never, ever, least: to my daughter Laura Berg, the gift of a lifetime: thank you.

INTRODUCTION

by Linda Venis

Welcome to *Inside the Room: Writing TV with the Pros at UCLA Extension Writers' Program*—the first-of-its-kind book on how to write on-air and original dramas and comedies and how to launch and sustain a TV writing career. Based on the renowned UCLA Extension Writers' Program's TV-writing curriculum and written by some of its most talented writer-teachers, it takes you, as the title promises, "inside the room."

Which means what, exactly? On the most basic and important level, "inside the room" refers to a literal room: a room full of writers (i.e., the writers' room) who work as a team to write and rewrite, often line by line, the shows we watch every week. This is a key fact about TV writing, and one that many people outside the industry don't know: It is a highly collaborative medium, not the domain of the individual artist. And when everything is clicking in the room, scripts are made stronger by creative input from all the writers congregated in that single space.

The Pros Take You Inside Writing for TV

Inside the Room embodies a similarly rich and collaborative spirit. Ten working TV writers have come together "in the room" of this book to teach you the kinds of lessons in the craft and business of television writing that have, until now, only been available in UCLA Extension on-site and online classrooms.

Reflecting a scope of professional experience that no single author can possibly duplicate, *Inside the Room*'s contributors collectively have had hundreds of hours of television episodes and pilots produced. Their credits include *House M.D., CSI: Miami, Battlestar Galactica, Pretty Little Liars, Homicide: Life on the Street, The Simpsons, The Wonder Years, Cheers,* and *Frasier.* They have won Emmys and Writers Guild Awards. They have been producers, supervising producers, consulting producers, and showrunners (*Medium, Mad Men, The Glades, The X-Files,* and *The Wayans Bros.,* among many others). They have created series (ABC/Touchstone's *Miracles* and Paramount TV's *Almost Perfect*). They are, in short, the real deal.

Inside the Room Brings You into the TV Community

There is a second layer of meaning that "inside the room" has for writers—particularly at the beginning of their careers. When they have the chance to hammer out scripts with a group of creative, talented peers, their own skills improve dramatically. Just as importantly, they learn that collaboration is vital to professional survival; as Alison Lea Bingeman puts it, "Knowing how to be an effective member of a writing staff is critical to your success as a writer in television."

In my many years as director of Writers' Program, I've had thousands of interactions with those very special professional writers willing to pass along their hard-earned knowledge to our students, and I've seen their facility for collaboration in action. At instructor retreats, they excel at being creative in a group; when they judge the UCLA Extension Television Writing Competition, they are expert in the art of give-and-take. And in particular, when they teach, they often conduct their classes as modified writers' rooms, in which students learn to break stories together, bounce jokes off one another, and offer feedback to their fellow "staff writers"/classmates. They listen respectfully, guide students to their best ideas, and chime in when helpful—thus modeling skills central to a successful TV writing career.

The same spirit infuses *Inside the Room*: Its contributors do a remarkable job of replicating—as much as prose alone allows—these lessons. Every chapter contains its own versions, its own permutations, of how to write well and work successfully in this community. If you tune in to this aspect of the book, you'll gain a whole new level of insight from it.

Writers' Program Success Stories: Who's "in the Room"

The phrase "inside the room" has a final meaning: It's a metaphor for being an insider in an elite, high-paying, high-stakes industry. As Joel Anderson Thompson puts it, new writers are "on the outside, trying to join the club."

To inspire you as you make your way through *Inside the Room,* here's a sampling of writers who studied TV writing with the UCLA Extension Writers' Program. Their talent, passion, dedication, *and* training helped them get inside the room:

Tucker Cawley (*Parks and Recreation, Everybody Loves Raymond*); Zoanne Clack (*Grey's Anatomy, ER*); Lee Eisenberg (*The Office*); Doug Ellin (creator, *Entourage*); Al Gough and Miles Millar (*Smallville*); Drew Z. Greenberg (*Buffy the Vampire Slayer, Dexter*); Alexa Junge (*United States of Tara, Big Love, Friends*); Melissa Rosenberg (*Dexter*); Kevin Williamson (creator, *Dawson's Creek, The Following;* writer/executive producer, *The Vampire Diaries*); and Ellen Byron, a staff writer and/or producer on twelve half-hour comedies, including *Just Shoot Me!* and *Wings,* who says of her training, "The caliber of the teachers and courses is stupendous. I can't imagine a better writing program in the country."

How to Use This Book and Get the Most out of It

Inside the Room is designed for writers at various levels to dip into and use according to their abilities and goals. Each chapter stands on its own as a resource for beginning and experienced TV writers alike.

There is only one "rule" I'd strongly suggest you follow: If you have never had any experience or instruction in writing for television, first devour the chapters that cover how to write on-air dramas and sitcoms, starting with the all-important story and outline. The almost 100 percent irrefutable answer to the question "How do I write for TV?" is by learning how to mimic the stories, characters, and style of an existing show. Doing so helps you understand the elements of how and why a successful show ticks—knowledge you need to sell scripts for existing shows *and* pilots. This is what we tell aspiring TV writers who contact Writers' Program from all over the world.

If you're a first-time one-hour-drama writer, **Joel Anderson Thompson** (chapter 1, "Writing the On-Air One-Hour Drama Spec: The Story and Outline") is your initial mentor. He tells you, "I promise not to tell anyone. You'll feel better once you admit it. You love TV," and then teaches you how to capture a show's stories, characters, plots, settings, tone, and style; work within specific television time slots, outlets, and genres; and come up with an outline—the all-important blueprint for an on-air drama. With a solid outline in hand, **Charlie Craig** (chapter 2, "Writing the On-Air One-Hour Drama Spec: The Script") assures you that "*writing* a script is actually *fun*—but it's a process." He then helps you refine your stories and make characters and plots come alive, and shows you how to maximize the power of each and every scene.

If you're a new sitcom writer, **Julie Chambers** and **David Chambers** (chapter 5, "Writing the On-Air Half-Hour Comedy Spec: The Story and Outline") take you through a step-by-step process to brainstorm ideas, develop stories (and complicate them!), and create a beat sheet and outline. In chapter 6 ("Writing the On-Air Half-Hour Comedy Spec: The Script"), they show you how to write and rewrite your script, learn to think in screen time, nail the essence of the characters, put in great jokes, and make act breaks pop.

Once you've fulfilled the basic TV writing requirements, you are ready to use *Inside the Room* as your "personal trainer." Flexible, versatile, and grounded in practical experience, this book helps you focus on your individual writing goals.

Of course, all TV writers, no matter how seasoned, need at least one original pilot in their portfolio. In chapter 3 ("Writing the One-Hour Drama Pilot"), **Richard Manning** says, "Be unique. Be bold. Be passionate. Be original. Above all, be *yourself*," and helps you discover how to tap into your one-hour drama "TV taste," choose a subject, develop a solid franchise, and create fresh characters. In chapter 7 ("Writing the Half-Hour Comedy Pilot"), **Phil Kellard** lays out how to write a sitcom pilot that conveys "*your* voice, *your* brand of humor, and *your* sensibility" and gives you suggestions for coming up with a Big Idea that can be sustained for one hundred episodes; for creating a cast of funny, memorable characters; and for pitching with style.

As you focus on improving your scripts, be they for on-air shows or pilots, *Inside the Room* provides you with more pro tips and strategies. In chapter 4 ("Revising One-Hour Drama Specs and Pilots"), **Matt Witten** begins by telling you that if you're ambitious enough to finish a spec or pilot, you should "take a moment to pat yourself on the back." He then hands you twenty-seven proven tools for rewriting it: six to prep yourself for the process of rewriting, and twenty-one nitty-gritty suggestions to get it done thoroughly and successfully. "Character rules" is the mantra of chapter 8 ("Sitcom Master Class: Creating Comedy through Character"), in which **David Isaacs** explores how character drives the story, conflict, and theme of the best half-hour comedies and shares his techniques for creating captivating and relatable comedic characters.

As every chapter in *Inside the Room* reiterates, the best of TV writing is a creative triumph (think *Modern Family;* think *Mad Men*), but within the overarching context that it is a business. Your scripts are products; they have a "shelf life" that expires quickly after a show goes off the air. When you write a sample script for an existing show, it's crucial to "think *in*side the box" in order to demonstrate that you understand the show's dictates. And while the pilot you conjure up from your own imagination demands a fresh perspective, "your task as a television pilot writer," as Richard Manning puts it, "is not to create something *utterly unlike anything anyone's ever seen.*"

Which brings us to *Inside the Room*'s singular chapters on the business of television writing. In chapter 9 ("Launching and Sustaining a Television Writing Career"), **Alison Lea Bingeman** gives you a mother lode of tips on branding yourself, building a portfolio of the right kinds of specs and pilots, networking, getting jobs that give you a leg up in the business, managing representation, and the necessity of loving what you do. In the final chapter, **Richard Hatem** provides an unprecedented glimpse into "The TV Year": an intimate and sometimes hilarious look inside the process of creating, selling, and getting a fictional (yet so real!) TV show made.

Bon Voyage and Good Luck!

Whatever phase you are at in your journey from TV fan to TV writer, my sincere hope is that *Inside the Room*'s practical tools, tips, strategies, insider advice, reality checks, and business savvy will make it easier, faster, and better informed. The first step to joining the amazing community of TV writers is to write, and you're now on your way!

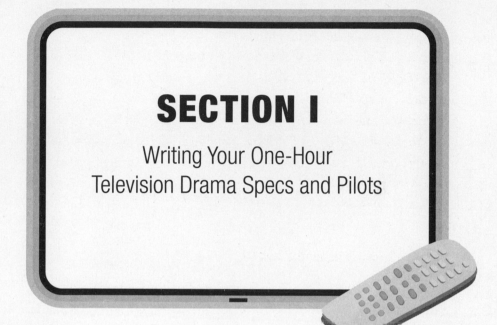

SECTION I

Writing Your One-Hour
Television Drama Specs and Pilots

CHAPTER 1

Writing the On-Air One-Hour Drama Spec: The Story and Outline

by Joel Anderson Thompson

I promise not to tell anyone. You'll feel better once you admit it. You love TV. For richer or for poorer, in sickness and in health, TV has always been there for you to make you laugh, cry, and sometimes, dare I say, even think. No doubt it was love at first sight. Yet it's now become far more than that. Being a fan standing on the sidelines doesn't cut it anymore. You're here and hungry because you want in on the game.

How Do You Become a TV Writer?

Television writers come from everywhere and have diverse backgrounds. However, there is one common thread among 99.9 percent of them: They wrote scripts for on-air shows for free as part of their goal of writing TV professionally. These noncompensated scripts, based on the characters, structure, setting, tone, style, and format of an existing show, are called "spec scripts," written with the hope or "speculation" that they will eventually be bought or lead to other paid writing assignments. In addition, the term *spec* can be used as a verb ("I'm going to spec a script") or as a noun ("The competition is accepting specs"). The takeaway is that a well-executed spec script can open many doors because it proves to agents, managers, and/or producers that a writer can mimic a given show and therefore is in command of the form.

Based on my ten years of experience writing on TV dramas like *Battlestar Galactica, House M.D.,* and *Falling Skies,* as well as selling pitches and projects to the networks, I can tell you that behind every strong spec is a strong story and outline. To learn and master the craft of creating these building blocks of a one-hour script isn't a fast process, but there are clear steps you can take to acquire the knowledge and skills you need to write a story and outline that executives might want to buy. It is my pleasure to be your coach and to pass along the same techniques and tips I teach to my UCLA Extension Writers' Program TV-writing students.

In this chapter, I'll cover what the story and outline are and why they're so important, how to choose an on-air show to spec and how to research it, and how to create an airtight story and outline. I'll share my step-by-step approach to understanding the inner workings of the characters, plot, setting, tone, and style of the show you want to spec; how TV's major time slots, outlets, and genres come into play with your story choices; and how to create a story and outline that observes the "house rules" of your show's structure and maintains your authentic vision.

Forty Percent of the TV Writer's Paycheck: A Strong Story and Outline

Story and Outline Defined

The *story* is an account of incidents or events in a particular order, with a beginning, or premise; middle; and end, or conclusion. In the TV industry, the story is brief: as succinct as four sentences or as long as a short paragraph. A story can also be used to establish, in broad strokes, what your idea for a TV show is about.

The outline is a detailed, expanded version of the story, generally ranging from eight to twelve pages, and serves as a blueprint for your script. The first step in creating an outline is to write a beat sheet, which is a list of your story's events, particularly its plot points (beats), which drive your story forward. The beat sheet is then fleshed out into an outline, which includes key bits of detail, scene locations, period of day, and in some cases, dialogue. In its final form, the outline serves as the bridge between your one-paragraph story and your fifty-six-to-fifty-nine-page spec script.

One of the most commonly asked questions from new writers is "Why write an outline when I already know my story?" For creative reasons, the outline is essential because it is the main tool the writer uses to order the events of the story and determine which incidents fit logically into the progression of the story. The outline is a "story stress test" and is critical to the scriptwriting process.

The outline is also critical for professional and monetary reasons. First, showrunners, those people with godlike powers responsible for the day-by-day running of the shows, place tremendous value on the outline because it allows them to see the details of a writer's story and how it fits in among the other episodes. It also gives the showrunner and writer a tangible way to evaluate and discuss the approach to writing the script.

Second, network executives, who as individuals wield power of the demigod variety and as a group can cut down a showrunner in his or her tracks, have the final say, and they sometimes reject or champion story ideas based on an outline. That's a big reason why the first 40 percent of a writer's paycheck for a one-hour script is tied to the story and outline. If both are strong, you're good to go. If not, there's no payday.

The Outline as Your Spec Script's Blueprint

Imagine being an architect trying to describe the house you intend to build to a general contractor and a bricklayer without blueprints. No matter how detailed your thoughts, no matter how well you can see the grand plan in your noggin, the three of you are going to share a long and confusing day. Odds are someone's going to get slapped around with a two-by-four, probably you.

The same scenario applies to the TV writing business: An outline keeps network execs—or "the suits," as they're affectionately called—informed about the story they've purchased and the episode they can expect to see produced. In most instances, the outline reduces the chances of any writer getting slapped around with a metaphorical two-by-four.

Selecting the Right One-Hour Drama Show to Spec

Selecting the show you are going to spec is a big decision. It's just like getting married, except without the drunken uncle who makes a toast that embarrasses everyone. Since you're going to be investing a large amount of time writing your spec, it's best if you love the show. That said, for those of you jonesing to write that killer *Sanford and Son* or *ER,* slow your roll. Actually, make that a full stop. Only shows currently airing are viable choices for specs.

For that matter, not all of the shows presently airing will get you read by a producer or an agent. For many reasons, your show selection can hurt or help, so how do you know which to choose? First, don't pick an obscure show that almost no one watches. Agents and producers need to be familiar with the program in order to assess whether you nailed it. Second, choosing a long-running show could be a misstep too. In most cases, by the time a hit show enters its fourth season, agents' offices are flooded with submitted specs for it, most of which are rejected.

Think of writing a spec as making an investment that has a shelf life. It's safest to choose a show no younger than the last third of its first season, and no older than three seasons. For the show that's in the process of completing its first year, verify that it's been renewed, because by and large, agents, managers, and producers will use the cancellation of a show as an excuse not to read a spec script. If you base your selection on the above criteria, you'll get the most mileage out of your spec. That said, if you have an idea for a spec in its fourth season that's so supercool it damn near writes itself, maybe you should give it a go. Only you can decide.

One trick to aid you in the selection process is to cold-call an agency or management firm. The assistants are on the front line of which shows are being renewed and accepted as viable submissions. Who better to give tips on the hot shows versus the not-so-hot than the gatekeepers themselves? Don't be nervous. You're not asking them out on a date. Some assistants go all day with no one asking them for their opinion. They might be happy that their advice is being sought. Just be polite and keep your questions short and to the point.

Know Your Show

You Only Think You Know Your Show

Once you've selected a show that's right for you, it'll be tempting to jump in and start writing. Even if you've seen every episode, writing a script without doing the research would be a classic rookie mistake. Here's why: You watched those episodes as a fan, which means that you were not actively assessing dialogue, style, story structure, theme, pacing, and character development. If you were, then, well, okay. You're a badass. However, I'll bet you only *think* you were observing those factors. In actuality, analyzing TV means that you are taking copious notes on every aspect of the show you are specing, making sure to look for subtle details and trends.

Insider TV note: When you're viewing something and your purpose is not limited to being entertained, it's called *screening*. Using this term will make you sound and feel more professional when you say to your spouse, girlfriend or boyfriend, significant other, or insignificant other, "Wow, I'd love to go with you, but I have to screen some episodes tonight." Depending on how you sell it, this strategy can also work well if you're avoiding an event you'd rather not attend.

How to Research Your Show

Weaseling out of social obligations aside, knowing your show backward and forward is crucial. The worst way to have a spec script rejected by an agent is if she deems that the writer failed to do "research." When agents read a poorly researched script, they think, *If this writer is too lazy to get his facts straight when seeking a writing job, how lax is he going to be if he's put on a show?*

Obviously, it's to your advantage to screen every produced episode of the show that you intend to spec. If you can't get access to all the episodes, the next best thing is to watch as many episodes as you can and then find a website that provides episode summaries and pore over them. One way to go about this would be to place the title of the show and the phrase *episode summaries* in your favorite search engine.

To Construct a Show, You Must First Deconstruct It

Now that you've selected and researched your show, it's time to get down to business and learn how to construct a story and an outline. When I teach "Beginning Writing for the One-Hour Spec Drama: Building the Story and Outline" at UCLA Extension, the students start by familiarizing themselves with all of the story elements that make up any dramatic television show and that are present in almost every form of storytelling: characters, plot, setting, tone, and style.

Know the Show's Main Characters and the Role of Supporting Characters

The protagonist is the lead character, and in most instances, there is only one per show. He or she is the person around whom the show revolves; the events in any given episode will affect him or her the most. Think of a protagonist as the front man in a band, and the remaining characters as backup singers or musicians. These supporting characters, as they are called, directly assist the protagonist in overcoming obstacles and are sometimes in a subplot (B plot or even C plot) that may dovetail into the main (A) plot.

For example, *House M.D.* features the challenges and exploits of a protagonist, not-so-coincidentally named Dr. House. As a member of the writing staff, I can tell you that the show's creator was tremendously thoughtful about his character's design. Dr. House is a brutally honest, sarcastic superintellect who's also spellbound by soap operas. He's phenomenally gifted at diagnosing mysterious rare ailments but blew a diagnosis on his own leg, which left him with a permanent limp and lifelong addiction to Vicodin. The creator's dedication to having irony course through House's veins heavily influenced how the staff writers approached this character as well as each episode.

An exception to the "front and center" protagonist in one-hour dramas is the ensemble show, which has a subtle lead and supporting characters. In *Southland,* Detective Lydia Adams tends to get the most screen time, but any given episode can feature a different character as the protagonist. Unlike *House M.D.,* in which Dr. House dominates every case, the supporting characters in *Southland* pursue their own cases even as Lydia works on the episode's most important homicide. What distinguishes Lydia as the main character is her dogged determination to catch bad guys by the book, her sensitivity, and her patience in living with a mother who has a far superior romantic life to her own.

He's a Character, but Does He Have Character?
It's All in the Arc

Your next job as the writer is to show a curved trajectory of your character's development. This growth is called the character's *arc,* and any successful show's protagonist, as well as key secondary characters, will experience it. The completion of the arc can be personal or professional; it can be subtle, humorous, or dramatic. The characters can experience a revelation about themselves, those around them, or the world. By the end of the show, for better or for worse, their opinions or philosophies have shifted. Perhaps this change is triggered by realizing the significance of an earlier event; it may also be pivotal and convey a character's arrival at a major decision.

For instance, among the many potent character arcs that course through the world of *Boardwalk Empire,* one of its most elegantly contoured and dramatic is that of Margaret, Nucky's common-law wife. She is introduced as a pious prohibitionist, but increasingly fed up with Nucky's physical and emotional absenteeism, she secretly begins to drink. Margaret's rebellion culminates in her affair with Nucky's right-hand man.

As you construct a character arc for your spec story, take the time to note what things mean to the character. As you screen episodes of your chosen show, keep a list of the protagonist's likes and dislikes, beliefs, philosophies, and values. While you are not tethered to this list, it might help you locate the launch point of the protagonist's character arc.

Know the Show's Plot and Its Premise

When my students say they're uncertain about what plots are, I remind them that they've been discussing them forever. Whenever people are asked what a book, play, film, or TV show is about, they usually retell the events as they unfold in the story—i.e., give a plot summary. Every plot has a premise, which is its starting point or circumstance that gets the story moving forward. If we dig a little deeper, we find that a plot is made up of three key sections: a beginning, a middle, and an ending, each with its own specific purpose.

The beginning of a plot functions to introduce the protagonist and the premise of the story. This area of the plot is traditionally known as the point at which the hero hears "the call" to act, or to embark upon the mission or journey. In the premiere episode of *House M.D.,* an elementary school teacher develops a mysterious illness that gets progressively worse. Dr. House has no interest in the teacher but becomes intrigued by the case once he learns that the standard treatments by other doctors have failed. The conundrum of the disease functions as Dr. House's "call" to engage in the mission. He must commit to a course of action. Otherwise, as any fan of *House M.D.* knows, the patient might die before Dr. House can fully berate her. And we can't have that.

The middle of the plot is where the hero has made some progress but discovers greater obstacles. In the majority of one-hour dramas, the hero's efforts to solve the problem yield a small victory, but then he encounters complications that make things worse and put everything in jeopardy. In *House M.D.,* this point frequently occurs when an initial diagnosis turns out to be incorrect. The patient's condition worsens, and Dr. House has to go back to the drawing board. In the show's first episode, the teacher is misdiagnosed with a brain tumor. Obsessed with figuring out her actual condition, Dr. House tries to learn everything about her, which entails coercing his colleague (neurologist Dr. Foreman) to break into her house illegally.

The end of the plot—called the conclusion—occurs when the hero confronts the greatest problems he has faced so far, and his perseverance pays off. In our example, failed efforts to find a cure for the teacher's illness put so much physical and emotional strain on her that she elects to end all treatments and "die with dignity." Dr. House reluctantly bonds with the teacher by revealing sensitive aspects of his past, and in so doing, he convinces her that there is no "dignity in dying" and wins her permission to perform a high-risk treatment. It's a success and the patient lives happily ever after.

In most one-hour dramas, with the exception of serialized programs (to be discussed later), the episode ends when the protagonist has risen above all obstacles to solve all problems and, by so doing, restores order to the world of the show.

Know the Show's Setting

Setting is the location, time period, and/or surrounding environment in which the story takes place. Some settings function as a way of focusing the viewers' attention onto the characters. The HBO series *In Treatment* primarily takes place in the confines of psychoanalyst Paul Weston's office. This setting's intimacy—literally, behind closed doors—intensifies the relationship between Dr. Weston and his patients. The surroundings seem to fade away as viewers mingle with the patients' raw and exposed psyches—their innermost thoughts, fears, and regrets.

Conversely, the setting of a show can be so prominent, rich, and textured that it is practically a character unto itself. Smoke-filled restaurants, offices stocked with hard liquor, and commuter suburban homes filled with dysfunctional families: The settings of *Mad Men* epitomize 1960s New York. They also set the stage for the era's casual displays of sexism, racism, and classism, and provide a prism through which the audience examines an aspect of where we once were as a society to measure where we are now.

Know the Show's Tone and Style

The tone is the attitude that dominates, permeates, and defines the show and is the unsung hero among the elements of television drama. Viewers tend not to appreciate a show's tone until it's gone or changed. Where would *CSI: NY* be without its gritty tone or *Parenthood* without its tone of whimsy and deep sensitivity? Imagine a *CSI: NY* episode in which Gary Sinise weeps tears of joy while hugging the medical examiner over a corpse. Or a *Parenthood* plot that hinges upon the discovery of a decapitated hooker in the Braverman house's Dumpster.

The style is the manner in which the tone is expressed. It can be visual, conveyed through wardrobe, hair, and color scheme. Most strikingly, style is manifested in a show's dialogue's pacing, vocabulary, and cadence. A classic example is *The West Wing*, which follows the political and personal lives of a fictional Democratic president and his intense and cerebral White House staffers. The show's clever, machine-gun rapid-fire dialogue, loaded with glib one-liners and rhythmic, almost poetic exchanges of lines, is its most defining feature and contributes strongly to the show's unique tone.

Keep in mind that the personality of the protagonist can tell you a lot about a show's tone and style. Enoch "Nucky" Thompson of *Boardwalk Empire* is unlikely to win a handsome-man contest, but he's smart, charming, and in addition, cunning, ruthless, determined, sarcastic, and cynical. Not coincidentally, the same can be said for the tone and style of the show itself. In a world of politics, corruption, affairs, murders, and bootlegging, Nucky, in appearance and in mind-set, embodies it all.

Tone and the Power of the One-Hour Drama's Humorous Moments

Many of TV's more sophisticated one-hour shows lace their serious dramatic content with humor and irony, which can amuse, charm, or even horrify its viewers. Humor can, for example, give the protagonist more dimensions or offer comic relief. By being alert to how a show uses humor, you can delve deeper into its range of tones and incorporate that into your own story and outline.

Consider how *Boardwalk Empire* oscillates between gritty drama and gallows humor. When Nucky makes jokes, they tend to be morbidly ironic understatements. When World War I veteran and tortured soul Richard Harrow attempts suicide in the remote woods, a stray dog wanders in from out of nowhere, steals his prosthetic half-faced mask, and runs away. When Richard puts down his gun and gives chase, it's all things morbid and funny.

Sometimes access to humor and irony is essential not only for the audience and show but for the writers as well. *Battlestar Galactica* probed human nature in the face of annihilation and was contoured to capture some of the tones of 9/11, but the show's subtle humor and irony gave us staff writers the freedom to tell authentically dark dramatic stories by balancing the bleakness of the subject matter. A prime example of how this dynamic worked was in the character of Dr. Baltar, a destructive, repugnant superintellect and the major culprit in the downfall of humanity, who, at the same time, was an oversexed coward and a prisoner of his own vanity.

Creating the Story for Your Spec

Time Slot, Outlet, Procedural Versus Character-Driven, and Genre

Now that you know how to break down all the dramatic elements of your show, there are several "must know" aspects of the sprawling TV landscape that will inform your story choice and help you stay within the show's established parameters: time slots, outlets, categories, and genres.

Time Slots

With the exception of Fox, with its limited prime-time hours, few hour-long dramas air at eight P.M. and nine P.M., primarily because many children watch TV at this time. While the ability to record shows has liberated viewers from scheduled viewing habits, the networks still must abide by the Federal Communications Commission (FCC) rules, which designate eight and nine o'clock as family viewing hours. The more adult-themed dramas are required to air at ten o'clock.

Outlets

The programming outlets themselves offer a way to gauge how "family or adult" in tone and style your story needs to be and what demographic it should serve. To offer a few examples: Among the free networks, CBS's demographic tends to be a little older and gravitates toward shows like *The Good Wife*, which has a relatively slow pace and a protagonist dealing with midlife issues in a realistic way. The CW, on the other hand, caters to teen and tween girls who want to see shows featuring young adult girls. That's why the CW, from back in the day, has aired shows like *Gilmore Girls, Gossip Girl, The Vampire Diaries,* and *Ringer*. By contrast, Fox's main target audience is boys and men, as indicated by flagship programs like *24, Prison Break, Alcatraz, Terra Nova,* and *Fringe*.

Categories

Knowing the two main categories of shows—procedural shows and character shows—is another tool to help you zero in on the key elements that your story must have to be successful. While the programming on free networks combined with that of cable channels runs the gamut of audiences, styles, tones, and settings, there are two main categories that all TV shows fall under: procedure-driven shows, or *procedural shows,* and character-driven shows, or *character shows.*

Procedurals are always driven by the protagonist's singular dramatic function: to solve the crime. We get to know very little about the main characters beyond the execution of this task, which follows a routine professional procedure—hence the term "procedural show." *Law and Order* is a perfect example of a procedural show, and the *CSI* and *NCIS* franchises, *Cold Case,* and *Without a Trace* all fall under this category.

In most instances, procedural shows, by the end of the hour, have answered all the questions and solved all of the problems pertaining to the premise of the episode. This type of episode design is called a *standalone,* which means that everything the viewer needs to know about the story and characters is self-contained within the one-hour time frame. On rare occasions, procedurals are serialized, meaning the viewer needs to see the whole series over a season to have a complete dramatic understanding of it; *24* is an example of a serialized procedural.

The second category is the character-driven show, in which we get to know a great deal about the protagonists. The central characters are motivated by something they desperately want or need on a personal level. This want or need is sometimes satisfied by the end of a single episode but is more typically part of the characters' ongoing quest throughout the season—or even for the entire run of a series. *Boardwalk Empire, Damages, Revenge,* and *Boss* are among the many one-hour character-driven dramas, and all feature protagonists who impose or externalize what is driving them internally (i.e., what they want or need) upon the world. How they overcome obstacles, coupled with the consequences of their actions, dramatically shapes each episode of the show.

Character-driven shows are almost always serialized. Even if all questions are answered and all the problems are solved within an episode, new questions and problems will be introduced. Unlike stand-alone shows, viewers screening a random episode of a serial show will find it difficult to follow. Imagine watching a single episode of *Lost;* you'd be just as lost as the characters.

Hybrids

Hybrids of character-driven shows and procedurals also exist. In *Homeland,* CIA agent Carrie Mathison copes with unrequited love, extreme loneliness, and paranoia. She also hides a mental disorder that both helps and hampers her professional efforts to use a procedure to track a terrorist. Carrie is driven by her internal wants, which are interlaced with high-stakes procedural goals. In *The Shield,* corrupt detective Vic Mackey cracks street-crime cases using a procedure, while lining his own pockets with stolen money by double-crossing gangs and organized crime. He does all this while struggling to keep his twisted brotherhood of cops and family together.

At this writing, the trend is for procedurals to be aired on the free networks, while character-driven, experimental-niche, serialized, and period pieces tend to reside on cable. For example, *Mad Men, Hell on Wheels,* and *Boardwalk Empire* would likely not be developed for the free networks. Likewise, *Homeland, Weeds,* and *Californication,* with their mature subject matter—including nudity, graphic violence, and profanity—and heavy focus on character would not be welcome on the free networks. Basic-cable networks such as FX allow limited profanity, while premium cable channels like HBO allow profanity as well as nudity. A writer would be remiss to not consider the audience for his spec script based on such segmentation.

TV Genres: A Quick Tour

Between them, procedurals and character-driven shows house the full spectrum of every type of TV drama; a TV show's type is known (as it is in all kinds of dramatic writing) as its *genre.* The most prominent TV drama genres are cop, crime, law, medical, fantasy, sci-fi, half-hour dramedy, action-adventure, and nighttime soap. Nighttime soaps are characterized by long story arcs about relationships, love, betrayals, and revenge. In particular, the nighttime soap is often combined with one other traditional genre to create a hybrid. For example, while *Grey's Anatomy, Battlestar Galactica, Boardwalk Empire,* and *Game of Thrones* are in the medical, sci-fi, crime, and fantasy genres, respectively, they are also nighttime soaps. Other such hybrid shows include *Gossip Girl, 90210,* and *The Vampire Diaries.*

The exercise of categorizing shows cultivates your feel for their dramatic nature and helps you assess which one speaks more to your sensibility, and if possible, knowledge base. Think of it as another way to kick the tires on a car as you walk around in the showroom of a dealership.

Harvesting the Idea for Your Story

The most accessible way to discover the premise for your story is to start with subjects that appeal to you politically, psychologically, or emotionally, and then figure out how you might embellish these interests to make them "TV dramatic." Keep in mind that challenging your own philosophical, political, and even religious views can be fertile ground for dramatic circumstances. We tend to embrace our outlooks and principles as if they're sacred virtues, but with respect to writing, virtues mean little until they collide with a challenge head-on.

While working on an episode for *Falling Skies,* I pondered what the dramatic circumstances would be for a doctor who, in the midst of a fallen society, struggles to remain a pacifist. What would have to happen to her so that she not only starts toting a gun but begins to like it? The doctor's character arc did not parallel my own politics, and that very fact made it stimulating to explore. Never be afraid to have your protagonist do something that might run counter to your own philosophy. If you maintain a logical path on the evolution of the character's principles and virtues, the drama will emerge.

There are a few spec story premises that are definite "don'ts." No characters should have birthdays, be raped, be seriously injured or killed, become pregnant, or have a long-lost relative show up. Perhaps you saw one or more of these events on the very shows you've been researching, but that doesn't give you, the new writer, permission to do the same. The writers who work on those shows are free to explore those situations. You, however, are on the outside, trying to join the club, so it's in your best interest to generate a fresh premise.

Whatever Your Story Idea, Know It Deeply and Maintain Its Credibility

Whatever elements you introduce into your story, be sure to make them credible. If you're writing a cop show and set the crime at a comic book convention, immerse yourself in that world. Read articles, watch YouTube videos, and if possible, attend a comic book convention. Know the demographic of its attendees: How do they dress, act, and interact? What are their quirks and patterns? How might their behaviors and dispositions help or hinder the investigation, or open them up to suspicion? This knowledge, combined with what you have learned about the structure and story elements of the show, will elevate your writing and demonstrate your willingness to work hard for the sake of writing a great story.

The Balancing Act: Respect the House Rules While Maintaining Your Authenticity

Fitting your authentic story into a one-hour drama's repetitive structure with its own creative rules can be a challenge. Think of writing a spec as being allowed to throw a big party in someone else's house while she's out of town. You can do almost whatever you want, so long as you maintain the owner's level of cleanliness and leave her furniture in the same place.

With respect to your spec, that means no cliffhanger endings and no marrying or killing off characters. If it's already been established that a character is coping with an ongoing problem, be it internal or external, you cannot resolve it. For instance, if the protagonist is a substance abuser in denial, your spec can't break the house rules and have him enter a rehab program. Even so, you have choices: You can show him indulging in or exhibiting the results of the substance abuse. You can also explore the addiction itself, introducing a fresh manifestation of the problem and how it impacts the protagonist in a way not previously dramatized.

Shows ranging from *House M.D., Nurse Jackie,* and *True Blood* to *The Wire, Californication, Battlestar Galactica,* and *Breaking Bad* all feature characters struggling with addictions, so it is possible that the protagonist of any current show you choose to spec will have one or more of them. On a more general level, any deeply rooted flaw, be it substance based, behavioral, or sexual, requires a skillful approach, and the best strategy is for your spec script to end with the same problem alive and well. An addiction remains an addiction; allies remain allies, and the same goes for enemies.

Research Your Show Once Again— This Time to Build a Modern Classic

When you watch an entire season of even the best-written shows, three or four episodes usually stand head and shoulders above the others. Zero in on your show's most memorable episodes and screen them multiple times with these questions in mind:

- Are there any common elements in the areas of tone and theme?

- Do the circumstances at play impact the protagonist on a more personal level?

- Do they reveal something about the protagonist that was not previously known?

- Does each classic episode involve the same character?

- Are there any underserved second-tier characters? If so, do you want to use them in the lead position of your B story (secondary story)?

- Are the stakes in the classic episodes much higher than in the others?

- What are the aspects that differentiate them from the run-of-the-mill episodes?

- Imagine people at work gathered around the watercooler discussing the classics. What would they be saying?

Write Your Story

Assuming your mind and gut tell you that your story possesses many qualities of the classic episodes, it's time to finalize it. Write up your story in four sentences or so (one small paragraph, maximum), with a beginning, middle, and end. Now you are ready to outline.

Create Your Outline

The Beat Sheet

The first step in developing an outline from your story idea is to create a beat sheet, which lays out all the events in a broad, logical order. The most important of these events are *beats,* also called *plot points,* which are *those specific events that drive the dramatic action forward.* Think of your beat sheet as the skeletal wood-beam structure of a house. There are regular beams, and then there are the all-important support or weight-bearing beams; if any of those are removed, a large portion of the house will collapse. The events are your story's regular beams; the beats are its support beams.

Here's an exercise using a fictitious show, *John the Cop,* to illustrate how to identify beats and distinguish them from events:

While off duty and suffering from a hangover, John accidentally knocks over the milk. As his baby girl throws up on him, his wife tells him that it was the last of the milk. John forgets his gun and goes to the store. Gunmen enter to rob the place, and John, unarmed, uses his wits to thwart them.

Can you find the beats? The baby throwing up on John is an event but it does not drive the story; therefore, it's not a beat. Likewise, John's hangover, while a character detail, doesn't drive the story and is not a beat. However, John's spilling the milk and gunmen entering to rob the store are definitely beats, because if you remove either, the rest of the story falls apart.

Fleshing Out the Beat Sheet

A plot point on a beat sheet consists of no more than one to two sentences and doesn't contain any scene description or, as is present in some outlines, dialogue. This lean structure makes it easy to see if each beat propels the protagonist through the story and yields a change in him, and if a compelling plot extends through the entire story.

Plot Points and Character

Let's pretend you're a writer on the above episode of *John the Cop* and I'm your showrunner. I ask you, "How does this situation affect John in his gut, in ways he doesn't want to talk about? Why do we care about him?" You'll ponder the impact the events are having on John and then pitch me an idea: *John's hangover is part of a drinking problem that he's in denial over. It's what made him forget his gun and hesitate in a moment that led to the gunmen murdering a hostage. Yes, he saves the day, but his guilt over that casualty makes him throw out all his alcohol and go to rehab. This leaves John a changed dude at the end.* You have taken a small character detail, the hangover, and generated a character arc.

Dramatic Acts, Plot Points, and Structure: "Building Progressively"

Teleplays are made up of dramatic acts, which are segments or units of drama, within which the featured characters take action. The number of acts that make up a one-hour drama script can have either five or six acts, and each act contains an escalation of action and dramatic consequence.

Accordingly, plot points must be arranged to build progressively, making the story more and more complicated and interesting all the way to the end, and in addition, the last beat in each of the acts should leave the protagonist with a question, complication, cliffhanger, or revelation. These beats are called *act outs* or *act breaks*. Each act break should be more dramatic than the previous one. Hence the idiom "and the plot thickens," which is exactly the kind of structure in an outline that will make your spec hot.

By the way, an easy way to cultivate an appreciation for how one act transitions to the next is to note how network television inserts commercial advertising between acts. A more challenging way to study act structure is to screen shows on the commercial-free premium channels such as HBO, where the act progressions tend to be more subtle.

Here is an exercise I do with my students to illustrate the "building progressively" principle. Once again using our trusty fictional show *John the Cop,* we start with a two-beat story. Plot Point A: A baby's kidnapped. Plot Point B: John the cop, dressed as a clown, captures the kidnapper and rescues the baby. As a group, we make the story longer, more exciting, logical, and satisfying. We retain Plot Point B as our conclusion and then create a series of events that relate logically to each other between points A and B. Remember that the events you insert as beats must drive dramatic action and build to a conclusion.

Break out some paper and give it a try. Start with Plot Point A: Someone kidnaps a baby. The original Plot Point B is moved to be the conclusion. My new Plot Point B: The parents get a ransom note from the kidnappers demanding cash. If the police are called, they'll never get the child back. New Plot Point C: After some debate, the parents decide to alert the police. New Plot Point D: John the cop is on the case and finds a clue from the scene of the kidnapping. New Plot Point E: The clue leads John to a shady character, whom he works over to get a tip on the kidnapper's identity. New Plot Point F—Formerly Plot Point B: John, not revealing that the police are involved, disguises himself as a clown in the park, where he captures the kidnapper and rescues the baby. If you removed any of the beats, the plot and the story would collapse.

Return to a Produced Episode of Your Show One Last Time

After you have established a few beats to support your story, put them in sequential order. This next step may seem repetitive, but trust me, after all you've done, you will see how it pays off for your own beat sheet and outline. Screen one more episode of the show you're working on. This time as you view it, keep track of the plot points. Write a beat sheet, a one-or-two-sentence listing of every beat that occurs within the teaser (a show's first sequence of scenes, which leads into a commercial or opening credits) and throughout each listed act. Now take this beat sheet of a produced episode and use it as a guideline for your own story, making sure to have the same approximate number of beats per act. You'll then be better prepared to compose an outline.

From Beat Sheet to Outline

Because a picture is worth a thousand frustrated expletives, I've screened the pilot to NBC's *Grimm* and created both a beat sheet and an outline of the first ten pages. These samples show you how each is constructed, particularly in the relative use of detail, and provide templates for you to use both tools. Do note that the outline below doesn't contain dialogue and its usage is optional, not required; the choice is yours.

Also observe several formatting conventions for writing beat sheets and outlines (as well as scripts) in evidence here. First, when characters are introduced for the first time, their names are always capitalized (e.g., NICK); once introduced, the names are no longer required to be in caps. Second, the slug line, which is the heading for a particular scene and/or plot point that indicates the scene's interior or exterior location, specific physical location, and time of day (for example, INT. C'EST LA VIE BAKERY—DAY), is always capitalized.

INSIDE the ROOM

Joel Anderson Thompson's Beat Sheet of NBC's *Grimm* Pilot

1. A young female jogger is attacked in a forest by something unseen.

2. NICK talks with his girlfriend, JULIETTE, at her job. Tonight's a big night because she'll be moving in with him.

3. HANK, Nick's partner—they're detectives—picks him up and takes him to a homicide they're assigned to investigate. En route, Nick's confused when he sees a beautiful girl passing by, who momentarily turns into a demon and reverts back to being human.

4. A sick woman, MARIE, drives defensively, as if she thinks she's being followed. A middle-aged man, HULDA, is following her from a distance in his car.

5. A FOREST SERVICE OFFICER shows Nick and Hank the crime scene in the woods where we saw the jogger attacked. As they gather clues, they see that the mutilation appears to have been done by an animal, but there are no signs of an animal attack, just a boot print.

6. At the police station, Nick and Hank check the databases. Nick sees a cuffed thug morph into a demonic owl and quickly revert back to human.

7. Marie takes medicine, enters a small Victorian house, and dons a scarf to cover her bald head.

8. While at the station, Nick and Hank get a call informing them that a university student never returned from jogging.

9. Nick and Hank interview the roommate of SYLVIE, the missing student. Via clues, they quickly deduce that Sylvie is the murder victim.

10. Juliette lets herself into her new home and is startled to discover Marie is already inside.

END OF TEASER

Joel Anderson Thompson's Outline of NBC's *Grimm* Pilot

TEASER

1. EXT. MCIVER PARK FOREST—DAY

A young woman, who's a student at the university, jogs in the beautiful lush forest while listening to her iPod and wearing a red hooded sweatshirt. Think Little Red Riding Hood. She's attacked and knocked into a ravine by something that moves so fast we can't see it. Amid the vicious snarling of her attacker, we hear her screams.

2. INT. C'EST LA VIE BAKERY—DAY

NICK BURKHARDT, 28, talks with his girlfriend, JULIETTE SILVERTON, 26, as she serves pastries to the patrons. He happily picks up bags that she had packed and has waiting for him. He can't wait to see her later tonight.

3. EXT. STREET—DAY

Outside the bakery, Nick meets with HANK GRIFFIN, late 40s. Pretty ladies pass by. Hank teases Nick about not being able to look anymore because of his new girlfriend, Juliette. Nick looks at the ladies anyway. One stares back and appears to morph into a demon, scowls at Nick, and reverts to normal. Nick shakes his head in disbelief. Hank informs him that they have to report to a call. A mutilated body was found in McIver Park. They get into the car and speed off with the siren blasting. They're detectives. Hank is his partner.

4. INT. SUV—DAY

A sickly and bald MARIE KESSLER, 49, drives an SUV and tows an Airstream. She continues checking her side-view mirrors as if she fears being followed.

5. INT. CORVETTE—DAY

Several cars behind Marie's SUV there's a Corvette following her. An overweight, balding, and middle-aged man named HULDA drives. He's following Marie.

6. EXT. FOREST/CRIME SCENE—DAY

Nick and Hank, wearing badges, follow the winding trail guided by a FOREST SERVICE OFFICER. He explains how the victim's severed arm, with a piece of the red hooded sweatshirt still on it, was discovered by other hikers. The large amount of blood spatter conveys that this was a violent attack. The remains are so unrecognizable that a discarded women's running shoe is the only evidence that reveals the gender of the victim. Forest Service Officer also explains that instead of the expected animal tracks, there is only a boot print. No human should have been able to do this. Too many pieces of the body are missing. A particularly happy song is on a continuous loop on the victim's discarded iPod.

7. INT. POLICE STATION—ROBBERY/
HOMICIDE—DAY

Nick and Hank run leads, check for DNA results, and scan database for violent predators in the area. Nick sees an ANGRY PERP sporting tats, handcuffed to a desk, being interviewed by a detective. Angry Perp stares back at Nick. His face morphs into a demonic owl and quickly reverts back to being human. This shocks Nick into running into SERGEANT WU and causes him to spill his coffee.

8. EXT. SMALL VICTORIAN HOUSE—DAY

Marie pulls the SUV and Airstream quickly up the long drive into the backyard of a run-down house. Now she's hidden from the street. Before getting out, Marie takes what looks like potent medicine and covers her bald head with a scarf. She exits the SUV with a cane. She finds a hidden key to enter the house. Finally, she has a smile born from relief.

9. INT. POLICE DEPARTMENT—ROBBERY/ HOMICIDE—DAY

Nick and Hank are at their desks, hunched over their computer screens. They discuss elimination of the usual suspects. A call comes in informing them that a university student went out jogging and never returned. Nick and Hank push back from their desks and head for the door.

10. INT. SYLVIE THE JOGGER'S DORM ROOM—NIGHT

Hank and Nick interview the possible victim's ROOMMATE, 18, who is worried sick. The roommate's description of the running shoes that SYLVIE, the missing jogger, wore is similar to the style found at the crime scene. The two detectives see photos of Sylvie and her roommate during happier times in their lives. Both of them wear the red hooded university sweatshirts. Nick and Hank conclude the murder victim is indeed Sylvie.

11. INT. SMALL VICTORIAN HOUSE—NIGHT

Juliette lets herself into the house. It's completely dark. She turns on the lights. GASP! Juliette gets the shock of her life when she discovers Marie standing before her.

END OF TEASER

Their Structure Should Become Your Structure

Be mindful that your outline should directly reflect the structure of the show you're specing. Count the number of scenes per act in a minimum of three episodes, and approximate this scene distribution within your outline. Follow this process within the teaser (again, a show's first sequence of scenes, which leads into a commercial or opening credits). Its purpose is to set a clear tone for the rest of the episode as well as to entice viewers to remain with the show and not change channels. While not all shows use teasers, the ones that do may have certain rules.

For instance, while most shows proceed linearly from the teaser into the story events, *Southland* does not. Its teaser is nonlinear and is used as a foreshadowing that plays out later in the episode. Some shows feature the protagonist in the teaser, some never do this, and others allow for both. In this respect, the teaser in your outline should emulate the show.

As with teasers, acts can have some variation as well. The easiest way to determine the separation of acts is to look for the commercial breaks. For premium cable, keep an eye on the clock. The rise and fall of the drama will convey a pattern revealing the act breaks. Some shows use a five-act structure and others have a sixth act. Your outline should reflect the same number.

Write That Outline!

Now it's your turn: Once you complete the beat sheet for your story, flesh out each plot point with light scene description, external and internal location, period of the day, and minimal choice dialogue. Voilà! You now have the first draft of your outline.

Welcome to the Team

Congratulations! By creating a story and outline for an on-air show, you have moved from sitting in the stands as a fan to joining that elite team of people who actually write.

Okay, stop high-fiving. That's only the first draft. Do a second draft. Let someone read it to offer notes on whether it seems logical and feels like the show. Implement the ones that sound sane. This will be your third draft.

Now that you have both a strong story and an outline, it's time to write the script. You will discover your outline needs changes. Don't panic. Revamping your outline in accordance with script demands is a part of the process for even the most experienced and gifted writers, and that's why the next chapter will guide you carefully through this new terrain. As you rework your outline and begin writing, you'll learn more about the truth of your story and acquire all the essential tools you need for a solid first draft. Trust the process, trust yourself, and most importantly, have fun.

CHAPTER 2

Writing the On-Air One-Hour Drama Spec: The Script

by Charlie Craig

Welcome and congratulations! Before we talk about what lies ahead on your quest to write a spec hour-long script, let's gloat a bit about what you've done so far: You've chosen an appropriate show, studied countless episodes, and spent days developing a story with a great teaser, gripping act outs, and tremendous forward momentum that builds to a satisfying climax. And better than that, it's all written down! There it is, right next to you: a well-crafted outline, clean and organized, seemingly begging you to type FADE IN and start writing.

Well, I've got some advice for you: *Don't.* There's still some work to do before you're ready to begin "generating pages" (a favorite euphemism picked up during my twenty-five-plus years in the business). You've already done the hardest part—compared to breaking a story and outlining it, *writing* a script is actually *fun*—but it's a process. A journey. And, like any journey, it can benefit from some last-minute preparation and planning.

In the first section of this chapter, "Before You Start Writing Your First Draft," we'll fine-tune elements like conflict, clock, and stakes, and go over your outline's structure to make sure your story flows and that the act outs are effective. You wouldn't want it any other way, right?

Our second section, "Writing Your First Draft," will provide a template to guide you through each scene of your script. Just as importantly, it will prepare you for the fact that your story will change as you dig into it; as your characters and plot come alive, it's inevitable that certain scenes or motivations won't make sense anymore. The good news is that the fixes you come up with will be better than what you originally had.

In "Writing Your Second Draft," you'll read your script for the first time, practicing techniques to help you gain perspective on the material, giving you the opportunity to make adjustments to the elements of the story that didn't end up working as well as you'd hoped.

Our final section, "Write—Write—Keep Writing!," addresses what to do when you're satisfied that your script is finished. How do you kick it out of the nest, and in what direction? *And what do you do next?* A scary proposition, but I hope this section makes it less so.

If all this seems like a lot of work—if you feel like you put all of this time into an outline, it reads perfectly, and you just want to *write*—I hear you. You're excited, you like your story, what's the holdup? I'll answer that with another question: Why are you writing a spec? The answer I get most often from my students at UCLA Extension is *to get an agent and a job.* That's a good one, but it's not the only reason you're devoting this much time to an episode of *Dexter* or *Breaking Bad* or *The Mentalist.*

You're also writing to prove that you have the tenacity and follow-through to actually finish a script. You're writing to prove that you understand what makes a good story and can come up with one on your own. You're writing to demonstrate your ability to capture the voice of a particular show and put it back on the page so it seems indistinguishable from the best episodes of that show.

This script is your first calling card; if you don't do everything you can to make it as good as you can, you're wasting your time. If, on the other hand, you give this script everything you've got, those who read it will be able to tell.

And they might just be interested in reading the *next* script you write.

Before You Start Writing Your First Draft

What I'm about to describe for you is a process I've gone through on every show I've written for (from *The X-Files* to *Invasion* to *Pretty Little Liars*) and every show I've run (from *Brimstone* on Fox to *Traveler* on ABC to *Eureka* on Syfy). Between finishing an episode's outline and starting to write the script, I review a series of questions I've been honing since . . . well, since forever. I share this process with my UCLA Extension class, and now I'm going to share it with you. I hope it causes you to come up with answers to some questions you never knew you had. If you can honestly say you already went over everything I'm about to discuss back when you were writing your outline, that's great. I'll bet your outline is better because of it.

Now let's do it one more time to make your *script* better. And let's start with something that should be obvious.

Turn on the TV

I'm sure you watched episodes of the show you've chosen to spec before you started on your outline. Well, guess what: *You need to keep watching.* If ever there was a time to become a student of your show, this is it. It's of crucial importance if your show is serialized, but even if you've chosen a stand-alone episodic it's really something you have to do. Why? *Because things change.*

Even your average closed-ended show has some low-level serialization: Will the leads of *Castle* or *Bones* finally sleep together? What have been the latest developments in *The Mentalist*'s quest to find Red John? What have we learned about the backgrounds of the characters in *Revenge* that might help us figure out what's going on? And if your show is truly serialized, you really need to stay on your toes: *Boardwalk Empire* ended its second season with the death of one of its two most important characters!

And it's not just the lives of the characters than can change overnight; regular sets and locations can change as well. Between the first and second season of *Eureka,* we tore down an entire soundstage of sets and started over again. The result was a whole new collection of labs and offices and meeting rooms that became our *standing sets*—the locations where most of our scenes took place. This change gave our show a dramatically different look than it had in season one; the observant writer would note this and set his scenes in the new locations, avoiding the ones that are no longer part of the show.

Lastly, *the entire structure of a series can change.* Partway through our second season, ABC Family decided to change *Pretty Little Liars* from a show with a teaser (the situation that compels the character to action and sets the episode's stakes) and five acts to a show with a teaser and six. Just like that. One day we finished cracking a T+5 episode; the next day we put an act 6 card up on the board and started a new story. Another opportunity for a shrewd writer to pick up on a change and adjust her outline accordingly.

So what's the bottom line? Things change—maybe a little, maybe a lot—and you need to be on top of those changes as you start writing your script. So keep the TV on, or fire up Hulu or one of the networks' own sites, and stay up-to-date with your show. You can always tweak your script as you write it, or even after. That proves you're paying attention. A failure to do so is an indication of a writer who's not hungry enough to be taken seriously.

Think Inside the Box

Now that you're up-to-date with any recent changes or developments to the flow of your show's season, it's time to take a final, closer look at the particular aspects of a single episode. I like to tell my students that although thinking outside the box is a good approach in many areas of life—none of us would be writing on Macs or standing in line to buy the latest iPhone if Steve Jobs hadn't decided to "think different"—when it comes to writing a spec, one needs to think *inside* the box. This is not the time to conceive of "a very special episode" of your show. There should be no major new characters introduced, it should not be Christmas, there should not be a wedding, and no one should *ever* wake up in bed and say, "It was just a dream."

Developments like those only occur on shows after lengthy discussions between the writers and the network and are, by definition, atypical. You're trying to write the exact opposite: a "typical" episode that will stand out not for its differences from its series but for its similarities, for how well it mimics the series while at the same time presenting a great and involving story.

So how do you go about giving yourself the best shot at achieving this goal? The answer, once again, is to compare your outline to a typical episode of your show. Actually, to as many episodes as possible. In as many ways as possible.

Franchise and Stakes

Let's start with the *series franchise*. I define that as "what happens in the show every week." If it's a police procedural, there's probably a criminal who needs to be stopped or captured. If it's a medical procedural, there's a life that needs to be saved. In a legal drama, there's a case that needs to be won. It may sound obvious, but your episode needs to have the same franchise as your series . . . and, going off of what I said above, your story should not be one where the killer gets away, the patient dies, or an innocent person goes to jail.

Closely related to franchise are your series' typical episodic *stakes*. How important is it to our regulars or guest cast that the story ends the way they hoped it would? In the three examples above, the stakes are usually life-or-death: We blow it and a murderer lives to kill again, or the patient dies, or a guilty man is exonerated of a crime he committed. In other shows—say, a high school or family or adult ensemble—the stakes may not involve physical survival, but to the characters, it usually *seems* as if they do: Will I get asked to the prom, will my kid get into the right school, will my mom ever stop judging me? Deduce the kinds of stakes that are raised in your series and make sure your outline's stakes are similar.

Conflict

Even more important to a series than stakes is *conflict*. You've heard the phrase "drama is conflict" for a reason: *It's true.* Without conflict in an episode of TV (*any* episode of TV, or any story, for that matter), there's nothing for the audience to care about. Why would there be, if the characters are going about their lives without a worry in the world, meeting no resistance to anything they're trying to accomplish? As much as we wish *our* lives were like that, you put that on TV and you're canceled before you're out of bed the next morning. Your spec needs conflict, and it needs to be of the kind your series has every week.

There are two other elements intertwined with conflict that you need to devote equal attention to: your characters' *goals* and the episode's *clock*. Goals are linked to conflict: The impediments that your characters face in trying to achieve their goals provide conflict. Take a look at your series and this convention will become readily apparent: Cops are lied to and shot at while trying to solve their cases; doctors come up with diagnoses that prove to be wrong while trying to save their patients; lawyers are ruled against by judges while arguing their cases.

In many shows, the clock is even more apparent. Something needs to be accomplished by the end of the episode or our characters fail to achieve their goals: The statute of limitations will run out, the disease will prove fatal, the perpetrator will leave the country.

Both goals and clock are easier to detect in closed-ended shows like *NCIS, CSI,* or *The Good Wife* (which, despite its serialized elements, usually has a legal case that's resolved within an episode). But even in *Pretty*

Little Liars—an extremely serialized show, and one set in high school, not a precinct or an ER—characters have goals in every episode and a clock running against them, making those goals even harder to accomplish: A wedding has to be stopped, a friend has to be convinced, a lie has to be told . . . *or else*. Make sure your characters have equally important concerns and drives.

B and C Stories

Does your series employ *B and C stories*? As compared to the A story—the main plot movement of an episode—B and C stories usually employ fewer beats and are often centered on characters less important to the A story. Almost all shows employ B stories to some extent, usually to give the show someplace to go while boring elements of the A story are taking place offscreen, or to provide comic relief, or to help reinforce the episode's theme (if it has one). C stories are, by definition, even less important and developed than B stories. Again, they'll be easy to spot in your series; just make sure that your story follows the show's pattern.

Theme

Since I've just mentioned *theme*—a general truth or main message—now's the time to make a last-minute check of whether your series usually has one. In some shows, the theme is quite overt: *Grey's Anatomy* and *Dexter* begin and end every week with narration that explicitly invokes that episode's theme. In other shows it's more nuanced, there just below the surface, appearing every once in a while like a stepping stone to help you cross a river.

That was our approach in *Eureka:* An episode in which an experiment had gone so terribly wrong that the only way to save the entire town was to risk losing it was paired with a B story in which the sheriff debated whether or not to ask a newly arrived coworker out on a date, and a C story in which his daughter worried about leaving for college. The theme?

"Sometimes you have to take a leap of faith." Take a look at your series and see if it relies on themes or not, and make sure your outline follows suit.

Framing

Speaking of narration, does your series employ any sort of *framing device* on a weekly basis? Does every episode begin or end in the same way or location, or focus on the same character? Framing like this is more typical in the half-hour world, but it shows up in hour-long dramas as well: Each episode of *Alcatraz* ends with a captured prisoner being locked up in that special underground prison. Every *Dexter* ends with the title character. *Law and Order* utilizes interstitial titles and the *bong-bong* sound. You probably already know if your series uses any elements like this, but if you're not sure, now's the time to double-check.

Finally, examine your series' *time frame*: Most shows tell their stories in a matter of a few days, if not less. The hallmark of *24* was that each episode took place over exactly the same amount of time—that is, twenty-four hours. No other series is quite that precise, but each show has its comfort zone. Find it and stick with it.

Okay. It's almost time to start writing! I wouldn't be doing my job, though, if I didn't (briefly) bring one last area to your attention. You want your reader to stay interested and focused on your script, right? Good. Then listen up.

Remember That Not All Acts Are Created Equal

Each act has a specific purpose in the hour-long drama, and before you begin writing it's worth a quick review of what each act should accomplish. The examples below apply to almost all one-hour shows, be they serialized or closed-ended. Of course, every show has its own twist on how its stories lay out, but when you start to study different series, you'll be amazed at how the writers pretty much construct episodes in the same fashion. The structure that I teach in "Beginning Writing for the

One-Hour Drama: Building the Story and Outline" at UCLA Extension is the one those lucky (and tenacious) enough among you will be using for the rest of your career. So let's make sure you're using it in your outline!

Teaser: *A situation is introduced that will compel your characters to act and the audience to watch.* A good teaser lets the audience know not only the subject of this week's story but also the episode's stakes. It should raise the viewers' expectations and curiosity: A mystery needs to be unraveled, a life needs to be saved, a problem needs to be solved. Dangers will be faced, time will be of the essence, stakes will be high. By the end of a good teaser, the viewers should be fully committed to sticking in their seats for the next hour—if they don't care what happens by page 5, the impact of the end of your show will be severely compromised. Does your teaser fulfill these requirements? It does? Onward.

Act 1: *All elements are put into place.* It's in act 1—usually the longest act—that the full ramifications and scope of the problem introduced in the teaser are realized. The main characters now grasp the severity and difficulty of the task that lies ahead and may have formulated their first plan to resolve it. The audience in turn feels fully aware of what impediments they expect the characters will face. Any B and C stories have been kicked off. Sound like your outline? If not, think about adjusting.

Act 2: *Things get progressively worse.* Our heroes thought they had a handle on things, and boy were they wrong. The patient's not improving, the informant has nothing, the witness has been murdered. Perceived forward progress has been revealed to be the opposite; the clock is ticking and the stakes are rising. This is roughly the middle of your script: Do your characters look like they're going to lose this one? Good!

Act 3: *One last element joins the mix and makes things worse.* Even the B and C stories aren't going the way the characters had hoped. This act combined with act 4 corresponds to the third act in a traditional four-act structure and presents new and unforeseen roadblocks. A simple metaphor: Act 3 is where the first shoe drops. In act 4, the other shoe hits someone in the head. Simply put, *things are getting worse for everyone.* Sound like your story?

Act 4: *You thought things were bad in act 3?!* Basically, by the end of the fourth act, one of two things has happened: Either the solution has become apparent but the characters don't have the time or resources to achieve it, or it appears that there's no solution at all. Either way, everyone's screwed. Except the writer, because he knows what's coming next.

Act 5: *Hey, there's a way out of this mess!* In the nick of time, the brightest minds come up with a way to save a life, a case, a family, a prom. Everyone lives to go through it all over again next week.

These guidelines illuminate the way almost every hour-long show works, whether the stories play out in the world of forensics cops or hot doctors or shrewd lawyers or crazy scientists or lying high school students. It's a formula your outline should follow. My guess is that by now it does.

My other guess? *You're ready to start writing.* So let's get to it!

Writing Your First Draft

So today's the day, huh? We've done everything I can think of to get you ready to write, and now there's nothing left to do but power up your laptop, open your scriptwriting program of choice, type TEASER, and have at it.

It's a scary prospect, isn't it? As much as there's a story in your outline waiting to be told, that blank page can freeze you. Think about it: There is an infinite number of ways you can begin that first scene. Who should talk first? What should they be doing *as* they talk? How many *other* people should be in the scene? Why are they there and where did they come from? Are they happy about being there, or do they wish they were someplace else? You could spend the rest of the day just answering these questions and not get anywhere at all!

Sounds like you could use a little advice to help you calm down. That's what this section of the chapter is for. First, I'll share some tips to help you get through your writing day without your head exploding—everyday guidelines that apply to any script you write. Then I'll lead you through a series of questions to ask yourself before you write each scene.

How do I know the questions work? Because I still ask them of myself before *I* write each scene. Let's get to it.

As You Write Your Script

The first piece of advice I'll give you—and I dispense it to every writer in my class—is trust your instincts. Your concept of this particular story and how it should play out is what got you this far, which is a real accomplishment in and of itself. You're going to hit plenty of walls in the next couple of weeks; don't give in to that little voice that says, "This was a stupid idea in the first place!" You wouldn't be here if that was true; you'd have moved on long ago. *You believe in this story, so believe in yourself.*

Trusting your instincts, however, does not imply that you should be rigid in your approach to your script and its structure. You need to be aware of the fact that *things will change.* You'll come to all sorts of realizations as you write: Certain scenes that made perfect sense in your outline—sometimes your *favorite* scenes—will no longer seem sensible, or even necessary, in the draft. Characters' actions that used to seem motivated will now strike you as wonky. Act outs that positively *sang* in the outline will now seem limp and anticlimactic. So what do you do? *Adapt.*

Take a moment, analyze why something isn't working, and *fix it.* If that sounds simple, it's not, but it's what you have to do. *Nothing is written in stone* is a phrase you'll hear applied to every script and outline you ever write. It's true. Embrace the concept (or as we used to say at Stephen J. Cannell Productions in the nineties, "Eat the reality sandwich"). *In change lies opportunity.*

With respect to the physical act of how you put your words on the page—your writing style—one of the most important suggestions that I can give you is *don't overwrite.* It took me a while to learn this lesson. I'm always very proud of how my words look on a page and take a lot of care in choosing those words . . . but let's face it: If your end goal is to produce words that will be appreciated for their meticulous sentence structure and painterly mise-en-scène, *write a book.* When you write a TV script, by the time it's passed through five sets of studio and network rewrites, the discerning eye of the director, the mouths of the actors, and three editing passes in post, you'll be lucky if any of your favorite script moments are even recognizable. Okay, it's not that bad, but the point here is that *the script is a tool, not a work of art*. It's a means to an end, and a well-written script, spec or otherwise, is constructed with that in mind.

Be Concise

So what does that mean, exactly, to "be concise"? For one thing, *don't novelize*. Don't take half a page of scene description to describe a character's entry, what he's wearing, where he's come from, whether he enjoyed his breakfast, and what he watched on TV last night. The audience is never going to know any of that anyway, unless it's important for that character to talk about, in which case it'll end up as dialogue, right? My rule of thumb is that no scene description should be more than three lines long. I'm not saying you have to write that way as well, but limiting scene description is a good way to make sure what's important makes it onto the page, and what's not stays off it.

Another good approach to keeping your work concise is to remind yourself of your role: *You're the writer*. You're not the director or the director of photography (DP). Don't take valuable space on the page to set up how you want a scene to look. No one needs to read, "The camera pans to find Bob in the doorway, then follows him to the desk, where he sits, under a lamp, revealing the open window behind him." That's just annoying; if you're lucky enough that your script makes it to the set, the director and the DP will figure out how they want to shoot the scene all by themselves. That's why they were hired. So no shots, no camera moves. You're in charge of the *story*, and that's what you need to be concentrating on.

Keep Up the Pace

Writing in a concise manner will help you with another area of concern: *pacing*. How often do you watch a show and complain that the story is moving too quickly? Hardly ever, compared to the times a show, or a script, seems to drag. The last thing you want is for readers to put your script down and pretend they will get back to it tomorrow, *because they won't*. That script leaves their hands, and you've lost them for good.

The best way to prevent this unfortunate fate is to *keep things moving*. Decide what the meat of your scene is and make sure you get to it sooner rather than later. In my scripts, I aim for the average scene to be between one and two pages long. Maybe once a script I'll approach three pages—usually a scene in which a character is both pouring her heart out and giving us information crucial to the resolution of the story—but that's it. Some of my scenes will be *less* than a page.

Do the math: Divide the page count of an episode of your show by the number of scenes—the average will be around a page and a half per scene. You need to get in and get out: Do characters really need to enter a scene, or can they already be there? How much of a conversation could have taken place offscreen, before the scene began? And does everybody need to leave when they're done, or can you cut out of the scene after a particularly provocative line? Put what you absolutely need on the page, and nothing more. It takes practice to learn how to pull this off. Start today.

Learn When to Reevaluate and When to Push Ahead

Okay. You're rolling. Pages are piling up. Scenes are tight. What happens when that juggernaut comes to a standstill? When you realize you've spent all morning trying to make a scene work and it's just not coming? This happens to me once or twice a script, and here's what I've learned: *If something's really not working, there's a reason*. What you need to do when you hit one of these roadblocks is stop trying to write the scene and start looking for the underlying reason it's proving so difficult.

Perhaps the scene, despite how well it worked in the outline, is no longer motivated due to modifications you've made to the story. Maybe the attitude you've chosen for a character isn't really true anymore. Maybe there's no real conflict—the scene is just relaying story information in a boring fashion—or the conflict you have is unmotivated. *Maybe you just don't need the scene anymore.*

Whatever the cause, if you're this stuck, the answer is to reevaluate the scene conceptually. Stepping back from the trees to take a look at the forest usually provides a solution and gets you back on track.

And on track is where you want to be. Writing a script is all about forward progress, pushing ahead. Make no mistake: This spec of yours is a test, an endurance contest to see if you have the mettle to finish. Toward that end, here's my next bit of wisdom: *Avoid reading what you've just written.* I know you're proud of that scene or act out; who wouldn't want to read it over just to remind himself of how smart he is?

There are a couple of reasons why this is a bad idea. For one thing, rereading is less productive than writing; you're wasting valuable time. More importantly, the less you go over your script now, the fresher it will seem when you're finished. You're going to need a critical eye when you begin the rewriting/tightening process, and if by then you're reading material you've already gone over countless times, your job will be infinitely harder. I can't stress this enough: *Leave it alone.* If that scene or act out is good, it'll seem even better in the context of an entire script. And your ability to judge it will be much more acute.

Two more quick bits of advice before we move on to some scene-particular tips. First: *Keep a pad and pen next to your bed.* Once you're really in the zone, your brain will keep working on your script whether *you* are or not. Ideas are going to come to you when you least expect them, so be prepared. Second: *Finish the script.* Of course you intend to—every writer intends to finish every project—but history and Hollywood are littered with half-completed scripts. You have no idea how many people have told me over the years that they could be writers, too, if they "only had the time." You know what that's code for? *They're not writers.* But you are. At least you will be, when you finish that script. *So keep writing!*

Scene by Scene: Ask First, Write Later

I mentioned above that we all hit points in a script where a scene just doesn't work. While embracing the fact that this *will* happen and realizing that your reaction to this curveball is where the real writing takes place, let me give you a series of questions to ask *before* you begin each scene that may minimize the number of times you find yourself squeezed.

I've been employing this list in one form or another since day one of my career. When I started out as a TV writer, I literally codified it into what I called "scene sheets," forms that I filled out before I attacked each scene in a script. By now the list is burned into my brain and I don't use the sheets, but to this day I look at the scene paragraph in my outline and make little notes: reminders, directions, and changes to help me write the best scene I can.

If it works for me, there's no reason it shouldn't work for you, right? So here goes.

Why does this scene exist? Does it reveal new information, thus advancing the story? Does it set up expectations for what's going to happen later in the script, and does it propel us into the next scene? Is the scene related to theme? Could the information it *does* contain be covered by dialogue in another scene? Most importantly: *If it wasn't here, would we miss it?* There are usually a couple of scenes in an outline that fail this test. Save them for your next script.

Are the characters in this scene necessary? This point seems obvious, but sometimes it's not. Just because two characters have been hanging out for the last couple of acts doesn't mean they still have to be together in this next scene. Just because a character lives with a roommate doesn't mean the roommate has to be home. Basically, if you find that characters are just standing around, not saying or doing anything important, get rid of them. I learned this lesson on the first show I ran, when I found myself trying to explain to an actor his function in a scene we were shooting. In fact, he had no reason to be there. But he was, so I gave him a gun and that made him happy. It would have been easier if I'd caught the fact that he was superfluous at the script stage.

Does the scene have adequate conflict? I know I've mentioned this before, but this question is one that I answer for every scene in every script I write. I literally write *conflict* next to the scene in my outline, then briefly indicate what that conflict is. Make sure each scene you write has conflict and that it's important to the story. Enough said.

Is it clear what the person driving the scene wants? This has to be clear for a number of reasons: We have to know what he wants in order to understand where the story is going; you have to know what he wants to put impediments in his way. On the set, the most common question you'll hear from an actor is "What's my motivation?" If you can't answer that at the script stage, you sure won't be able to answer it on the set. And giving the actor a gun doesn't always fix the problem.

Where is the scene located? Is the scene you're about to write in a typical and appropriate location? Is it in a set that's used often? If it's out in the "real world"—in a place necessary to your script but not a location your show normally visits—is the location fully taken advantage of? To show you really know what you're doing, try to get back to that location one or two more times during your story. You'd have to anyway if you were shooting so that the production company could justify the expense of traveling there. *Write like a pro and someone might mistake you for one.*

Is the scene an act out? If so, does it leave the reader hanging, barely able to contain her enthusiasm until she turns the page? Does it raise the stakes? Does it truly propel the story into the next act? If not, you need a better act out!

Is the scene part of a B or C story? If so, is it related to the A story by theme? Does it reinforce or provide insight into other elements of the A story? If the answer is no—if it's a freestanding story line—is it balanced correctly against the number of A story scenes? Usually, a B story, and especially a C story, will only have one scene per act. At most, two.

Is there something surprising about the scene? This question is my favorite. It's not really a formal aspect of scenes you hear talked about very often, but it's worth a thought. Another way to put the question would be: Is there something you find particularly cool about the scene?

Something you think the reader will remember later? Or is there a *reversal* in the scene: Did you skillfully lead the audience into thinking one thing was going to happen, then surprise them with a different outcome? It's not a goal for every scene, obviously, but it can make a *good* scene.

There you have it—the sum total of what I can tell you about writing the first draft of your spec. Stop paying attention to me and get back to writing. I'll see you on the other side.

Writing Your Second Draft

Time for another round of congratulations! You did it. You *really* did it: You wrote the script. And you know what you get to do to celebrate?

Write a second draft.

These words leave a bad taste in most working writers' mouths, because they're associated with notes and calls from studios and networks and subsequent pained attempts to make sense of what was said while at the same time trying to remember what made you want to write the script in the first place. In this instance, however, you should move forward without trepidation: The only notes you're going to get are coming from yourself. But first things first: You have a very important task to undertake before any reading or rewriting takes place, and that brings us to the subject of our next section.

Gain Some Perspective

Now, I know you followed my advice and avoided the temptation of re-reading your script as you wrote it. *Now's your chance to try again.* Put your script in a drawer. Go away for the weekend. Get back to the gym. Again, not being on a show, facing a deadline, means you have the luxury of gaining some precious distance from your script, and this will make a critical difference when you finally read it. It's a well-known fact that it's easier to identify areas of concern in other people's scripts than in your own; putting your script down for a couple of days will help you be (a little) more objective when you pick it up again.

The good news is, I have something for you to do in your time off: *Watch more TV.* Specifically, check back in on your show and make sure nothing big has happened while you were off writing. I know I sound paranoid, but humor me. Get back up to speed. Then, when you can't take the suspense any longer, take a deep breath . . . and take the next step.

Read Your Script!

At last, the long-awaited moment is here. Find an hour, close the door, and pick that baby up. Make sure you have the time to read it all in one sitting, and make sure you have a pen in your hand. You're going to want to make some notes.

The first thing you're liable to notice is that the script is too long. Most first drafts are—there are usually more beats in an outline than are needed. If you had a showrunner or network they might even have told you that, but with the story all crammed in your head, it's often hard to separate the wheat from the chaff. At this point, though, its being long is actually an advantage. Why? Because you're going to want to trim and tighten, and that will drop page count. Making a script better usually involves making it shorter. Funny how that works.

So read your script. Write little notes—trims, dialogue improvements, inspirations—right on the script as you go. Bigger ideas can go on the back of the last page: If a character went *here,* you could drop the scene where he went *there;* there are too many scenes without the lead in the third act; that romantic attraction seems forced—stuff like that. Work your way to the end, then sit back and ask yourself how you enjoyed the read. I hope you think the script was pretty good. Most writers like their first drafts; the tormented-writer thing you hear so much about comes later in the process. And, honestly, if you hate it, then the issues are more fundamental (perhaps a career in accounting doesn't seem so bad after all). So let's say the script was pretty good.

Now you need to evaluate your notes. If they're mostly the ones you wrote on the pages, then have at them, remembering that your constant goal is to *tighten,* to cut the scenes down to the bare minimum that keeps the story moving. Could you enter a scene later or leave it earlier? Could some of your dialogue be left unsaid? Keep one of my favorite writing words in mind: *velocity*.

When it comes to the larger notes, the ones you wrote on the back, I suggest you sit with those for a day. If some of them are fairly substantial structural changes, or ones involving adding or dropping characters, you might even want to go back and move things around in your outline, "seeing" how things would look before you actually tear into the script. My guess is, though, that your structure is solid—we've certainly spent enough time going over it—and that your bigger notes have mostly to do with scenes that somehow just "don't work." They feel unsatisfactory—boring, or confusing, or out of character. In that case, I suggest you go back to the categories we discussed earlier in the chapter. Whether you're looking at the entire act or just a scene, ask yourself those questions again:

Why does this scene exist?

Are the characters in this scene necessary?

Does the scene have adequate conflict?

Is it clear what the person driving the scene wants?

Is there something surprising about the scene?

If the scene is an act out, is it a cliffhanger?

When you're done answering the questions, it's back to the script again. Implement your notes. *Do that rewrite*. Remember your goal: This script should seem like a "lost episode" of the show you chose. Don't quit until it does.

Write—Write—Keep Writing!

I only have two more pieces of advice for you, and they both concern what you should do when you're finished with this spec. *Really* finished, as in you've gotten feedback from everyone you know, written one or two or ten more drafts, spell-checked the heck out of the script, and released it into the wild. What do you do then?

First, the long answer: *Continue to learn your craft.* Luckily, part of that means watching a lot more TV, but you also need to read scripts—lots of them. The Writers Guild of America website can point you toward some, and so can Google. You would also be well served to find some other writers to hang out with: A lot of people I've worked with have at one time or another been members of writers' groups. Ex-students of mine have formed them after every class I've taught. And speaking of classes—take some! UCLA Extension Writers' Program is a tremendous resource; in the hour-long drama field, you can take ten-week classes devoted to any and every step of the TV writing process, from outline to script to pitch to pilot.

That was the long answer. My guess is you already know the short answer: What do you really need to do next? *Write.* In my career, that has always been the answer to problems I've faced. Too much work to do in too short a time? *Write.* Stuck writing crime shows even though your real interest is sci-fi? *Write.* Been out of work for a year? *Write.* Want to break into the business? *Write.* I hope this chapter has helped you on that journey, and I'll see you in Starbucks.

CHAPTER 3

Writing the One-Hour Drama Pilot

by Richard Manning

Now that you've taken the lessons of chapters 1 and 2 to heart and written an excellent one-hour spec for an existing one-hour drama series, it's time to relax, take a deep breath, enjoy a beverage . . .

. . . and start thinking about writing a *one-hour pilot*.

Why? Because you need more than one sample in your portfolio . . . and more than one kind of sample.

Consider the readers of your samples: showrunners, agents, producers, and executives. Some will prefer "originals," some will prefer episodic specs, and some will want to see both. (When I'm looking to hire writers, I always like to read both.)

The more samples you have, the better, especially when you're starting out. Let's say you've found a producer willing to read your stuff, so you offer to send the brilliant spec episode of *Homeland* you've slaved over. Here are some possible responses:

- "I'd rather read an original. I can't tell much about a writer from an episodic spec. What else ya got?"

- "Well, okay, I'll read it, but I'm not at all familiar with that show, so . . . what else ya got?"

- "*Homeland*? Nah, I can't stand that show. What else ya got?"

- "I love *Homeland*. Send it." (Reads it, then:) "Terrific script. You nailed it. It really felt like a *Homeland* episode. But *my* show, a sci-fi action romp, is nothing at all like *Homeland*. What else ya got?"

(Or:)

- (Reads it, then:) "'Solid script, but I've read three other *Homeland* specs just as good, so I'm on the fence about you. What else ya got?"

If your answer is "Nothing," you're at a disadvantage. The producer might think, *One script's all you've written? That's not much practice. Yes, it's terrific—but for all I know, it took a year to write, and I need writers who are both talented and fast.*

But if your answer is "I've also got a pilot," you're proving that you aren't a one-hit wonder.

(Of course, it's better still if you can reply, "I've got a pilot and two other episodic specs and a feature!" The more prolific you are, the more you demonstrate that you're a hard worker who's serious about this writing stuff.)

A pilot allows you to show off *your own voice as a writer*. With an episodic spec, you're demonstrating that you can write someone else's show and harmonize with someone else's voice—but an original pilot is 100 percent you.

In this chapter, I'll guide you through the creation of a one-hour dramatic pilot. I'll share some of what I've learned not only from creating a television series, writing three pilots, and writing/producing shows such as *Farscape, Star Trek: The Next Generation, TekWar, Sliders, Fame,* and many more, but also from the TV writing courses I've taught at UCLA Extension. I'll help you choose a subject, brainstorm ideas, develop a franchise and a premise, and create fresh and original characters—all the ingredients you'll need to write your pilot.

Let's begin!

Writing Your Pilot

The first question, of course, is:

What Should I Write?

Hey, it's *your* pilot! Write anything you like.

Yes, I know that doesn't help much. How about this: *Write something you can get excited about.*

That might seem like "Well, duh" advice, but trust me—plenty of pilots out there read as if they were written by Marketplace-Analyzing Robots. "Hmm. Procedurals usually do well. Spunky young heroines with attitude and tattoos are all the rage. And several studios are developing postapocalyptic shows, so networks must still be buying them. I therefore conclude that a series about a young, tattooed woman who analyzes crime scenes in a near-future *Hunger Games*–type world is precisely what I should write."

Now, maybe you're thinking, *Hmm, call me crazy, but I actually kinda like that idea! That show could be cool if they did it right!* But that's my point: If you can truly get excited about the idea, then—by all means—go and write it!

However, if the idea doesn't get your heart racing, and the main reason you're pursuing it is that you've coldly calculated that someone *else* might like it, chances are that attitude will show through in your material, and it'll read as flat and manipulative.

Remember Jean Giraudoux's classic quote: "The secret of success is sincerity. Once you can fake that you've got it made." The problem is that *very few writers can successfully fake sincerity.*

Why even try? Write honestly. Write from the heart. Write what you want to see, not what you think others might want to see. *Come up with ideas you can get excited about.*

Note that I've phrased it "ideas you can get excited about" rather than "ideas that excite you right on the spot." Not all ideas jump up and grab you the moment they're born; often, a new concept needs to be developed before it sets your imagination on fire.

That's a phenomenon I call "there's something there, but." An idea's caught my eye and I'm interested . . . but I'm not in love with it yet. Maybe it sounds too vague, or too ordinary, or too familiar, or too uninspired. . . .

Don't discard those half-baked ideas. Set them aside, let them marinate in your subconscious for a while, and come back later for a fresh look. What is it about the idea that appeals to you, however slightly? What's the "something there" that seems to have possibilities? Toss that "something" around in your head. Mix it up with other ideas. Push it in several different directions.

Take a walk or grab a coffee with a friend or significant other and kick the idea around between you; a fresh perspective might help you make a vague idea click into place. I can't count the number of times I've sat in a TV writers' room with several other scribes, all fussing over an idea that seems promising but isn't there yet. Sooner or later, one thought will sound half-decent, and that'll spark someone else's thought that sounds better still, and that'll inspire yet another thought that winds us up, and faster and faster we go until—*snap!* Now we've got it! That's what we were looking for! What a terrific idea!

Talking over an idea with someone, even if they have nothing to contribute but a sympathetic ear, will often help you clarify what you like (and don't like) about the idea. I know that sometimes writers think, "My work is my art and my soul, hence I must do this entirely alone, or else I'm cheating." Untrue . . . and particularly untrue in television writing, which is as collaborative as it gets.

What's *your* favorite pilot idea? What does it need to make it "click" for you?

Help! I Have No Ideas! Not One!

Really? Not *one* idea? Not one faint glimmer of a hint of a concept of a notion?

(Or are you actually saying, "Well, I've come up with a few ideas, but they all *suck*." If so, skip to the next section: "Help! My Ideas All Suck!")

Okay, let's prime the creative pump with a few brainstorming techniques.

(A caveat: These are *techniques*. Not rules, not commandments, and most definitely not the Only Officially Approved Methods. Try them—but if they don't work for you, no worries; try something else.)

The first vital step: *Turn off your inner critic*. Silence that voice in your head that comes up with reasons why something's no good and won't work. It's easy for the inner critic to shoot down every notion the creative side of your brain comes up with—and when that happens, it's also easy for the creative side to get discouraged and quit trying.

Don't let that happen. Ignore your inner critic. Your goal is to generate *as many ideas as you can*—good, bad, or indifferent. When we brainstorm, we're after quantity, not quality. Come up with a ton of ideas, and at least a *few* of them might have possibilities—but you won't get to those good ones unless you give yourself permission to churn out a lot of not-so-good ones first.

Make a document with two columns. Label the left-hand column "Favorites."

In the "Favorites" column, list all the current TV shows you enjoy. Nobody's going to see this list but you—I promise I won't peek!—so be honest: Don't just list shows you think are "good" or classy or Emmy-worthy; list what you actually watch and like.

Add to the "Favorites" column all the TV shows no longer on the air that you used to watch and enjoy. Again, be honest; don't leave anything off because, for instance, you were only twelve then and you're sure you'd think it was horrible if you watched it today. Indeed you might—but this isn't about quality. This is about what hooked you.

For good measure, also list a few of your all-time favorite movies, books, plays, graphic novels, operas—any dramatic works in any medium that have stayed with you.

Now label the second column "Elements"—and for each item in your "Favorites" list, ask yourself, "Why did I like it? What appealed to me?" Maybe you watched it for its clever banter . . . or its intricate plots and unpredictable endings . . . or its rousing action . . . or its dark, gritty tone . . . or because it felt so emotionally real . . . or because it felt so mind-bendingly unreal.

Isolate the specific elements you latched on to. They won't necessarily be the show's primary elements, or what it was best known for, or what the critics liked, or what made it popular. Keep it personal. This is about your likes. Jot down those elements in the second column.

When your "Elements" list is complete, look for patterns. Some will be obvious: "Yeah, I'm a sucker for sci-fi, especially with space battles." Some might surprise you: "Gee, I never noticed, but all the stuff I like best has characters who are seriously screwed up."

Start a fresh list entitled "Rough Ideas," making sure your inner critic is still on "mute," and then . . . Mix and match. Take two or three items from your "Elements" list, stir them together, and voilà! There's a possible idea for a pilot. Write it down.

For example: What if you had two seriously screwed-up characters *something like* the ones in your favorite shows A, B, and C . . . in an interstellar navy *something like* the one in show D . . . but with *something like* the harsh, realistic tone of show E instead of the campy action-adventure tone of show D . . . ?

I've emphasized *something like* because I'm not suggesting you simply copy-and-paste together a Frankenstein's monster that obviously rips off other shows. This is an idea *generator,* not an idea recycler; it's meant to spark inspiration, to start you down paths of your own.

When you find combinations that pique your interest even a little—"there's something there, but . . ."—try mixing them up even more. What if you make the two lead characters both female? Both male?

One young, one old? Teenagers? Gay? Rich? Formerly rich, now poor? Not human? Best of friends? Mortal enemies?

And/or . . . what if the interstellar navy is . . . mostly aliens, and humans are in the minority?

And/or . . . this navy isn't the good guys, it's the *bad* guys, and our main characters soon realize they're on the wrong side?

And/or . . . our main characters are in two opposing navies, kind of like brother against brother in the Civil War. . . .

Keep jotting these combinations down. The longer your "Rough Ideas" list, the better.

For each combination, ask yourself what appeals to you about it, and see if you can tweak that aspect to increase its appeal. "Hmm . . . I really like the brother-against-brother-in-wartime notion . . . but what if it's a *husband and wife* on opposite sides? Still in love, but forced to be enemies? Yeah. That could be cool. I could do something with that."

Do I hear an objection from the balcony? "That method just sounds like a way to mash up old ideas. Isn't it better to create *new* ideas?"

Here's the thing. Combining "old ideas" in innovative new ways is how "new ideas" get made.

Your task as a television pilot writer is not to create something *utterly unlike anything anyone's ever seen.*

Songwriters don't invent new tonalities, new musical instruments, and new languages for the lyrics. Restaurant chefs don't create meals from entirely unfamiliar ingredients. We don't expect anyone to reinvent the wheel. It's the particular *combination* of ingredients that makes a creation new.

Look at the shows you consider "freshest and newest" on your "Favorites" list. What was "new" about them? Break them down and you'll likely find old ideas combined in new ways.

Take, for example, *Homeland.* Your mileage may vary, but I'd certainly describe that series as "fresh and unique." But at its core, it's a blend of two far-from-new Hollywood tropes: the brilliant-but-troubled Defective Detective and the hero-who-might-secretly-be-brainwashed Manchurian

Agent. (See www.tvtropes.org for more about these and many, many other tropes.)

Another example: Countless TV shows have dealt with the drug trade. What sets *Breaking Bad* apart? The drug-dealer protagonist is a high school chemistry teacher—middle-aged, married, and (at least in the pilot) meek.

New combinations of old ideas *are* new ideas. What are your favorite "TV ingredients" that *you* can mix and match?

Help! My Ideas All Suck!

Now that you've got a long list of pilot ideas, pick out and develop the ones that appeal to you the most.

What's that you say? *None* of them appeal to you? Not a single one? Why not? Too vague? Too familiar? Too unclear?

You're not letting your inner critic talk you out of any ideas, are you? We're still at the "no negativity, anything goes" stage; keep that inner critic quiet!

"I don't *hate* my ideas," you may be saying, "but I don't love them either. Some seem okay, but none set me on fire."

Fair enough; in that case, let's try a few more idea-generating techniques.

"Someday . . ."

If you've ever thought to yourself, "Someday, they'll make a TV series in which [fill in the blank] . . ." then what are you waiting for? Go write it yourself!

If "someday" seems a long way off because the idea is way out there or the subject matter's controversial or any such variation on "TV's not ready for this yet"—all the more reason to write it *now* and beat everyone else to the punch!

Given the explosion of cable channels that produce scripted series— and the success of so many "way out there" shows on cable—TV just might be ready for your series *now*.

I mean, c'mon. We've seen TV dramas about mobsters, serial killers, advertisers in the 1960s, sex addicts, Roman gladiators, meth makers, polygamists, and Prohibition-era Atlantic City . . . and nearly all those shows won Emmys! So tell me—what exactly isn't TV ready for?

Besides, even in the unlikely event that your pilot is "too far out" for TV at the moment, it could still be a superlative writing sample. Risk-taking, boldness, and originality get attention. Playing it safe? Not so much.

"My Dream Job Would've Been . . ."

What's your all-time favorite series that's no longer on the air, the one you wish you could travel back in time and write for? Let's call it *Dreamshow*.

Pretend a Big Network Executive says to you, "We've acquired the rights to *Dreamshow* and we'd like you, its biggest fan, to write a pilot for a new version of it. How would you update it and make it relevant to to-day's audiences yet still keep its original appeal? You can do whatever you want—continue the original; do a *Dreamshow: The Next Generation*–type sequel; reboot it from scratch like *Battlestar Galactica* . . . anything."

You eagerly set to work, have a huge amount of fun, and bang out a sparkling pilot script for *Dreamshow Revisited*. The Big Network Exec says, "It's brilliant! We want it to go to series and pay you a zillion dollars to run it. However, there's a snag: Turns out we *don't* have the rights to *Dreamshow* after all. But we still love what you did with it and we want to produce it! Can you change the names and the setting and the other recognizable *Dreamshow* elements enough so that we don't get sued but still keep the stunning excellence of your script intact?"

In other words: If you loved *Dreamshow,* why not create a series in the same vein, but different enough so viewers say it's "kind of an updated version of" or "seems inspired by" or "has delightful echoes of" *Dream-show* rather than being a "blatant rip-off" of it.

"Why Don't They Make Shows like _____ Anymore?"

Also known as, "In my opinion, TV needs more musicals/space operas/ westerns/whatever."

Consider the western. In 1959, when there were only three TV networks, twenty-six western series aired *every week* in prime time. *Bonanza* ran for fourteen seasons, *Gunsmoke* for twenty. But that was long ago, and audiences have moved on . . . right? The genre's old-fashioned and played out; every possible permutation of every conceivable western plot has been done to death. You'd be nuts to pitch a western now . . .

. . . or would you? *Deadwood* ran on HBO for three seasons starting in 2004 and won eight Emmys. It was a gritty, profane blend of fiction and history—and although it was a western through and through, it didn't look like any western that had come before.

That's the challenge: to invigorate a beloved but tired genre by taking it in a fresh new direction. What kind of series would *you* like to see return to television? Come up with a unique way of doing it—and give it a shot!

"It's an X Dressed Up as a Y"

Another way to make an old genre new again is to dress it up as something else—transplant some of its elements into a different time and place.

Justified, for instance, is a western dressed up as a cop show. Its lead character is a hat-wearing, quick-drawing US marshal . . . in present-day Kentucky. Although the setting is contemporary, the themes are pure western.

Firefly was also a western, but dressed up as space opera. *Once Upon a Time* and *Grimm* are fairy tales masquerading as a soap opera and a police procedural respectively. *House M.D.* was a mystery cloaked in a medical drama.

The influences don't have to be large or obvious. I wouldn't say *Castle* and *Bones* are romantic comedies dressed up as mysteries, but there are certainly strong *elements* of romantic comedy in both.

How will *you* take a favorite genre, blend it with something else, and come up with an appealing new hybrid?

What About Trends?

While searching for pilot ideas, some writers look at what's currently "hot" on TV and attempt to capitalize on the latest trend. For example: "Vampires are hugely popular; I'm going to dream up a vampire series!"

Three cautions here. First, as mentioned earlier, a shameless attempt to pander to the marketplace often looks like just that. Producers and agents read thousands of scripts. They see right through gimmicks and hype. They can tell when you're faking it. *Don't fake it*.

Second, by the time a trend becomes clear, it's already too late to join the bandwagon. If something's a hit, networks and studios instantly jump on it and develop more copies than will ever see the light of day. Your vampire pilot will be lucky to get noticed amidst the crush; it'll have to work *really* hard to stand out.

Third, when the trend inevitably burns out, your pilot will seem stale. Why invest time and effort into writing something with a short shelf life? Why not create a pilot that won't expire once everyone's moved on from vampires to zombies to whatever's next?

Don't follow a trend. *Start* one.

What's My Franchise?

The next step in developing your pilot idea is to choose/identify your *series franchise*. What's the engine that drives your series? What's the primary story-generator? In short, what the heck will everybody be *doing* week to week?

Usually, the franchise refers to the occupations of the main characters. The three top TV drama franchises are cops, lawyers, and doctors. (And *cops* can be broadly defined to include "any crime-solver with a gun, badge, or license," such as FBI agents and private detectives.)

Why are these three franchises so perennially popular? Several reasons:

- **They deal with life-or-death situations.** Will a murderer be caught and convicted? Will a patient be saved?

Drama, conflict, and suspense are inherent in each franchise.

- **There's a built-in supply of stories.** Crimes are constantly committed. Cases constantly go to trial. Illnesses and accidents constantly strike. The writers don't have to concoct ways to involve the protagonists with each week's story; stories come to the protagonists instead of the other way around.

- **Each franchise is open-ended.** The job's never finished; there's always another problem on the way.

Cops, lawyers, and doctors date back to the beginning of television. A fourth franchise that's become popular is what I'd call *survivors,* in which the characters' primary goal is simply to stay alive in a hostile (often postapocalyptic or postinvasion) environment. Some examples: *Revolution, Lost, The Walking Dead, Falling Skies.*

But not all franchises deal with life-and-death subject matter. Look at *Glee* and *The Secret Life of the American Teenager,* where the franchise is high school . . . or *Parenthood* and *Downton Abbey,* where the franchise is family conflict . . . or *The Newsroom,* where the franchise is right there in the title.

The measure of a good franchise isn't how "big" or "significant" it is, but *how well it propels the series as a source of stories.*

The corollary: A not-so-good franchise is one that doesn't generate a whole lot of stories. For instance, I doubt that a drama series set in, say, an accounting firm would work, simply because I can't imagine very many compelling stories springing from an accounting firm.

You disagree? You have a terrific idea for a drama set in an accounting firm? Excellent! Go write it and prove me wrong . . . and I'm not being sarcastic. I was almost as skeptical about the franchise "a Madison Avenue advertising agency in the sixties" . . . yet, at this writing, the multiple-Emmy winning *Mad Men* is entering its sixth season.

The moral of the story? A good franchise is important, but what's more important is what you *do* with it, which leads to the next question.

What's My Premise?

Time to zero in on whatever it is that *makes your series unique* . . . your personal "take" on the franchise. We'll call it your *series premise*.

Ideally, your premise should be "pitchable" in a simple sentence or two (the *one-line* or *logline*)—clear, concise, and catchy. It answers the question "How does *your* cop (or whatever) show differ from the nine billion cop (or whatever) shows already out there?"

For example, let's start with a franchise: *cops*. Specifically, *detectives*.

Let's narrow the franchise further: *civilian detectives*. Further still: *amateur detectives*.

Now, here's an idea using the *amateur detectives* franchise: *A writer of murder mystery novels helps the police solve actual murder cases.*

Is that a premise? No, not yet . . . because it's not unique. It could describe the Ellery Queen novels and TV series adaptation as well as the long-running series *Murder, She Wrote.*

So let's give that idea a very specific take: *A male writer of murder mystery novels teams up with a female NYPD homicide detective to solve actual murders; they butt heads at first but develop a partnership, friendship, and romance.*

That's the premise of *Castle*, currently in its fifth season. Anything new about the franchise? Nope. Any new elements in the premise? Not really . . . "murder-solving novelist" isn't new, nor is "female homicide detective," nor is "male and female lead characters who don't initially hit it off but slowly find romance." The novelty is in the mix, not the ingredients.

What's the recipe that'll make *your* pilot unique?

What Are My Arcs?

The *arcs* of a TV series are the story lines that continue across episodes.

In a series with a strong overall arc, the episodes are like chapters in a book. They're not meant to be viewed individually or out of order, but sequentially as parts of one long story.

Conversely, in a series with zero arcs, each episode is a pure "stand-alone" with a self-contained story. Episodes can be viewed in any order.

Few series are either 100 percent arc or 0 percent arc. "Non-arc" shows generally portray *some* character changes over the life of the series, often in the characters' romantic relationships. "Heavy" arc shows usually structure each episode with *some* dramatic payoff, either to one aspect of the ongoing plot or to a smaller story self-contained in the episode.

Most drama series today blend arc and non-arc elements. Let's look at *Castle* again. It's non-arc in that there's a new murder each week that the regular characters solve by the end of the episode. But it also contains arcs dealing with the unsolved murder of Beckett's mother as well as the slow-blooming romance between the leads.

A "semi-arc" series like *Castle* shoots for the best of both worlds. Its stand-alone episodes can be enjoyed individually, even by a new viewer who knows nothing about the show. At the same time, its arcs allow the writers to develop characters, evolve relationships, tell more intricate stories, create suspense, and keep long-term fans hooked.

You may be thinking, *Hold on. I'm just writing a pilot here, for a series that'll be semi-arc at most. Do I need to figure out every last detail of my show's arcs in advance and set them all up in my pilot?*

Relax; you don't need to do that. However, you might want to give thought to possible arcs for your series as well as possible episode ideas; doing so will help you figure out what your series is about, and that in turn will help you map out your pilot.

If a particular arc has a grabber of a beginning that's too good not to include in your pilot, then put it in! But if it's merely backstory—planting seeds that won't sprout until later—don't include it just for the sake of completeness.

You can also *hint* at an arc to follow. In the *Castle* pilot, Castle intuits that Beckett has a traumatic, unsolved crime in her past, but we don't learn the specifics until episode 5, and the arc doesn't kick into high gear until several episodes later. Castle's discovery in the pilot adds depth and motivation to Beckett's character—worthwhile even if the series never followed it up. But it also teases the audience with the notion that Beckett's mystery may get explored later in the series.

How much does *your* series arc, and how much of that arc do you need to plant in your pilot?

Are There One Hundred Episodes in My Series?

Network executives frequently ask during TV series pitches, "Does this show have a hundred episodes in it?"

A bit of history: In the Olden Days of Television, a series usually wasn't profitable for its producing studio until it had made one hundred episodes. A series with fewer episodes than that was far less lucrative in the syndicated TV market, because shows in syndicated reruns often aired five times a week. One hundred episodes would last for twenty weeks without a repeat, but a show canceled after twenty-four episodes wouldn't even last five weeks.

The first-run and syndication markets have changed drastically since then, so the hundred-episode benchmark is now neither as significant nor as accurate; eighty-eight is a more frequently heard "magic number" today. But regardless of the number, the underlying question is the same: *What is the natural lifespan of your series?* Is it a rich enough franchise and a solid enough premise to generate several seasons' worth of episodes, or will it run out of steam after a season or two?

Don't fret; nobody's expecting a list of all one hundred stories. And many series concepts are inherently so prolific that the question's easily answered. (The *Law and Order* "ripped from the headlines"–type shows won't run out of stories as long as there are headlines.)

But there are plenty of series concepts where it isn't immediately obvious how (or if!) the show will yield a hundred episodes. For that matter, there are pilots out there that deliver excellent writing, intriguing characters, and compelling drama—but give little or no clue what the series will be like over the next six episodes, much less a hundred.

Here's one way to test the "longevity" of your series premise. Set aside an hour and brainstorm episode ideas. Nothing fancy, nothing elaborate—just simple, one-line concepts. Don't worry if they're any good. Don't worry if they're original. (In fact, *go* for the "obvious" stories. Our brains often need to churn out all the obvious ideas before they can get to the less-obvious ones. Besides, an "obvious" idea might freshen right up with a little mix-and-match . . . later.)

Just come up with as many "story starters" as you possibly can. For example, let's say the series premise is "humans establish a colony on a distant planet." Off the top of my head:

- Severe drought. Crops die. Food rationed. Tensions mount.

- Second ship brings more colonists. Our colonists, already struggling, don't want them.

- Colonist is murdered. Colony splits over what to do with alleged murderer.

- Discover that the "uninhabited" planet isn't. Alien life forms pop up and say "go away."

- Scientist claims planet's sun is about to go nova. All must evacuate. Most don't believe and refuse.

- Plague lays most colonists low. Healthy few are over-worked, overstressed.

- Alien shape-shifter invades colony.

- Evil megacorporation "buys" planet, wants to evict colonists.

- Interstellar war breaks out; planet is in a strategic location; colonists want to stay neutral but are pressured to take sides.

- Colony strikes "oil" or equivalent; everyone becomes rich.

- Alien bacteria in water supply alters colonists' behavior. All turn violent. Or . . . all lose inhibitions. Some get violent, some get romantic, etc.

- Colonists discover (too late) that an alien plant is a highly addictive drug.

And so forth. Yes, they're vague, obvious, derivative, you name it; that's not the point. The point is that in less than ten minutes, I was able to spit out a dozen of them—and, good or bad, any of them could be hammered into a workable episode. This indicates that the premise has "legs."

Let's try the same exercise on another premise: "An elite squad of mountaineering rangers patrols Rocky Mountain National Park." Hmm. Well . . .

- Squad performs thrilling rescue of a stranded mountain climber.

- Squad must find and rescue lost climber/hiker before nightfall/freezing temperatures.

- Squad deals with avalanche.

- Small plane crashes into mountain; squad must find/ rescue.

Dunno about you, but I'm already struggling. How many variations are there on "daring mountainside rescue"? I can't see twenty episodes here, much less a hundred . . . and if this premise went to series, I suspect it would soon get radically changed to "open it up" for more stories. ("Squad encounters Bigfoot! Squad finds lost city of Shangri-la! Squad gets transferred to Malibu to become surfer lifeguards!")

See how many episode notions you can come up with for *your* series. If you can't hit double digits within an hour, take a second look at your premise to see what's holding you back.

Who Are My Characters?

Pilots live or die by their characters, because so does television. Series characters become family. You invite them into your home each week; you care about their conflicts. You don't necessarily have to like them—a depraved villain can be just as fascinating as an upright hero—but you *must* want to see what they do next.

Strong, distinctive, quirky, recognizable, surprising, watchable characters will keep an audience solidly hooked even if the stories are overly familiar or weakly plotted. Fresh, unique characters make old stories new again—because even if we've seen a particular plot a hundred times, we'll still be interested to see how it will affect *these specific people.*

This is why, for example, the "oddball detective" genre stays popular. By and large, the audience doesn't tune in to see what clever clues and intricate mysteries the writers concoct every week; they tune in for the fun of watching that particular detective solve the case in his/her own inimitable fashion.

(Here's a thought experiment: take a mystery plot—any mystery plot—from any show at random. Now imagine that same plot as an episode on other detective shows—*Castle, Elementary, Monk, Bones, Columbo, Psych*—pick your favorites. Same crime, same clues, same solution—yet the resulting episodes would be as diverse as their protagonists.)

Your characters are the most important ingredient in your mix-and-match. Bring them to life. Make them demand our attention. Make us believe in them and *care* about them—and you're halfway home.

How Do I Develop Characters?

There's a school of thought that says before you can write your characters, you must know their backstories inside and out. Some people suggest you fill out character sheets listing their family histories, places they've lived, college majors, political leanings, religious affiliations, employment histories, favorite foods, books, music, clothes, pets . . . you name it.

Try it. If it works for you, great!

But it's not the only way to bring your characters to life. Personally, I don't find that assembling a long list of facts helps me know my characters any better, and here's why:

I'm writing television. Unlike a novelist, I can't get into my characters' heads (well, not unless we hear their thoughts in voice-over, and that gets old fast). In a script, I can only describe what a character says and does. As a result, when I create characters, I focus on just that: what they'll say and do in a given situation.

Example: Let's create a character named Sam. A lawyer, age thirty, single. First scene in our hypothetical pilot: Sam comes home to a modest downtown apartment in a big city, drops briefcase on sofa, kicks off shoes, and pours himself a drink. (Sam's just been ignominiously fired from the law firm, but we don't want to reveal that until a later scene.)

You ask, "What does Sam drink? Beer, wine, whiskey? And what brand?" I respond, "Well . . . does it matter what Sam drinks? Do we get much insight into Sam by knowing the beverage and the brand? I'm more curious about *how* Sam drinks. For instance, let's try it two ways. . . ."

Sam enters kitchen. Opens a wine refrigerator full of bottles. Looks them over judiciously. Carefully removes an expensive vintage from a lower shelf. Opens it with a corkscrew—and takes a long, deep swig right from the bottle.

Or flip it around: Sam enters kitchen. Takes crystal wineglass from cupboard. Notices spot on glass; meticulously wipes it clean. Opens wine refrigerator. It's empty. Opens regular refrigerator. Nothing but milk, eggs, leftover takeout boxes. Rummages in pantry; finds a tiny airline-size bottle, opens screw top, pours red wine into glass. Swirls wine in glass, holds it up, eyes its color, gives it a sniff. Looks out window, raises glass to city skyline in a silent toast. Takes a sip, savors it, swallows.

Two variations on the same basic scene: Sam drinks red wine. However, describing *how* Sam drinks (not just *what* Sam drinks) gives us different insights into the character.

Another method of creating distinctive characters: Think of real-life people—friends, family, acquaintances, or even people you've only encountered once. Who sticks in your mind? Who among them could you write into a scene?

For example, maybe you've got a distant cousin you rarely see but vividly recall because she's so gleefully outspoken; she'll say anything to anyone, and usually does. Sometimes you wish you had her devil-may-care fearlessness; other times you wish she'd grow up.

Now drop your cousin into situations and imagine how she'd respond. Some jerk yells catcalls at her? She'd verbally cut him to ribbons. Some bureaucrat tries to wrap her in red tape? She'd stand on his desk and become such a pest that she'd get her way. She's supposed to say a few brief words at a funeral? She'd deliver an honest, impromptu eulogy both hilarious and touching.

And even though you may not know much about your cousin—her college major or her favorite music or what jobs she's had—it doesn't matter. You can imagine her speech and behavior well enough to write her in any of those scenes, and they'd be entertaining to watch. Despite not knowing the underlying psychological reasons why she's the way she is, you can picture what she'd say and do in various contexts.

When you need an outspoken character, imagine your cousin—or, more precisely, those facets of your cousin's behavior that you can transplant onto your character. They may be vastly different people—your cousin might be young, skinny, tattooed, and blue-collar, whereas your character might be male, white-collar, gay, whatever—but if they have similar *attitudes and actions,* thinking about your cousin will help you bring your character to life.

Help! My Characters Are Flat!

We talk of making our characters "real" and "rounded" so that they "pop off the page." One way of doing that is to acknowledge that people have many sides and many personas; they're never just one thing. Writing simplistic stereotypes does your characters and the audience a disservice.

You can combat this by considering your character's traits—and adding a *but* to each. Fred's a corrupt, greedy politician—*but* he genuinely loves his family and would die to protect them. Kristin's a shy, introverted lab technician—*but* she writes steamy erotic fan fiction under a pseudonym. Yoshi's a vegan and a peace activist—*but* she becomes dangerously aggressive behind the wheel of a car.

People are complicated. Characters shouldn't be one-note.

Even your most minor character should be distinctive. Any character important enough to speak is important enough to give a personality and an attitude. Generic characters are dull characters.

Every interaction between two characters, no matter how small, presents an opportunity to reveal new information about them both. Why squander those opportunities?

Let's return to Sam, our laid-off lawyer. Later in our pilot, Sam goes to a bar to meet a potential (and desperately needed) new client, who never shows up. While waiting, Sam has too many drinks, which leads to a stupid move by Sam in the following scene.

The bar scene could start like this:

Sam sits at the bar. A BARTENDER asks, "What can I get you?" Sam replies, "Scotch. Straight up." Bartender: "Right away."

Quick, simple, and utterly boring. It's the sort of bland setup scene that gets edited out after the first rough cut. Try it this way instead:

Sam sits at the bar. The bartender—BRIANNA, 40ish, friendly—grins. "Sam! Long time. How goes the ambulance chasing? You want coffee? I'll start a fresh pot." Sam barely looks at her: "Scotch. Straight up." Brianna's taken aback: "You sure?" Sam repeats, "Scotch. Straight up." Brianna shrugs, heads to the well. "Comin' up."

Yes, it's longer, and it's still a nonessential scene we might trim out later—but at least the bartender's now a character instead of a prop, and we imply that Sam used to be on the wagon but has now fallen off.

Drama is about characters—their goals, challenges, virtues, and flaws. Richer characters make richer drama.

Premise or Nonpremise Pilot?

You've got a solid franchise, an intriguing premise, an overview of your show's arcs, and some fascinating characters. Now you need to decide if your pilot will be a *premise pilot*.

A premise pilot explains how the series premise gets started. It's your show's origin story: How the Superhero Got His/Her Powers . . . or How All These People Crash-Landed on This Island . . . or How a Nerdy Salesman Began a Life of Espionage and Adventure . . . or How Holmes and Watson Met and Became a Team.

If it must be the first episode aired because it sets up all the others, it's a premise pilot.

In contrast, a *nonpremise pilot*, also called a *prototype pilot*, doesn't delve into origins; instead, it's a typical episode of the series, with the franchise, premise, and characters already up and running. It doesn't have to air first; it could just as easily be episode 3 or 4 or 6 or 8.

There are huge advantages to writing a nonpremise pilot. Because a premise pilot is busily setting up the series, it isn't a representative episode of the show. By jumping right in, a nonpremise pilot is a much better sample of the series.

Moreover, premise pilots are often less interesting than what follows. They're like driving to Disneyland: No matter how entertaining the journey might be, the *real* fun doesn't begin until we arrive. In a nonpremise pilot, we're already there, riding Space Mountain.

Ask yourself, "What's the heart of my show? What's the fun, the 'good stuff' that my audience will tune in to see every week? And in my pilot, when does that good stuff start?"

If the good stuff doesn't start until the end of your pilot—or, worse still, episode 2—rethink your pilot.

If your pilot *must* be a premise pilot, *get to the good stuff as soon as you can.*

Don't sneak up on it. Don't obsess about the setup. Don't feel you have to introduce every single character before the fun starts. If your pilot story kicks off the series by turning your main character's world upside down, spend *as little time as possible* setting up the character's ordinary, right-side-up world.

Cut to the chase. The best way to do that is to write a nonpremise pilot. The second-best way is to write a premise pilot with *absolute minimal setup*. If it's a fish-out-of-water pilot, get your fish out of the water *fast*.

Time to write!

Okay, I'm Writing. Any Tips?

Well done! You've got your premise and your characters firmly in hand and you're writing away. A few suggestions:

- **Reread chapters 1 and 2.** Plotting a story and writing a teleplay are the same processes whether it's your own series or someone else's, so I won't repeat what's been so ably covered already. Well, actually, I'm lying, because I am going to repeat *one* thing from chapter 2:

- **Rewrite.** Rewrite, rewrite, rewrite. Get plenty of feedback, take what's useful, and make your script better. Resist the temptation to send it out when you know it still needs "a little polishing." Your scripts are your calling cards. Don't be sloppy. *Get them right.* The following chapter, "Revising One-Hour Drama Specs and Pilots," will give you strategies the pros use to improve their scripts. And speaking of feedback:

- **Have fresh eyes read your teleplay.** I would hope you have several trusted "beta readers"—fellow writers willing to read your work and give you clear, honest reactions. Perhaps you'll invite a few to help you break your pilot story; perhaps you'll run your outline past them as well. My advice: Keep one or two of your beta readers out of the process until the teleplay stage; their feedback will be much more useful if they know nothing whatsoever about your series before they read your pilot script.

- **Come up with a great title.** It's the first thing readers see when they pick up your script. Put some effort into it. A distinctive title that grabs attention is much better than a generic title that could apply to a thousand other works. Short, sweet, and intriguing is also better than long and on-the-nose. (For the series *Justified*, I'll bet titles like *Raylan Givens, US Marshal,* and *Deputy Givens,* and *My Old Kentucky Home* were considered and discarded. The show's working title, by the way, was *Lawman*.)

Conclusion

An episodic spec shows that your writing is professional . . . and a pilot shows that your writing is *unique.*

Be unique. Be bold. Be passionate. Be original. Above all, *be yourself.*

In the writers' room, once a story's been broken and an outline's been network-approved and a writer's being sent off to write a teleplay, the showrunner's parting advice invariably includes the suggestion to "have fun with it!"

Fun? thinks the writer. *We're over budget and behind schedule; the story break was rushed and the outline's got problems; I've got to grind out a teleplay in less than a week—and I'm supposed to have* fun *with it?*

Well . . . yes! When you're slogging through a recalcitrant act 2, it's easy to lose sight of the fact that you're *creating a television show*! Telling stories, concocting plots, giving birth to characters, spinning worlds of make-believe—it *should* be fun, shouldn't it?

Therefore, my parting advice to *you,* fellow writer, is to work hard, get it right . . . but at the same time, don't forget to . . .

"Have fun with it!"

CHAPTER 4

Revising One-Hour Drama Specs and Pilots

by Matt Witten

So you've finished your first draft and even done some rewriting. Mazel tov! My advice to you now is:

Don't change a word! It's perfect!

Just kidding. The only TV writer who does perfect first drafts is David E. Kelley, who created *Ally McBeal, Boston Legal, Harry's Law,* and a zillion other TV shows. Not only that, he's married to one of the world's most gorgeous women. And if that weren't annoying enough, he's reputed to be a nice guy.

But for the rest of us mere mortals, life doesn't work that way. In my ten years of writing for TV shows like *House M.D., Law and Order,* and *Pretty Little Liars,* I've never seen a first draft that didn't need revising. I've seen very talented writers turn in dreck. I've done it myself. So join the party!

My serious advice, which I've given to hundreds of students at UCLA Extension, is: Do take a moment to pat yourself on the back. You've written a complete draft. The world is full of people who call themselves writers but don't write. You, however, are now officially a writer (definition of *writer:* one who writes). Finishing a draft of an hour-long show isn't easy, as you're fully aware at this point, but you've done it.

Now what?

I'm going to give you twenty-seven suggestions. The first six are about process—how to prep yourself and think your script through before you even sit down at your computer. The next twenty-one are nitty-gritty suggestions to guide you during the actual rewriting.

The Writer's Process *Before* Rewriting

These six suggestions are fundamentally about ways to help you get a new perspective on your script.

1. Take a Break

Put your first draft aside for a while. You want to come back to it fresh. Otherwise, you'll find yourself spending hours debating whether or not to delete a comma. You won't be able to look with a new perspective at the larger issues in the script. Some people need only a day for their brains to rest; others need a week. Give yourself as much time as feels right.

On the other hand, some of my Writers' Program students have been procrastinators who have trouble finishing things. If that's true of you, then I strongly suggest that you don't wait longer than two weeks, because you might lose your momentum. Get yourself back to the computer. Turn off the Internet. Turn on some Encouraging Music.

2. Get Feedback

Imbibe other people's fresh perspectives. You're looking for folks you can trust to be honest about what's not working. Ideally, they're writers too, or they have experience critiquing writing, or some related experience like acting or directing. But good advice can come from anywhere. One of my best readers is a friend of my wife who's never worked in the entertainment biz but happens to be smart, watches a lot of TV, and doesn't worry about hurting my feelings. (In fact, she seems to enjoy it!)

Give your script to friends and acquaintances to read. Invite them over for pizza and have them read your script aloud. Read it out loud yourself, from beginning to end, and to a loved one (again, if you trust him to be honest). Bring your script to your writers' group. Give your script to a writer who's more experienced than you.

You don't have to do all these things, obviously. But do at least two of them; that will probably be sufficient. Your goal is to attain a clear enough understanding of the problems in the script so that you'll be propelled and compelled to go back to your computer. Sometimes having just one insightful, simpatico reader will do the trick. She'll say, "You know, your main character doesn't seem all that active," and suddenly the light will go off in your head and you'll be ready to rewrite immediately.

When you get feedback that seems inane, don't respond immediately. Don't defend yourself or your script. Take a deep breath. Try to hear what your critiquers are really saying. Maybe if they keep talking, they'll say it in a way you understand better. Or maybe you won't get it right away, but tonight, when you're in the middle of brushing your teeth, it'll start to make sense.

If somebody says something in your script doesn't seem real, don't respond as a colleague of mine at *Law and Order* did to the head writer: "But it *is* real! I read it in *The New Yorker*!" For this response, the writer got fired. To quote an old aphorism, "Reality is not a defense for drama." If something doesn't *feel* real, then it doesn't matter if it is real.

Everybody has his own style of giving comments. One person might say, "I think the script could use a little cutting," and it means he thinks you need to cut a quarter of a page in act 3. Somebody else—like my TV writer friend Laurie, who is so nice that she tries to sugarcoat things— might say the exact same words and mean she thinks your script is an utter bore and you should ditch half the darn thing. It's incumbent upon you to probe a little and get your critiquers to be as specific as they can.

Be alert to people's biases. For instance, if you've written a great script about zombies and you give it to me, I'll hate it. Sure, I'll try to be objective, but I'll bet even if it were the best script ever written in the history of television, I'd still hate it. Zombies? Who needs 'em? You want to show your script to people who are on your wavelength.

Often critiquers, especially inexperienced ones, will offer solutions without clearly stating problems. Someone will say something totally out of left field, like, "How about if the main character's love interest has really bad PMS? Or maybe she's a dwarf." Before you throw this person out of your house for offering aggravating non sequiturs, try to figure out where she's coming from. Maybe this comment is her ungainly way of saying the love interest is too utterly perfect to be believable.

Giving criticism is hard. It's intellectually challenging and emotionally fraught. Your critiquers are acutely aware, as are you, that by sharing your script with them, you've just pulled your pants down and revealed your most private parts. Try to make the process as easy on all of you as possible. Have some Cherry Garcia handy. Send your readers a thank-you e-mail afterward, or a gift certificate to iTunes—even to those who might have hated your draft. As long as your readers are being honest, that's all you can ask for.

3. Listen to Your Inner Voice

So here's a common scenario:

The writer, at dinner, asks her boyfriend, "I've been thinking about that scene on page eighteen. Do you think it really works?" Boyfriend, having heard this question at dinner every evening for the past two weeks and wanting to make her happy so he can get lucky that night, replies, "Yeah, I think so."

But the writer is only mollified momentarily. Later, as she's taking a walk through the neighborhood, that darn scene pops into her head again. She thinks about it while going to bed. The next morning there it is, like a chipped tooth. She may find herself saying, while she's alone in the car, "It's probably fine." "Joe says it's fine." "I think it's okay."

You know what? That scene doesn't work. If you have to keep trying to convince yourself something works—a scene, a character, a plot point, whatever—it almost certainly doesn't. Sorry. Go back to the drawing board.

4. Visualize Every Scene—and Every Character

The next time you're out walking or biking, or waiting in line at the supermarket, think about your script. Start on page 1 and visualize every scene. Say to yourself, "What's cool about this scene? Why would I enjoy seeing it on TV?" If you can't think of an answer, then you've got a problem you need to address.

Sometimes if you do this exercise, you'll find it takes you a minute to remember what scene comes next. Danger sign. The reason you couldn't remember it? It's a boring scene.

The flip side of this, the more positive aspect, is that you may find yourself saying, "Wow, I've got a lot of great scenes." You'll be energized to get back to your computer.

Another thing to try: Consider all your characters, one by one. Do they each have a unique voice? Are they in scenes that are entertaining or moving? In a story you enjoy? If you were an actor, would you love to play this character, or would it be just another paycheck?

5. Watch TV

If you're rewriting a spec of an existing show: Watch a few episodes. Yes, I know you've already watched a whole bunch. But now watch them again, or watch some new ones. Armed with the experience of writing a first draft, you'll watch the show you are specing in a more sophisticated way. You'll have whole new insights. You'll realize your character wouldn't really say some of the things you have him saying. You'll get inspired to add a new thematic element to your script.

If you're rewriting a spec pilot: Watch a few episodes, including pilots, of shows that are similar to yours. It will get you thinking afresh about tone and pace.

6. Stay Loose

Yes, rewriting a script can be stressful, but have fun too. Now that you've finished a first draft and the bones of your story are in place, you're free to explore. Take things to the limit. Instead of your characters kissing or shaking hands, let them have wild sex. Instead of people arguing verbally, have them whip out .357 Magnums and start shooting. Have your main character fall off the cliff and land on his head. See what happens.

Raymond Chandler said that sometimes when he was writing and wanted to shake things up, he'd have two guys burst through the door with six-guns; then later he would figure out who they were and what they were doing there. Get some of that spirit in your own process. If you're going too far, you can always pull back. Even if you keep only 3 percent of the wacky stuff you throw in there, it's time well spent. Let those brain juices flow.

And now . . .

The Nitty-Gritty of Rewriting

Okay, so you've taken a break, you've gotten feedback, and you've been thinking deep thoughts. Now it's time to get cracking! Here, as promised, are twenty-one practical suggestions that I share with my students—and use in my own rewriting process—for both specs and pilots.

1. If You're Rewriting the Same Scene Over and Over Again . . . Red Alert!

You have one scene, or one part of a scene, or one speech, that you keep rewriting over and over again. You know it's not quite working, but you figure if you get the dialogue just *perfect,* you'll be in business. Maybe if you change the word *that* to *this,* it will all come together. Or if your character says, "I love you, Joe," instead of "I love you," will that give your scene the resonance it needs? Or maybe if you cut that one sentence . . .

no, maybe it would be better to leave it in . . . no, maybe take it out . . . or maybe put it back in . . . no, maybe take it out . . .

Here's the reality. Speaking for myself and other professional writers I've consulted about this nasty phenomenon, nine times out of ten, if we're going nuts trying to fix a scene or a speech, obsessing over it endlessly, the problem isn't something that can be fixed with slightly better dialogue. The problem is more fundamental.

Maybe the plot point is wrong. The reason you're having so much trouble writing the scene where Sally leaves Joe is because it's not real. In reality, Sally wouldn't leave him. If you're writing a spec of *The Good Wife* in which Alicia and Eli have a one-nighter, and you're having trouble getting their romantic scene just right . . . Well, the reason you're having trouble is because those two characters would *never* get romantic together.

Maybe the tone is wrong. You're writing a spec of *Homeland,* and you interrupt a tense chase scene with some jokey stuff. But the scene's not working. Do you need to cut *all* the jokes? Or just some? Or what about *keeping* the jokes and getting rid of the chase?

My advice: Stop rewriting that cursed scene. Get up from the computer, take a long walk, and figure out the deeper problem. Which leads us to . . .

2. If the Scene Isn't Working, the Problem May Lie Earlier in the Script

You're writing a scene in which your lead character, a farmer, is deeply upset. He can't pay his mortgage and he's in danger of losing the farm that's been in his family for over a hundred years. Obviously an emotionally charged situation. You write the scene. You write his big heart-wrenching speech. You give it to friends to read.

And one by one, they tell you, "You know that scene where the farmer was upset about losing his farm? I didn't really care that much."

You're outraged. You tell your friends, "Are you kidding me? He's losing his farm! His home! His heritage! His whole sense of self! How can you not care?!"

Nevertheless, you trudge back to your computer. By God, this time you're going to bring tears to your readers' eyes. You rewrite the farmer's big speech. You rewrite it again. And again . . . and again . . . and again . . .

Then you give your new and improved script to another friend. He says, "You know that scene where the farmer was upset about losing his farm? I didn't really care that much."

You take to drink. You rage to your wife. You decide your friends are shallow idiots. And besides, they're city people. They've never lived on a farm. What the hell do they know?

But finally you storm back to the computer. You rewrite that goddamn speech . . . again . . . and again. . . .

You give the script to your one last friend who hasn't read it yet. And he says, "You know that scene where the farmer was upset about losing his farm? I didn't really care."

You can't take it anymore. Before he even finishes the sentence, you grab a bread knife. You stab your friend in the heart. You end up in prison—five to seven years for involuntary manslaughter. You get off with a light sentence because, luckily, your judge was an aspiring TV writer too, so he took pity on you.

Now that you're in prison, and sober, and with plenty of free time to look at your script with a new perspective, you realize what the problem was. There was actually nothing wrong with the scene. It was a darn good scene. And that speech was totally kick-ass. The problem was with what came *before* the scene—or what didn't come before.

You needed to have an earlier scene, or even two or three, where you showed the reader how deeply your farmer cherished his farm. A scene where the farmer, as a young boy, learned how to milk a cow from his beloved father. A scene where the farmer's eight-year-old daughter holds a newborn calf lovingly in her arms. A scene where the farmer promises his teenage son that no matter what happens, they'll always be okay; their family will never lose the farm.

Once your reader truly feels how invested this man is in his farm, she'll care if he's going to lose it.

Now, I realize the above scenario is hypothetical; most of you folks who are reading this are not currently in prison for a screenwriting-related crime. But in order to ensure that this tragic fate does not befall you: If a scene or a part of a scene isn't working, and you're starting to obsess over it, check to see if the problem lies earlier in the script. There's a good chance you'll discover your scene hasn't been set up properly.

3. Two Problems, One Solution: Bingo!

Any time you can take care of two or more problems with one solution, you can be pretty sure you're on the right track. Try not to look at your script problems in isolation, but as part of a whole.

For example: You're writing a spec of *Bones,* and you're having three problems. One: Your murder mystery isn't twisty enough. Two: Brennan is missing from act 3. Three: Brennan doesn't do anything superbrilliant in your spec. If you can come up with a solution in which Brennan figures out a cool, surprising clue in act 3 . . . then you'll have addressed three different problems in an elegant way, with one solution. I'll bet you fifty to one it will be the right solution.

I always keep this principle in mind when I'm rewriting: Can I come up with the solution for two or three problems at one stroke? It's a surprisingly accurate guide to what will ultimately work and what won't.

4. Look to Cut or Combine Characters

Do you have two characters with the same gestalt? The same attitude toward life? Do they root for the same baseball team and eat the same brand of chocolate? Then do your best to cut one of them. Or combine them.

The main reason for this is that these two characters will make your script feel a little repetitious and confusing. The reader will think, *Wait, did I see this guy already in act 1? Or was that some other guy?* Also, if two different characters express the same feelings in more or less the same way, the reader will lose interest. She's read that stuff already from one character; why does she need to see it repeated by somebody else?

Also, sometimes combining characters will help you make connections you didn't expect and add another layer to your script. So . . . in that spec pilot you're writing about the werewolf district attorney, you check your character list. You suddenly realize that the waitress who testified in court in act 1 feels very similar to the janitor in act 4 who cleans up the hairy, bloody mess the attorney made after he changed into a wolf. Now is a good time to wonder, if the waitress and the janitor were combined into *one character*, could she notice something in the mess—the attorney's necklace, say—that she also noticed in the act 1 scene? And could that lead to additional jeopardy that your attorney's big werewolf secret will be discovered?

If, for some reason, you feel that you absolutely can't cut or combine your two similar characters, then figure out a way to differentiate them. Change genders. Give somebody a limp. Make her a Zoroastrian.

5. Make Sure All of Your Main Characters Appear in Each Act

This is a rule—yes, I'd go so far as to call it a rule—many beginning TV writers break. Even seasoned professionals screw up on this sometimes. You have so many characters to think about that one of them slips through the cracks. I recall being in the writers' room at *Pretty Little Liars* at the end of a long day, and we were all feeling pretty good about the story we'd just broken and ready to go home—and then we suddenly discovered we'd forgotten to put Aria in acts 2 and 4. *Oops!*

This is an important rule, because out of sight is out of mind. Your reader will stop caring about the character if she's gone. Even worse, he may forget who the character is. Readers, and TV viewers, are fickle that way.

There are a few exceptions to this rule:

- Not every main character has to appear in your teaser.
  (Although your big star characters should.)

- Not every main character necessarily has to appear in your final act, especially if it's very short. Use your judgment. (And again, all your big star characters should appear here.)

- Sometimes you can get away with a semi-main character not appearing in one of your middle acts, if you have the other characters talking about him and thereby "keeping him alive," to use a cliché I've often heard in writers' rooms. However, this strategy is to be used judiciously. It's often not ideal.

There may be other exceptions that escape me at the moment. But again, as a general rule: Ideally, all of your main characters should appear in each act.

6. Make Sure All of Your Stories Progress in Each Act

You're rewriting your pilot about a sex-crazed but kind urologist from Mars who's eager to return to his home planet. In your A story, he's desperately trying to cure somebody's major urinary tract problem. You've got a B story where he's constructing a spacecraft out of an MRI machine. Your C story is about his attempted romance with a cute manicurist who finds him intriguing but thinks a right hand with eight fingers isn't sexy.

Go through your script. Make sure you've got something about each story in each act. As I said above: out of sight, out of mind. If the story disappears for too long, your reader will forget about it. She'll figure it must not be important. Then when the story reappears, she'll have trouble caring about it. All that brilliant, poignant writing about your urologist's longing for the manicurist in act 4 will go for naught if he hasn't been mooning for her in acts 2 and 3.

Not only should each story *appear* in each act, but ideally, it should move forward in each act. Stories are like sharks; if they don't move forward, they die.

Exceptions to these rules:

- Not every story has to appear in the teaser, especially if the teaser is short. (But the A story should be in the teaser.)

- Sometimes you can have a story end in the next-to-last act, especially if the last act is short, or if the A story in your last act is so suspenseful and page-turning that your reader would get frustrated if you pulled her away to waste time on some comic C story. Maybe your act 5 urinary tract operation is so thrilling the reader doesn't want to hear about any cute manicurists.

- Sometimes you have a story that's a "wraparound"—i.e., it wraps around the episode. It appears at the very beginning and the very end, but during the middle, maybe never. So for instance: Instead of doing a full-on B story about constructing a spaceship out of an MRI machine, maybe you just want to do a wraparound and show your hero working on the MRI machine at the very beginning and the very end.

By the way, this example may sound ridiculous to you. That's exactly how I feel about zombie shows!

7. Do a Pass for Each Character

One great way to do this: Sit down at your computer and read all of a single character's lines out loud. Don't read anything else; don't read the stage directions or the other characters' responses.

You want to make sure that in every scene, each character *wants* something from the other characters in the scene. That's fundamentally what makes for good drama—or comedy, for that matter. In *CSI: Miami,* when the CSIs are looking at clues together, they're not *just* looking at clues (at least, when the scenes are well written). Calleigh wants to get approval from Horatio, or Horatio wants Delko to focus on the job because he's been slacking off lately, or some other interpersonal *want* is happening.

As you read out loud, you'll also be able to hear if your character sounds too passive. Or if she repeats herself, saying basically the same thing in act 3 that she did in act 1. Or if she's just plain boring.

By the way, I've noticed over the years that when a character asks a lot of questions in a row, there's a good chance she's a passive character, existing mainly to illuminate the lives of others. My basic rule of thumb is that if a character asks three questions in a row, that's not necessarily bad, but it's a definite warning signal. Even if your character is a detective questioning a suspect, make sure she isn't just getting information and that her own unique personality, needs, and point of view are coming through.

8. Check Your "Act Outs"

When I use the term *act out,* I am referring to the last moment in an act. (Some writers use this term in referring to the last scene in an act.) Regardless of what definition you prefer, the key ingredient of a good act out is: Stuff gets worse.

Usually stuff is getting worse for one or more of our heroes. This is not always true; for instance, the act out to act 1 of *Law and Order* was almost always that our heroes busted somebody. So stuff got worse for the suspect.

But in general, since we care most about our main characters, you want stuff to be getting worse for one or more of them. If you're writing an *In Plain Sight* spec: Mary Shannon is in charge of transporting a deranged serial killer to prison—and he escapes. Or you're writing a pilot about a caring surgeon who just got married—and at the end of act 1, he discovers his new bride is secretly a vampire. Or a Republican. Stuff is getting worse.

Another way I've heard people define a killer act out is, "Everything the TV viewer thought he knew is suddenly turned upside down." This type of act out is most often found at around the halfway mark of a show. Your surgeon hero discovers his wife is not only a vampire and a Republican, but she's also secretly smuggling rare man-eating Tasmanian tulips into the US. Now there's an act out.

A more serious version of a world-turned-upside-down act out: Your hero discovers his happy marriage of twenty years is a sham when he comes home and his wife has cleared out all her stuff and disappeared, leaving behind only a short note on the bedroom pillow.

It's not an absolute requirement, but if you have one act out where the world suddenly turns upside down, it will help your script tremendously.

By the way: The one TV show that doesn't follow the normal conventions on act outs is *Mad Men*. That's a whole other kettle of fish. If you can write as well as Matt Weiner, feel free to write any act out you want. You can end your act with a close-up of a glass of milk and it will somehow be absolutely perfect.

But if you're not Matt Weiner, remember: Stuff gets worse, usually for your heroes.

9. Take an "Emotional Juice" Pass

Read your script. Have you gotten as much emotional juice as you can out of every scene? Are your characters saying things that would get more of an emotional wallop if they kept quiet and just communicated with a look? Conversely, are they *not* saying things that, if they did, would give your reader an emotional jolt?

Don't get corny, of course, but don't leave anything on the table. If there's a scene where you might be able to make the audience cry . . . go for it! In the writers' room at *Women's Murder Club,* with every episode we'd ask each other, "Where's the scene where the music swells and the audience gets teary eyed?" Even on *Law and Order,* a much grittier show, we'd often ask ourselves the same thing.

10. Take a "Fun" Pass

Read your script. Are you missing any opportunities for more fun? Could you take the comedy a little farther?

11. Take a "Long Speech" Pass

Go through your script and look at any speech over three sentences long. Chances are good that a lot of them would be better if they were shorter.

12. Change Up Your Writing Habits

As you do your rewrite, you want to stay fresh and keep looking at your script from new perspectives. An easy, painless strategy for achieving this is simply to write in a different way. A friend of mine who wrote for *CSI: Miami* did his first drafts at a desk and his second drafts sitting in an easy chair. Another friend who worked on *House* did first drafts in the morning and afternoon, but generally did rewrites at night.

I am currently revising an ABC Family pilot, and I'm using a pink pen as a way to access my inner teenage girl. Hey, whatever works! So if you did your first draft on your computer, try doing some of your rewriting longhand. If you customarily write at home, hit Starbucks. If you usually listen to Miles Davis while you write, switch to Adele. All of these things—posture, time of day, surroundings, music—will change the way you think.

13. Check for Scenes That Can Be Tossed

Are there any scenes that don't add much? If so, bye-bye, scene. Even if the scene is well written, if it doesn't move your story forward and/or illuminate your characters in an exciting way, cut it. Keep the show moving.

To quote Elmore Leonard, "Try to leave out the part the readers tend to skip."

14. Check for Cuts at the Beginning and End of Each Scene

Look at each scene. Would it work just as well if you cut the first couple of lines? How about the last couple of lines?

The basic rule to follow is to get into the scene as late as possible and get out as early as possible. That way, you'll keep your show clipping along at a fast pace.

15. If You're Writing a Spec Pilot, Make Sure Your Descriptions of the Continuing Characters Are Colorful

You want your reader to *get* your characters instantly and be intrigued by them. So when you introduce a character for the first time, describe him in a way that makes him come to life immediately. Hit your reader with both barrels. For instance, here's the initial description of Byron, Aria's father, in the pilot script of *Pretty Little Liars:* "Aging well, he's the handsome professor that the college girls on campus all talk about when they get drunk and horny." Marlene King, who wrote the pilot, could simply have described Byron as "a good-looking professor." Instead she had fun and made the character and the milieu vivid.

(But please, please—here comes my pet peeve—don't write "Men want to be like him, and women want to be with him." I've read versions of this in five thousand different pilots, at least. When I read it now, I don't know whether to laugh or puke.)

One other thing: remember to type each character's name in all capital letters the first time she appears. This way your reader will pay closer attention. And when your character reappears an act later, your reader will be more likely to remember who she is.

16. Check for Pages with No Stage Directions

I started out as a playwright. Like most playwrights, I was very spare with my stage directions. I'd write whole pages with nothing but dialogue. But when I switched to TV writing, I learned that doesn't always fly. If you have a whole page with no screen directions on it, just dialogue, it looks funky to some people. If I'm your reader, it won't bother me. But somebody else—like Stephen Zito, who was the showrunner at *JAG* for most of its run—will be bothered by the lack of stage directions. So my advice is, play it safe. If you have a page of dialogue with no screen directions, then throw in a screen direction or two.

17. Get Your Script the Right Length

"What is the right length?" you ask. I know you're asking, because all my students, without exception, have wanted to know the answer to this question.

For a spec pilot, shoot for fifty-three to sixty-four pages. Ideally, sixty or fewer. If your script is under fifty-three or over sixty-four, your reader will have a quick hit of negativity before she even starts reading. It's not a deal breaker, but still.

For an episode of an existing show, shoot for fifty-one to sixty pages. Ideally, fifty-two to fifty-nine.

By the way, different shows have different script lengths. I once wrote a script for *JAG* that was seventy pages long. But the episode came in on time because it had a lot of airplane action, and some of those pages took under twelve seconds of screen time. On the other hand, when I wrote for *Supernatural,* the head writer wanted the scripts to come in at forty-two to forty-four pages. *Supernatural* had a lot of slow, spooky scenes, and also a lot of music between lines of dialogue, so that number of pages turned out to be just right.

Most shows have scripts that run from fifty-one to sixty. Possibly there are shows on the air right now with forty-two-page scripts, though I'm not aware of any. Even so, I wouldn't write a forty-two-page spec for any of those shows. Most of your readers won't realize forty-two is actually the right number, and they'll think you messed up.

So now, what do you do if your script is too long?

The best option, by far: Cut!

Sometimes students ask me if it's okay to screw around with the margins. I'm not a fan of this strategy. For one thing, it makes the script look cramped and a little funky. If your script has half-inch margins at the top and bottom, or your dialogue keeps going an inch farther to the right, I believe the reader will sense something is off, even if he doesn't consciously notice it. Each page will take a little too long to read, and the script will seem slightly boring in consequence.

I don't mean to sound too dogmatic about this. If my script has a "widow"—a page at the end of an act with just one or two lines on it—then I'm not above futzing with the margins.

But don't overdo. Cut!

18. Get Your Acts the Right Length

And now you ask, what's the right length for an act?

Just don't make them too short. Don't have any acts that are shorter than six pages—except for the teaser (if you have a teaser) and possibly the last act.

If you're writing a spec episode of an existing show: Copy the act lengths of the scripts you've read, give or take two or three pages.

If you're writing a spec pilot: Pilots often have very long first acts, even as long as twenty-three pages. That's because the first acts of pilots have a lot of work to do. They have to set up the A story for the episode, set up the basic idea for the series, and establish the main characters. So if your first act is running long, don't sweat it too much. Do try to hold it down to twenty pages, if you can.

19. If You're Writing a Spec Episode of an Existing Show: Copy Minor Style Points

It's possible that some of the folks who read your script will have read actual episodes of the show. So copy the ways that the staff writers do things. It will make your script feel a little more professional to these folks. You don't have to copy every tiny detail obsessively. But if they have SMASH TO BLACK at the end of each act, then what the heck, you might as well write SMASH TO BLACK too.

20. Proofread for Spelling, Punctuation, and Grammar

Okay, I confess. I'm shallow. If somebody gives me a script and it's missing commas, or the writer uses the word *lay* in a screen direction when it should be *lie,* I instantly think worse of the script. I won't necessarily say the script has a strike against it, but it definitely has one-tenth of a strike against it.

I'm aware that some of the greatest writers in the world can't spell worth a darn. I actually try not to care about spelling and grammar. But I can't help myself.

And everybody else cares about this stuff too.

Before you turn in your script, proofread it. Even better: Have a trusted friend proofread it. Offer to wash his or her car in return.

21. When You Are Finished, Stop

Okay, so now the million-dollar question: How do you know when you're finished?

Actually, according to an old saying, "art is never finished, only abandoned."

Speaking for myself, I know I'm finished when I look at the changes I made the day before and realize that half of them, or more than half, are no good, so I change them back.

I'd say when you hit that point with your script . . . you're done! Once again: Mazel tov! Congratulations for completing your rewrite!

And now, as a special bonus, I am going to give you one more piece of advice.

Now that you've finished your rewrite, put it in a drawer for a few days.

Don't give it to your important contacts—your uncle whose new wife is an ICM agent, your old friend from high school who works for Greg Berlanti—just yet. Don't submit it to that major contest. Sit on it.

Because if you do give it to these folks right away, you may find that in a few days, you suddenly realize there's something you wanted to change. And then you'll feel tortured: Should I send my new draft to the agent and tell her not to read the old draft, or does that make me look unprofessional? Bottom line, it does look a little unprofessional, but you'll probably do it anyway, after spending three hours trying to figure out how to word the e-mail properly. And then you'll kick yourself about the whole thing.

And don't just sit on your rewrite; give it to a couple of people to read. People who didn't read your first draft, so they can come to it fresh. See what they have to say. You may decide you want to do another rewrite.

I know it's hard—you're probably kind of sick of your script at this point—but hang in there and take one more pass at it. After all, you don't want your script to be "okay." You don't want it to be "pretty good." You want it to be . . .

Freaking great!

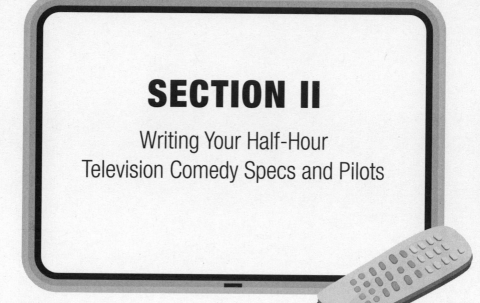

SECTION II

Writing Your Half-Hour Television Comedy Specs and Pilots

CHAPTER 5

Writing the On-Air Half-Hour Comedy Spec: The Story and Outline

by Julie Chambers and David Chambers

Writing a great spec script for a show that is currently on the air is an absolutely necessary component for getting into the world of television comedy. It's the way you say, "I'm interested in writing television for a living, I'm good at it, and here's the proof." It's your calling card.

What exactly is a spec script? It's a script that no one is paying you to write, but you're writing it on your own to prove you're good enough to be paid to write. It is written not for money, but on speculation, hence the term *spec script*. And the key to a successful spec is first to put together a strong, well-worked-out story, and then to lay it out, in outline form, scene by scene and event by event *before* you start writing.

Lining up your story is, in the opinion of everyone we know who has ever written for television, called the "heavy lifting." Network and studio executives have actually told us that with a well-plotted outline, the script practically writes itself. While in our combined over forty years of writing for half-hour comedy shows like *The Wonder Years, Frank's Place, Hangin' with Mr. Cooper, Becker,* and *The Simpsons,* we have never once had a script write itself, there is a nugget of truth in this statement. The fact is that we've never known a single writer, no matter how talented or how experienced, who wrote a good script without at least a rough outline. Everyone needs a road map to get to the destination.

In this chapter, we'll take you step by step through the process of creating a story and outline that we've taught hundreds of half-hour comedy writing students in UCLA Extension Writers' Program. We'll start with the "who, what, and whys" of writing a show that's currently on the air and the importance of knowing your show. You'll learn how to brainstorm general ideas, develop those into jumping-off points to a story, create complications that arise in the middle of the episode, and figure out what happens from beginning to end. Finally, you'll learn the basics of creating a beat sheet and expanding it into an outline, which sets you up to write your script more easily, faster, and more successfully.

Getting Started: Five Questions You Must Know the Answers To

1. Who Are You Writing For?

You're writing for yourself, obviously, to prove you can do it, and maybe for your friends and family, who might enjoy reading your work. But the real audience for your spec script is the people who can help you become a professional: other writers who are already there, as well as agents, managers, producers, and executives. Each of them is what we call a "Savvy Reader." They know what it takes to write solid and funny half-hour comedy. They know what they're looking for and what tells them a writer does or doesn't really get it. As we discuss putting together your story and outline, the Savvy Reader will continue to make occasional appearances.

2. Do You Have to Write a Show That's on the Air Now?

Savvy Readers are not going to read a script written by someone outside of the business if it's not a current show. They want to know you have a contemporary sensibility and that you're up to speed with what's going on right now. They read lots of scripts and will be able to gauge your abilities as a writer, comparing and contrasting your script with the many others they've read. As great as *Seinfeld* and *Friends* were, no one is going to want to read a spec script for a show that's no longer made.

3. Why Is a Spec Script Such a Peculiar Type of Writing?

Almost all forms of creative writing—novels, films, short stories, stage plays—are original to the writer, who creates the world and the characters inhabiting it. A brilliant novelist may not, and probably will not, have a ghost of an idea of how to write a really funny episode of *New Girl*. But in a spec script for an on-air show, this world and its characters already exist. You must devise and write a story inside that world. A network or a cable channel orders a given number of episodes, and each story fills that order. Ultimately, you are trying to demonstrate that you can be an effective order filler.

4. What Are You Trying to Prove with Your Spec?

Prove You Know Your Show

You're proving that you can devise and write a story full of funny situations and jokes that feel exactly like a typical episode of the series. You are parking it in the middle of the space of what they normally do on the show, not on or outside the lines. If they usually have one main story (the A story) and a lesser story (the B story), you do too, and you weave them together the way they do on the series. If they have three equally weighted stories, so should you. If they generally have some kind of running joke throughout an episode, you should think of one, too. If they most often start each episode in the apartment or the office . . . well, you get the idea.

Don't test the limits of the show, even if you have a funny idea for it. And conclude the show back where you left it. You end with a return to normalcy, not a new situation that isn't where the show on the air is this week. Your job is to write a typical episode, not a so-called special episode, and absolutely no two-part episodes.

Prove You Know the Characters

You're proving you can write in the voices of the regular characters and that you understand their relationships; they're not your characters to do with as you wish. The characters should sound, behave, and relate to one another in your script just as they do on the series—don't give them new backstories or significant traits. You may have a funny idea about two of the regular characters starting a romance, but as hilarious as your notion may be, there's one problem—it's a terrible idea for a spec. Okay, you may be watching the series on television six months from now and see those two characters get romantically involved. So, you did have a good idea. But the writers on the show can do that idea; you cannot.

Prove You Know the Lead Character

You're proving you can write a funny story about the show's lead character, which is who most episodes, and certainly typical episodes of the series, revolve around. Definitely do not write a spec script about the second banana, giving her the driving action and all the good jokes. That may happen occasionally on the series, but it's a bad strategy for a spec. Frankie is the star of *The Middle,* and Peter Griffin is the star of *Family Guy.* Even if it's hilarious dialogue, the Savvy Reader will not think much of your spec.

Of course, there are a few "buddy" shows that have dual leads, like *2 Broke Girls* or *Mike & Molly,* and if you're writing for one of those shows you need to make sure the two leads are equally weighted in your episode. (The occasional exception to writing for the lead character is a true ensemble show like *Modern Family,* which deals with a story for each of its three family units every episode. In that case, you'll need to make sure that every couple—Phil and Claire, Cam and Mitch, Jay and Gloria—is significantly involved in the story.)

Prove You Know the Format and Limitations

You're proving you get the format and flavor of the series—how many acts there are, how many scenes they normally have, what kind of pacing they employ, what storytelling devices they typically use.

You're also proving that you understand the limitations of shooting a show in production. Your episode should take place mostly, if not entirely, in the show's regular sets and locations, like a living room, bar, or workplace, and shouldn't include a raft of outside sets (i.e., sets that are not always up and standing on the soundstage). For example, if you're writing a multiple-camera show, which is shot in one day on a studio soundstage in front of a live audience (like *The Big Bang Theory* or *Hot in Cleveland*), you should limit yourself to no more than one or two outside sets. If you're writing a single-camera show (like *Girls* or *Suburgatory*) shot over five or six days, you have some more flexibility, because even though most of the scenes will be shot on their regular sets, they do not have live audiences and often use outside locations.

Why is minimizing the number of sets important? The budget. If you write a multiple-camera episode where the characters go to the top of the Empire State Building, a crowded nightclub, and a tractor pull, that show will never get made. Why? They can't fit that many sets on a soundstage, not to mention it's way too expensive to build three massive sets that would never get used again. This prohibition against too many outside sets applies, to some degree, even to animated shows, since it's costly to pay animators to create too many new background locations from scratch. The Savvy Reader will know whether your episode can be made within a reasonable budget.

What you are ultimately proving is that you can take the show out for a fun ride, bring it back where you got it, and park it in the middle of the spot.

5. Which Show Should You Pick to Write?

You need to write a show that you like a lot, that you feel comfortable with, and that is currently on the air. The best candidates are successful shows that haven't been on the air for too many seasons. For one thing, they have done fewer episodes, so it's easier to come up with an original story. But more importantly, sooner or later, all shows go away, usually through cancellation (though sometimes because the creators or the actors are just ready to move on). The longer a show runs, the more likely the current season will be its last. After a show is gone, the Savvy Reader may continue reading specs from that show for six months—maybe even up to a year. But then, that's it. Your script will be past its expiration date.

At the other end of the spectrum, it's a bit dangerous to try to write a spec for a show that's just premiered. As much as you may like the show, most series take a few episodes to find their storytelling rhythm, have their characters fully mesh, and reveal their backstories. The other reason is that a brand-new series is on a short leash with the network. If it doesn't perform well enough with the viewers, it may get canceled before you finish writing your spec, and no Savvy Reader will ever look at it.

A reality check: The writers and producers on the series you choose will almost certainly *not* read your spec. The legal departments at the studios don't want you, two years down the road, to sue if the series winds up doing an episode that has elements that could have come out of your script. The only exception to this "no reading" rule is if you're close to someone working on a show who might be willing to look at your episode.

Knowing Your Show

Discover Your Show's DNA

Once you've chosen the series you want to spec, you need to stop being a fan and start being an analyst and scientist. You are trying to clone the DNA of the show, so you have to look past the entertaining surface and see into the underlying structure: its skeleton, musculature, and pulse. How do you do that? You watch the show—a lot! Watch it until the funny fades into the background of your mind and the architecture of the show starts to reveal itself fully. Even after you've started putting your story and outline together, keep watching episodes of your show. You never know what subtleties you might learn that will inform your own writing.

What's also helpful is to watch one of your favorite episodes multiple times. The underlying scaffolding of the storytelling will more clearly reveal itself, and the nuances of the show's comic tone and the specific flavor of each character's humor will become obvious to you. Another helpful exercise is to listen to an episode without watching it. When you concentrate simply on hearing what the characters say, it helps make individual speech patterns clearer in your head.

Count how many scenes there are in each episode you view. You want to get an average of how many scenes are in a typical episode. Your outline should be constructed so that the number of scenes is within the show's normal range. (In case you're wondering what exactly constitutes a scene in a television show, any change of location or change of time within the same location is a new scene. When the story goes from the office to the kitchen, it's a new scene. If the characters walk into a bar after work, and then you dissolve to hours later and they're closing the place down, that's a new scene.)

Time the scenes. This will give you a better sense of the pace of the show. Are there a lot of short scenes, a few longer scenes, or a mix of shorter and longer scenes? You want to devise a story that flows the way typical episodes do on the series. If the show uses almost all short scenes, you don't want to have a big, long scene—no matter how funny it is—in the middle of your episode. It won't feel like the series.

Closely Observe How Stories Are Told on Your Series

Pay strict attention to what types of storytelling devices the show uses. If there are fantasy sequences, voice-overs, flashbacks, documentary-style interviews, graphics, signage, cutaways to tangential jokes, and/or a lot of contemporary music, then you can put those in your story, too. By the same token, stay away from any devices not commonly employed.

Observe the time frame in which the series tells its stories. You'll need to have the events in your episode happen in a believable time frame; don't cram more events into a day than would be realistic. And make sure the events in your episode occur in a time frame appropriate to the series; each series has its own kind of temporal rhythm. The episodes of some series take place over a single day, or perhaps two. Other shows will run a graphic saying "Six Months Later" and then come up on the characters after a lengthy period of time.

Of course, the series you want to write may have an episode or two that departs from the normal pattern of the show. But just as in the case of writing for the lead versus secondary characters, the writers on the show can do that because they have the gig.

Beyond Watching the Show: Do Your Research

Investigate your show online. Each series has an official website and often multiple fan websites. You can learn a lot from those. For one thing, you need to look at synopses of episodes they have already produced and aired. This is important! When we went in to pitch for *The Simpsons,* the show had already made hundreds of episodes, and we didn't want to pitch a story that was too close to something they'd already done. It took a long time to plow through all those synopses, but when we went to our meeting, we were confident everything we pitched was in a reasonably fresh area. (Reviewing each episode can have the additional benefit of teaching you about your main character. Perhaps you missed the episode where it was established that she is scared of parrots, so maybe now you find a funny use for a parrot in your story.)

You want to make absolutely sure your story does not repeat one they have already made. The Savvy Reader may well know if your story is too close to one that's been produced and presume you're a plagiarist, even if you have no idea that your show idea has already been done. (The good news is that if you came up with the exact story, you clearly have a great feel for the kinds of episodes they do! The bad news is that now you have to think of another story.)

What if the story idea kicking around in your head is uncomfortably close to one that's been produced? You may be able to salvage it, but you'll need to make adjustments. Change the emphasis; transform your main story (the A story) into a secondary story (the B story), but alter it enough so that it's not the same story.

For example, we pitched to *The Simpsons* the idea that Bart encounters a homeless man and coaches him on how to look more pathetic and play better on people's sympathies to improve his income as a beggar. Bart's suggestions work so well that the man gives Bart a cut of his proceeds. Other homeless people ask Bart for advice, and he winds up becoming a beggar pimp. But the show wanted us to explore a different idea for Bart, so our Bart story was given to Homer, who wound up working part-time as a beggar to supplement his income. Our A story was given new life as a B story on the episode "Milhouse Doesn't Live Here Anymore."

Find scripts for the show. Numerous websites have them, and even if they charge you, it's money well spent. You want your story to match the format that they use on the series. So, if you're writing a show that has three acts, don't write an episode that has only two acts. If your show starts with act 1, breaks for titles, then finishes act 1, don't write a Cold Opening (the brief scene at the beginning of many shows) and then go to a commercial break. Copy the show's format exactly in your outline.

Finally, and as silly as this may sound, it's important to spell the characters' names correctly. Is it Hayley or Hailey? Is it Jerry or Gerry? Is it John or Jon? Few things will make you look like you're an amateur more than spelling a regular character's name incorrectly.

Creating Your Story

Where Does Your Story Come From?

Stories come from anywhere and everywhere. Ultimately, the story you're going to write has to be shaped inside your own head, so start by brainstorming ideas: What would be funny for your show? What kinds of stories would you like to see on it? Also, bouncing ideas off of someone who knows the series can be helpful. (Professional television comedy writing is almost always done via a group process, i.e., the writers' room.) Your ideas don't need to be fully formed when you first start; a complete episode is unlikely to spring out of your head like Athena from the brow of Zeus. The little ideas that are germs of story making are what we call *spitballs:* suggestions of possible funny areas for a scene, a character's attitude, or a story.

An area that's always particularly rich to mine is your own personal experience, something that happened to you or someone you know that can be fashioned into a story. For instance, when Julie was a rebellious young teen, she snuck onto a field trip for a class she wasn't enrolled in to hang out with her best friend. That germ of an idea was behind the "Heartbreak" episode of *The Wonder Years*, which David wrote, and which depicted Kevin working his way onto a field trip with Winnie.

There are plenty of stories every day in newspapers, in magazines, and on the news. Maybe one of them can be adapted to fit into your story. Perhaps a phrase or a situation hits you as funny. One caution about using true events, whether drawn from your life or the outside world: Beware of too much fidelity to what really happened. The event has to serve the story; the story can't just be documentary reporting on the event. "But it really happened that way" is a bad excuse for overloading a story with unnecessary details or tangential occurrences.

The plotting of classic comedies can sometimes be adapted into a story for your show. Shakespeare has been pillaged countless times for stories, and the Bard himself often adapted stories he'd read or heard to create his timeless comedies and dramas. Classic characters can give you attitudes that could work for your story too. Think of the miser, the misanthrope, the hypocrite, and the hypochondriac from Molière. If a character on your show has any of the comic traits of classic characters, look for ways to milk their comic flaws by observing how the greatest comedy writers have done it.

Another time-honored way to think about your story is to start with the question "What if . . . ?" Use the comic traits of the characters and milk those with a "What if . . . ?" question. For example, on *The Big Bang Theory*, Sheldon is well established as an obsessive-compulsive germophobe. So, what if Penny gets a new armchair Sheldon thinks is extremely comfortable, until he discovers she got it off the street? They did that on the series, and Sheldon's story in that episode had him going through comic contortions as he obsessed about doing everything he could to get the defiled armchair out of Penny's apartment. If you think of your series and the characters' comic flaws and ask "What if . . . ?" questions, you may find some very funny and workable material.

As soon as you begin to ruminate about what your story might be, a little bit of self-congratulation is in order—you've taken the first steps in creating your outline. Just make sure that you are prepared, since you never know when a funny notion will hit you and the muses rarely visit on a defined schedule. Carry a notebook around so you can jot things down, or make notes in your cell phone. Few things are more aggravating than having an idea that's so good you know you won't ever forget it, and then when you go to write it down a couple hours later you've forgotten it.

You Don't Have to Reinvent the Wheel

Mine the History of Comedic Stories

Since you've watched a lot of situation comedies over the years, you know certain stories turn up again and again because those stories are common human dilemmas that are imbued with comedic possibilities and can be twisted and turned to fit into many different series and situations. Sometimes it's useful to consider those tried-and-true story areas and see if you can put a fun spin on them. Here are a few examples.

"What Happens in Vegas Doesn't Stay in Vegas"
A lead character discovers a secret and, though sworn to secrecy, blurts it out to someone or inadvertently reveals it. Once he does, things get

increasingly complicated with cover-ups, dissembling, and other ruses as he tries to avoid responsibility for revealing the secret.

"Liar, Liar, Pants on Fire"

A lead character tells a lie during a weak moment, perhaps to impress someone, or cover up something, or avoid being caught in a compromising situation. This generally leads to the spinning of more lies and the lead character's being caught in that web. It may be resolved with the truth being revealed, or perhaps not. Sometimes a clever twist allows the character to escape with his dignity.

"Wait, I Thought You Said . . ."

A lead character misinterprets something she is told or something she overhears and acts on that misunderstanding. The audience is way ahead of the character and enjoys watching her make things worse.

"Decisions, Decisions"

A lead character must choose between two very bad (or two very good) things and goes through comedic convolutions figuring out what to do. Often there's a moral dilemma involved, and while she might make the right choice, in today's sitcom, she just might make the wrong one.

"Trust Me, What Could Go Wrong?"

The lead character gets involved in a surefire scheme to make money or solve some pressing problem. The audience knows what could go wrong—just about everything. And when things start to go wrong, bad decisions and foolish risks follow as surely as night follows day.

"The Boat Rocker"

Something upsets the lead character's equilibrium. An incriminating e-mail or old letter is found, or a disliked relative threatens to visit. Whatever it is causes panic, and questionable choices follow.

"The Clock's A-Ticking"

The lead character gets into a predicament in which she has to accomplish or avoid something by a certain time. The harder she tries, the farther away the goal seems to get.

"The Corpse"

The lead character is stuck with a dead body (or more likely, something incriminating or embarrassing that's a bit shy of a real corpse). He has to get rid of it without linking it in any way to himself.

"Role Reversal"

The lead character is stuck in a situation where he has to behave exactly the opposite of how he normally would. The contortions and discomfiture he experiences create the comedy.

"The Green-Eyed Monster"

The lead character finds a reason to be jealous of someone, or she is the object of someone else's jealousy. Naturally, the reason driving the jealousy proves to be false or at least misapprehended. But in the meantime that jealousy, or the reaction to it, drives the comic behavior of the lead character.

"Mr. Fix-It"

Something is broken in a seemingly trivial way and the lead character decides to fix the problem. Unsurprisingly to the audience, the fix only makes the problem increasingly worse before it ultimately gets better—maybe. (Note: We don't recommend using a physical problem—for example, broken plumbing, electricity, or a car—for your spec, because that kind of story depends so much on physical comedy, which is in stage directions, not dialogue. But if you have a really funny take on the physical problem and can work a lot of funny dialogue in, then go for it.)

These are a few examples of classic story areas. You may be able to come up with more on your own. We don't recommend you just choose one of these and simply replicate it, though that can certainly work. But think of how to mix and match them in fresh ways. Recombine them, play with them, or go against the grain of how these stories are usually told.

Structuring Your Story

Whose Story Is It?

What did you notice about each of the classic comedy stories we just ran through? For one thing, they conform to the basic necessities of all stories: A lead character decides to pursue a goal and then encounters multiple obstacles along the way. The lead character's actions drive the events, and the lead is who the story is really about. We can't emphasize that enough.

Turn Your Spitballs into Springboards . . . and Listen to Aristotle

Now it's time to take your spitballs, the basic nuggets of ideas that will yield comedy gold, and turn them into springboards. A springboard is the episode's premise, or core idea, which leads into the heart of the story. It kicks off the beginning of the story and indicates what kind of funny stuff will be going on in the middle but doesn't necessarily tell you how the story ends.

For example, here's a springboard for the "Soda Tax" episode of *Parks and Recreation,* which is based on a real news story: Mayor Bloomberg's law concerning large-size soft drinks in New York City. The lead character, Leslie Knope, wants to make a splash in her first action as a new city councilwoman in Pawnee, Indiana, and decides to advocate a tax on large-size sugary soft drinks, believing it will help stem the rise of diabetes.

Once you have the springboard, you then figure out how the story moves ahead and finally resolves: In short, create its beginning, middle, and end. In the *Poetics,* Aristotle stated that a story has "a beginning, middle, and end. It will thus resemble a living organism in all of its unity." The old Greek has been right for twenty-five centuries. There is a deeply rooted human hunger for stories, and fans of half-hour comedies are no exception.

Kick Off Your Beginning with the Inciting Incident

As you've already learned, you inherit an on-air show's "normal world," so your first order of business is to create an event that upsets the balance of that world, for good or ill. This is called the "inciting incident," something that causes the lead character to take advantage of an opportunity or try to set things right, and it should happen almost immediately. In our *Parks and Recreation* episode, Leslie's decision to propose a soft drink tax at her first city council meeting is the inciting incident and is established within the first fifteen seconds on-screen.

Be Sure the Story's Action Rises in the Middle

What Leslie thinks is a great move to boost the citizens' health, however, almost immediately goes south, as the restaurants in town oppose her plan. There you have the kickoff to the A story and the middle complication. (Although they won't be discussed in this chapter, the episode also has a B story and a C story, which is typical of how that series works. Depending on the series you choose, you will probably have to come up with multiple springboards to fill in your show.)

Here's where the complications and obstacles set in, what's often called *rising action.* Suppose Leslie proposed the tax and it passed without any trouble. She sets a goal and meets it; hooray for her. But there is no story, so the main character needs to encounter some resistance to her idea, and that's what happens: Leslie meets with a representative of the restaurants in town who tells her that her proposal will cause a hundred people to be fired. How will Leslie resolve her dilemma as a politician?

She must make a tough decision: Is she willing to risk the loss of jobs in order to help the overall health of the town?

That's a complication to the lead character's plan, but a single complication followed by a clear, effective choice doesn't add up to a satisfying story. In the world of successful half-hour comedies, the action must continue to rise; things must grow more complicated. When Leslie comes into the city council the next morning to vote on her proposal, she's a wreck. She's been up all night, stewing about her decision, and drinking lots of sugary soda from a supersize cup. (Leslie's been established as a bit of a sugar freak herself.) When the vote comes up, what does she do? She vomits into her huge plastic soda cup and then requests a recess. It's funny, she's humiliated, and she still doesn't know what to do. The action of the story does indeed rise.

Move the Story Ahead with Each Scene

Even after you've set up rising action in your episode, you want to make sure that each scene moves the story forward. Professional writers have no qualms about getting rid of scenes if they slow down the story. You must do the same. Maybe there's a scene with a couple funny jokes you love, but if it doesn't move your story ahead, cut it. Maybe you can find a home for those jokes in a scene that does.

Bring It All Together

In an hour-long show or a movie, there would probably be further complications. But in television comedy, you only have twenty-one minutes and change of story time to work with, and here's how this episode of *Parks and Recreation* goes: Leslie's at a loss and needs to make a decision. She seeks advice from her old boss Ron, who tells her that she's so annoying he almost fired her four different times. But he always stopped short because he admired her determination and the fact that she wasn't "a wishy-washy kiss-ass." Her morale boosted, Leslie returns to the city council meeting and provides the decisive vote to pass the soda tax.

This is a fairly typical episode, so let's review its basic storytelling elements. It begins with an inciting incident (Leslie's desire to make her mark as a new city councilwoman), followed by the lead character's having a plan (Leslie wants to pass a tax on large sugary sodas), then encountering resistance (restaurants say the tax will cost jobs), which forces her to make an uncomfortable decision. Next, there's anxiety about what she should do (she stews all night while drinking sodas), and when we expect the situation to resolve, it doesn't, but actually becomes worse for the lead character (Leslie humiliates herself by throwing up and asking for a recess). Yet the problem still needs a resolution, so Leslie seeks counsel (Ron tells her she's annoying and disagrees with her, but he admires her conviction), which leads her to resolve the problem in a way that is true to her character (she provides the decisive vote for the soda tax).

As you look ahead to putting together your outline, make sure each story in it has these necessary *plot points,* the events that push the story forward: an inciting incident, a character making a plan, the plan running into an obstacle, the character trying to come up with a new plan or making a clear decision, some further obstacles or indecision, and then finally resolution—that is, a satisfying ending. As our old friend Aristotle said, the best endings are both surprising and inevitable. The viewers don't see it coming, but when it happens, they feel it makes perfect sense. In "Soda Tax," this happens when Ron, who's well established on the series as someone who hates government, is the one who inspires Leslie to vote for further government regulation.

Don't Neglect the Emotional Story

When you put the building blocks of story together, it's important not simply to think of what would be funny (as important as funny is), but also what will get the audience emotionally engaged with the characters.

Emotion is the bridge between the audience and the characters, and even if the viewers don't approve of a character's particular actions, they have to feel for her and be invested in her achieving her goals.

If you lay in an emotional arc for a character—that is, provide some emotional growth from the beginning to the end of the story—the audience will be satisfied. For example, on the "Mike Likes Lasagna" episode of *Mike & Molly,* Molly wants them each to write their own wedding vows. Mike is panicked, but Molly is a bit smug since she was an English major. Yet as Molly tries to write her vows, she only comes up with flowery and overcooked prose. Mike, who's a cop, shares his fears with his partner, Carl, who asks Mike to tell him about the lasagna at a restaurant he really likes. When Mike waxes poetic about the dish, Carl tells him to substitute Molly for the lasagna. At the end of their story, Mike shares his vows with Molly, and she's impressed but must confess she has nothing. They then work on her vows together.

So, Mike begins the story fearfully and Molly begins pridefully, but by the end, Mike is confident and Molly is humbled, yet happily so as she and her fiancé work together on their wedding vows. Both lead characters followed an emotional arc to a satisfying conclusion.

It's good to remember that all good comedy writing requires the study of human behavior. Not just the funny behavior, but all of it. Comedy isn't just about jokes, per se. It's also about being able to portray recognizable behavior in humorous (and sometimes not so humorous) situations. If you wander too far afield from how humans actually behave, you lose the "willing suspension of disbelief" necessary to sustain the audience's attention. Believable emotions provide the support system that gives comedy life.

We Know It's Comedy, but Logic Counts

Focus on both the story and character logic of your episode and make sure it is airtight. One of the biggest mistakes aspiring writers make is to bend the story logic or ignore the logical glitches that inevitably come up whenever they are trying to fashion a story. A second big mistake new writers make is to distort the way a character would behave in order to make the story idea work. Both these gaffes in logic are convenient for the writer, but they neither serve the show nor work for the spec script. So be certain that the story unfolds and characters behave just as they do on the series.

Ordering Your A Story, B Story, C Story, and Runners

In addition to matching how many stories your series uses in a typical episode, it can be helpful to figure out your A, B, and C stories separately. The next step is to figure out how to routine them—that is, how you will order the scenes for each story in your outline. A rule of thumb as you're putting the scenes in order is that you don't want to put together back-to-back scenes from the B story or the C story. You can have two or three straight scenes from the A story, but if you're running together scenes from the secondary stories, unless it's for an explicit comic purpose that can be done no other way, the episode will feel out of balance.

Also, many shows often employ *runners,* or *story threads.* These are small running story lines or jokes that may never truly resolve as stories but provide a few intermittent funny bits along the way. If your show uses these, you should, too.

Don't Neglect Your B Story

While constructing a solid, funny A story that's true to the show is absolutely critical, one thing we hear from Savvy Readers is that the difference between a good script and a great script is often found in the secondary stories. A fair number of writers can come up with a solid A story, but to make your whole script jump to the top of the Savvy Reader's pile, take the time and effort to come up with an exceptionally funny and surprising secondary story.

For instance, on the *New Girl* episode "Fluffer," the main story is about Nick's acting like a "boyfriend without benefits" for Jess, while the B story is about Schmidt's discovering that an attractive girl thinks he may be one of Mitt Romney's sons. (The episode was very topical, airing during the 2012 election season.) She's a big Romney supporter and Schmidt plays it for all it's worth. He's about to seduce her when two of her friends, also Romney supporters, show up abuzz with questions for him. When Schmidt's memories of his "dad" strike a false note, they begin to get suspicious of his claim and find a Romney family picture on the Internet. Schmidt is exposed. The emotional story for Schmidt concludes with Cece urging him to call his own father, from whom he's estranged, to try to reconnect.

The hard truth is that to be noticed enough to get into the business of TV comedy, you will need to write your spec at a higher level than many of the episodes you'll see on the air. Making all of the stories in your episode strong and funny is one powerful way to reach that higher level.

Theme: It's Not an Essay You Write in High School

As you get rolling on creating your episode, it's very helpful to discern the theme, otherwise known as the message or main idea, underlying it. Your goal should be to make this theme a unifying element among your episode's comedic stories, which makes for more satisfying storytelling as well as strengthens the emotional core.

In the *Modern Family* episode "Someone to Watch Over Lily," Mitch and Cam wonder who should be Lily's legal guardians if anything happens to them. They secretly evaluate other family members to see who would be best. They observe Jay being overly strict with Manny, Claire secretly taking Luke to a child psychologist because she thinks he's turning out too much like Phil, and Alex and Haley at odds. No one seems right. But then Jay listens to what's bothering Manny and changes his approach. Phil and Claire sort out their issues, and Alex and Haley reconcile. Cam and Mitch realize no one's perfect and that acceptance of the imperfections of others is an ingredient essential to love. Acceptance of human imperfection is the unifying theme.

As you can see, the theme doesn't have to be anything earthshaking.

Usually, it's pretty simple and common, like "family's the most important thing in life," or "lies lead to more lies," or "be true to yourself." The same theme may be replayed in different episodes; since comic characters don't really learn or change, yours need not be unique. But if you have a main message for your stories, you'll find that jokes come more easily and more organically.

Putting Together Your Outline

A Beat Sheet Helps You Crystallize the Story

In the professional world, a beat sheet is usually written preparatory to writing the outline and consists of a short scene-by-scene list of the essential *story beats,* or plot points, of the episode. In brief, telegraphic descriptions, you write out the specific events that drive the story forward, listing them in the order they occur, and (since this is comedy) possibly throw in a joke or two. Often these plot points are bullet-pointed and not written in paragraphs, and short phrases are used instead of complete sentences. The beat sheet is a document that gives you an overview of the organization of your story, a structural blueprint of cause and effect that's the basis for building your outline.

The plot points, or story beats, need to build progressively so that the rising action we discussed earlier is in place. As you continue to watch episodes of the series you're writing for (and continuing to watch episodes of your series is the first item of homework listed for *every* class session on the syllabus we give students when we teach "Beginning Writing for the Half-Hour Spec Comedy: Building the Story and the Outline" at UCLA Extension), try to chart what the plot points are in a few episodes. Don't worry so much about the tangential things, the character tics and the jokes; focus on what events happen that are necessary to drive each story forward.

For instance, if a man asks his wife for help with a crossword puzzle, and she can't figure out the word either, but their nine-year-old daughter gives him the correct answer, that is not necessarily a plot point. But the plot point would happen when in the ensuing conversation the parents learn their smart daughter is failing English. That information is what's necessary for the story to move forward. Now the husband and wife need to discover why the daughter is failing and will have to go see her teacher.

So a beat sheet for this scene might say:

Int. Kitchen—Day

—Husband and wife learn their smart daughter is failing English

—They call her teacher, set up an appointment

The crossword puzzle is the means by which you get to the important story beat that pushes the couple into the following scene of seeing the teacher, but there are many ways to get to the revelation of the plot point that the daughter's failing English. The mother could find a report card the daughter's hiding, or the teacher could call the house. Some writers may wish to include how to get to those critical plot points on the beat sheet, and that's okay, too. Those details, like the device of the crossword puzzle, can make the story flow more gracefully and capture the writer's thoughts about how the scenes should be shaped.

But just make sure as you work out your beat sheet that you can clearly see what information you need in each scene to drive the story forward. When the couple goes to see the teacher, then something else will happen they didn't expect (the girl suddenly becomes a disciplinary problem, or the teacher's related to the husband's boss, or whatever it is), and that will drive the plot to the next level. (By the way, if you have a scene that doesn't have any true plot points, there's a high likelihood that you may not need that scene in your story.)

Many students are puzzled about what a beat sheet looks like, so the following is an example of how the Cold Open might have been laid out in a beat sheet for the "Party of Six" episode of *Happy Endings*.

(Incidentally, "INT." indicates an interior scene that's shot indoors and "EXT." indicates an exterior scene shot outdoors.)

Sample Beat Sheet for a Cold Open
COLD OPEN

INT. BRAD AND JANE'S LIVING ROOM—NIGHT

—Penny's birthday, gang waiting for her

—Discuss Penny's bad birthday luck

—Alex says last year Dave caused the bad luck by bringing a teenage date

INT. BAR—FLASHBACK

—Graphic: "Penny's 29th Birthday"

—As the gang toasts Penny, Brad accidentally hits her, knocks her out

INT. A NONDESCRIPT ROOM—FLASHBACK

—Graphic: "Penny's 26th Birthday"

—Max keeps a dog at bay with a long stick, the gang looks on terrified

—Penny's gift puppy's a monster

EXT. PARK—FLASHBACK

—Graphic: "Penny's 7th Birthday"

—A bunch of seven-year-olds crowd around a Clown lying motionless on the ground

—The Clown's being shocked back to life by two Paramedics

INT. BRAD AND JANE'S LIVING ROOM—THE PRESENT

—Alex suggests Penny's birthday is cursed

—Jane says they must reverse the curse

—Penny arrives and they've planned her birthday dinner at Big Dom's

—Penny can't go there. She and her ex-boyfriend split up the restaurants they used to go to; he got Big Dom's

—Max and Dave let out that they think Penny's birthday's cursed

—Penny denies it—the lights go out. Max is leaning on the light switch

—They'll go to some other restaurant—but no one can think of one

This is just the Cold Open. The writer would then go through, scene by scene, and lay out the rest of the episode in that beat sheet. Note how short and telegraphic the descriptions of what goes on in each scene are. If you watch the episode, you'll see that a lot of the jokes and tangential riffs that characterize the series are left out of this beat sheet. But the essence of the story, the necessary plot points to get from point A (the beginning) to point Z (the end), starts to get laid out.

Turning Your Beat Sheet into an Outline

After you've constructed your entire beat sheet and identified the specific plot points you need to drive your story from start to finish, it's time to write your outline. In the professional world, outlines are written in complete paragraphs of smooth prose. For example, the outline of the beginning scene in the Cold Open of the "Party of Six" episode of *Happy Endings* we just looked at might read like what follows.

Sample Outline of First Scene
Cold Open

INT. BRAD AND JANE'S LIVING ROOM—NIGHT

Jane and Alex wrap presents. Brad wonders where Penny is and who shows up an hour late to her own birthday party. Jane says Penny's on time because she told them all to come an hour early. Alex complains that Jane shouldn't go around "daylight-savings-timing people."

Dave appears and asks if his solid green shirt makes him look too much like a tree. Max adopts a New Yorker's accent and jokes that Dave looks like a "tree outta ten at best." Then Max can't get rid of his New Yorker accent and says he's "stuck in a Pacino. Hoo-ah!"

Jane tells them she doesn't want a repeat of Penny's birthday last year, the one that was ruined by Dave and Alex. Alex says it'll be fine if Dave doesn't bring a date from Degrassi Junior High. Brad points out that Penny's had a lot of bad birthdays.

At that point, the Cold Open goes into flashbacks of Penny's previous bad birthdays. But you see how the brief descriptions of the beat sheet are filled in. The main plot points are that it's Penny's birthday; she's had so many bad birthdays they wonder if her birthday is cursed; Alex accuses

Dave of ruining last year's birthday by bringing a teenager as a date (who will happen to show up later in the episode and drive the story forward); and Penny says they can't go to the restaurant they planned to. Those things are absolutely necessary to the story, and that's what's in the beat sheet. But in the outline, the characters are all given attitudes, jokes are inserted, and a fuller sense of how the scene would play out in the script is achieved.

For instance, Jane's lying to everyone about when to show up is utterly typical of her controlling character. Alex, who plays the most intellectually challenged in the group, is given a "dumb joke," and some funny and characteristic byplay between Dave and Max is inserted. Elaborating on the characters' traits, inserting examples of jokes that fit the characters, and lightly filling in the scene is what you need to do as you move from the basic plot points (the beat sheet) to the fuller exposition of the episode (the outline).

Here Comes Your Outline!

Okay, you've gone through the process. You got to know your show intimately, then came up with spitball ideas and developed them a bit more into springboards. Next you took on the really hard part, breaking the story, figuring out how your beginning leads through the middle and gets to the end. Now you've written your beat sheet, hashing out the important story beats (or plot points) and knowing what will happen scene by scene. You're ready to write the outline. You will revise whatever you find doesn't flow quite right in the beat sheet, and you'll fill in the scenes more fully, adding some of the jokes and details.

And now it's up to you. We've shared with you what you need to know and detailed the process that works for us, for the professional writers we've known, and for the many students we've taught. It's your outline, so now write it. May the force (or farce) be with you, have fun with it, and we'll see you in chapter 6!

CHAPTER 6

Writing the On-Air Half-Hour Comedy Spec: The Script
by Julie Chambers and David Chambers

Congratulations! You have an outline. Seriously, hurray for you. Patting yourself on the back may feel a little awkward, but quick—while no one is looking—do it anyway. Like we told you in the previous chapter, you've done the heavy lifting. Now you can go to script. Of course, you'll always need to make adjustments as you go along, alter story beats, squeeze in jokes, but that's part of the fun. It's a puzzle, and since you already have most of the structural pieces in place, it will be a lot easier to put it all together.

Before You Start Writing Your First Draft

So, now you're ready for that fun part—writing the script—right? Almost.

Before you start, there are a few things to consider. Here's a checklist of what we discussed in chapter 5 that you might want to review. Use it to make sure you are ready to move ahead to writing the script from your outline.

✓ You're writing an episode for a show that's currently on the air.

✓ You've watched the show *a whole lot*.

✓ You've investigated the show online.

✓ You've found scripts for the show.

✓ Your outline has a similar number of scenes as a typical episode of the show.

✓ You minimize the use of outside sets.

✓ Your main story is about the lead character on the series.

✓ You avoid changes in the dynamics of relationships on the show.

✓ You do not use significant outside characters.

✓ Your episode is self-contained.

✓ You have a clear beginning, middle, and end to your story.

✓ The story is fully motivated. Both the story logic and character logic make sense.

✓ Your episode occurs in a believable time frame that's typical to the series.

✓ Each scene moves the story forward.

✓ Your use of A, B, and C stories and runners matches how the series works.

✓ Your story has rising action.

✓ You begin the way the series episodes typically start.

✓ You have a theme to your episode.

✓ You've spelled the characters' names correctly.

Start Writing Your First Draft!

Now that you've looked over your outline closely and made any adjustments to your story so that you've fully dealt with our first checklist, you're ready to write the script.

Set Yourself Up with the "Write" Schedule

What's the first thing you do? Make sure you set yourself goals. When you work on a series, it's easy enough to do. It's your job and you're getting paid. Having between us written for over twenty prime-time half-hour comedies, we know and appreciate the structure that offers. On a series, you have deadlines, colleagues who depend on you, and you get it done. The necessity of getting a show written and on the air provides a sense of urgency. When we teach half-hour comedy writing classes at UCLA Extension, we give our students deadlines and assignments, too. They know they have specific goals to reach by certain dates. It is very helpful to students to push themselves and their work forward.

If you're not getting paid, in a class, or in a writers' group, then it's up to you to motivate yourself. Of course, in a sense every writer has to do that, since no one gets into the game without producing really good material before he ever gets paid for it.

Which goal should you establish first? Simply try to put aside a certain amount of time—per day or per week (everyone's schedule and personal obligations are different)—to write. Tell your spouse, your roommate, your mom, your friends, your kids—anyone in your regular life whom you need to clear out time to write. You're not being antisocial or turning into a hermit, but you have something you are passionate about and want to do, and they need to understand that. The next goal is to get a specified amount of work done in each writing session. Today you say you'll finish the third scene. But if you don't finish the third scene, don't worry so much about it. Maybe you were being too ambitious, or maybe there was a tricky complication to the end of the scene that you need a little more time to figure out, or maybe your dog got sick and you had to take him to the vet. Don't beat yourself up. Just try to reach that goal the next time you write.

Think and Write in Screen Time

As you write, always remember to think in screen time. You are writing specific actions in a visual medium. Those actions take place on-screen in less than twenty-two minutes. If you're writing a novel, you can say, "She came home and opened a bottle of champagne." That takes two seconds to read. On-screen that takes two minutes, and no one wants to watch it (unless there's a lot of witty dialogue going on at the same time). Visualize exactly what pictures you want to see on-screen that will accompany your dialogue. If you don't think in screen time now as you write, when you rewrite you'll have to rethink a lot of what you put down.

Don't Novelize

Going hand in hand with thinking in screen time is this: Do not novelize. Remember that all information is conveyed to the audience either visually or through dialogue. No one watching a television show is reading the stage directions. So do not write into your stage directions things like this: "Clarice enters. She's Gretchen's best friend from high school, and they used to have so much fun together, until they had that bad falling out over a guy. They haven't seen each other in a few years, lost touch for a while, but both are hoping to repair their old friendship."

It's great for you, the writer, to have that in mind about the relationship between the two characters, but there is no pamphlet that comes with the episode for the audience to read. You have to get the information about their relationship into your dialogue and your visuals. If you always remember that those are the only ways you communicate with the audience—through dialogue and visuals—then you won't have to go back and root out a lot of novelization as you rewrite.

Keep Up the Pace!

With each scene you write, try to remember this mantra: Start late, get out early. You want your script to zip along, have drive and momentum, and pull the reader forward. One of the best ways to do that is to eliminate whatever is unnecessary. You may be in love with a joke and it may be a killer laugh, but if it takes three-quarters of a page to get to that joke before the scene really starts, if it doesn't drive the story forward, you should probably lose it. If you have a funny run between two characters that really cracks you up, but it takes up a page after the point of the scene is really over, you should seriously consider letting it go.

As the noted funnyman William Faulkner reputedly said, "In writing you must kill your darlings." It's true. One of the signs of mature comedy writing is being willing to cut great jokes and funny material if it gets in the way of the most streamlined way to tell your story.

Motivate Your Characters' Movements

As you enter and exit characters, make sure they have a motive for coming or going. They cannot just flit in and out of a scene for the convenience of the writer. They need a reason to enter or to exit a scene. They also need a reason for being in the scene if they're present when the scene starts. Why characters are where they are, and why they come and go, has to be true to character logic and story logic, not just your desire to get them where you, the writer, need them to be for your story to work.

Don't Try to Be the Director

Minimize your stage directions. The truth is that stage directions are not read very carefully, occasionally not even by Savvy Readers (i.e., agents, executives, working writers). What people do read is the dialogue, so don't clog up your episode with lots of stage directions. And if you keep your stage directions sparse, many might even get read.

Avoid camera directions. You're the writer, not the director. There are very few exceptions to this. One is if you need to see something important to your story that the camera is not going to be able to read in a normal shot (like the title of a book, a picture in someone's wallet, etc.). In that case, call for a close-up in a separate paragraph of your stage directions. Another exception is if you have an important joke that requires a particular camera shot. Again, if so, then call for it (like a tilt-down to his unzipped fly). Another is . . . well, we can't think of any others. So, avoid camera directions.

Adjust as You Go Along

Don't be afraid to make a few departures from your outline as you write. Your outline, as good as it is, was not brought down from a mountaintop inscribed on a stone tablet. If you find you've discovered a better and funnier take on a scene, or a different and cleverer way to work one of the story lines, go ahead and pursue that.

Before you jump ahead with a lot of alteration to the story, though, you may want to chart out how the revised story line would play out. You don't want to write yourself into a funny situation that you can't find a way out of. So, think it through. It's not necessary to go back and do a whole new outline, but a little effort spent figuring out if your brilliant new idea will carry through to the end is time well spent.

Don't Obsess over Jokes Right Now

Don't overworry about jokes right now. We know you're writing comedy, but don't obsess about jokes as you work your way through your first draft. In fact, feel free to write your scenes dramatically. That helps you write naturalistic dialogue, without concerning yourself about cramming in jokes. Once you have written that baseline of realistic conversation, where the characters are speaking with genuine emotion, then on subsequent passes through the script, the jokes will flow much more naturally out of your dialogue.

If you start writing by thinking only of setup, joke, setup, joke, then it may be difficult as you rewrite to get your script to read smoothly. The Savvy Reader may find your finished product "too jokey," meaning there are plenty of jokes in the script, but the dialogue does not flow naturally.

Jokes are great and absolutely necessary, but the story is what really pulls the reader through the script. To paraphrase the mantra in *Field of Dreams,* "If you build the story, the jokes will come." When your story is working, and you know the show and the characters you're writing, the jokes will not be that difficult to discover. Of course, if you have jokes you want to put in along the way, by all means go ahead and do that. But on your first draft, do not worry so much about jokes. Does that take a load off your mind? (We'll have more to say about jokes later.)

Write to "The End"!

Keep moving forward. You want to write "The End." One of the classic ways of not getting a script finished is to start on page one every day and rewrite from there. The problem with that method is that you usually don't go too far. A lot of people who follow this pattern will never get to the end. Remember, this is your first draft, not perfection. You may approach perfection, but it won't be until you've rewritten your script a few times.

Legend has it that another well-known funnyman, Ernest Heming-way, claimed that, "The first draft of anything is shit." You first must write badly to write well in the end. A great script does not spring out of your mind and directly onto the page. You have to get something less than perfect on the page, something that can be worked, massaged, and improved into a script that's good enough to ask another person to take the time and effort to read.

That being said, it's okay to start each new writing session by going over the work that you did in your previous writing session. That can help get the juices flowing and ease you into the flow of where you are in the script. But just make a few adjustments to what you did the last time and use that momentum to push you forward. If you're in the second act and have a brilliant idea about something that should go in the first act, by all means go back and make a note of it; perhaps even write in the dialogue so you don't lose it. That sort of story tweak may affect what you're going to do later in the second act, so it can be a good idea to get it in there in its proper place.

But do not make a practice of backtracking to put in everything you think of that will fit in earlier than where you're scripting right now. Make a note of your new idea, and then trudge back to the coalface, which in your case is the blank page ahead.

Sit Down and Do It

Okay, now sit down with your preferred writing mode—legal pad, computer, stone tablet, whatever. As the noted wit Dorothy Parker once said, "Writing is the art of applying the ass to the seat." So, start writing!

The Chambers "Start Writing Your First Draft" Checklist

 Set goals for yourself.

 Think in screen time.

✓ Do not novelize.

✓ Start scenes late, get out of scenes early.

✓ Motivate each entrance and exit with character logic, not authorial desire.

✓ Minimize stage directions and avoid camera directions.

✓ Don't be afraid to make a few departures from your outline.

✓ Don't obsess about jokes now.

✓ Keep moving forward.

✓ Apply your ass to the seat and write.

After You've Written Your First Draft . . . Write the Second

Congratulations again! You finished your first draft and typed "The End" (which may be the only words you don't change when you rewrite). Getting to the end is very important. Johnny, tell us what prize you get for finishing your first draft . . . The chance to improve it greatly by writing a second draft!

Problems Can Be Opportunities

As you go back over what you've written, look for problems and opportunities. Problems must be fixed, and comic opportunities should be exploited. Many times, a problem *is* an opportunity, not only to fix that particular problem, but also to make you think and ruminate, finding better ways to tell your story, ways that will elevate your script to a higher level.

Keep Following the Footprint of the Show

What's your page count? After you get your second draft finished, you're going to want that number to be consistent with the average for an episode of your series. Each series is different, but generally, a single-camera show will be around thirty to thirty-two pages and a multiple-camera show will be around forty to forty-five pages. The series you are writing may vary from those numbers, but just be sure you are in tune with the page count of your series. Under no circumstances should your single-camera show exceed thirty-five pages or your multiple-camera show exceed forty-nine pages.

The very first thing every Savvy Reader does when looking at anyone's script is to turn to the last page and check the page count. If you're a little long now, that's good. We're sure there's some stuff you can cut or compress. If your page count is short after your first draft, then your story probably needs a further complication and you'll have to think hard about adding another difficulty or two along the way that your characters will have to deal with.

Sprint off the Starting Line

Does your story get off to a fast start? You don't have to establish the "normal world" like you do if you're writing a screenplay. The audience knows the "normal world"—they've seen the show, so don't tread water in the normal world of the series for very long at all. You need to get your inciting incident in early and kick off your story.

Do you have at least one really good joke on the first page? We told you earlier not to worry too much about jokes as you write your first draft. Okay, now you need to think about jokes, and that first joke on page 1 is very important. If you don't have something funny right away, the Savvy Reader may not even bother to turn to page 2. Now, if you don't have a solid joke there just yet, don't worry. But you definitely must try to think of a good joke, or two or three, to start off the first page of your show.

You can't let up after that either. The old rule of thumb in a multiple-camera show was three jokes per page, and while that may not be exactly how the series you're writing works (especially if it's a single-camera show with more subtle smiles than big belly laughs), it's not a bad thing to shoot for.

Smooth in the Exposition

Writers have a name for putting in the story exposition; they call it "laying pipe." In a house the pipe's behind the finished drywall. It's working, but it's not visible. Have you laid your "pipe" skillfully? It's fine if the exposition is pretty baldly stated in your first draft, but as you go back through it, think of how you can reveal it as naturally as possible. (For instance, a character shouldn't blurt out, "Now I have to go to my mom's to feed her dog that always bites my leg." Instead he might be walking funny and his friend asks if he's okay. He explains he's fine but is wearing three pairs of jeans, then has to explain why—so when his mom's dog bites his leg it won't break the skin.)

Be True to the Characters

Have you done what writers call "servicing" all the regular characters on the series? Those actors get paid to show up each week and all have their comic functions on the show. Make sure each one has something to do, and a good joke or two. (The only exception to this is the rare show that has a huge roster of characters, like *The Office,* or *The Simpsons,* which over twenty seasons on the air has populated an entire town of people. So, if you're writing a show like that, you don't have to have a line for Meredith or a story involving Flanders.)

Do the characters sound like themselves? If you listen carefully to the speeches of the regular characters, you'll find that each has particular quirks and modes of expression. Some speak with proper grammar, some use double negatives, some speak in monosyllables, some use complex sentence structure, some use large words, some misuse words, some are proper, some are vulgar. Some characters have catchphrases, like Jay on *Modern Family* saying, "Of course you did," or Michael on *The Office* saying, "That's what she said." (Beware of overusing catchphrases, however, since it can sound like you couldn't come up with your own joke.) As you rewrite, shape the characters' dialogue so that it sounds the same way they speak on the show.

Check Your Act Breaks

Are your act breaks spaced as evenly as possible? If your show is in a two-act format, is the act break near the middle? If it's a three-act format, are the acts of approximately equal length? There's a fair amount of wiggle room in this, depending on how best to tell your story, but a twenty-three-page first act and a seven-page second act would definitely be out of balance and a red flag to the Savvy Reader.

Does your act break pop? Ideally, each act break is a cliffhanger and a big joke. But act breaks really do need to be at least one or the other of those. Why? Because the show goes to a string of commercials out of an act break. Viewers can change the channel, and often do, or they may go get a soda and snack. You want them to be sure to change the channel back, or hurry away from the kitchen, because they want to see what happens next on your show. A cliffhanger—what's going to happen now?—or a big joke is the surest way to hold your audience through the commercial break.

For example, in the *Modern Family* episode "Starry Night," Mitch and Jay drive out in the country to go stargazing. Mitch takes a walk in the woods to have some time all alone but comes back shouting that he was sprayed by a skunk. That's the act break. The joke is in his being sprayed and his hysteria, but we also are curious about what happens next. Will an army of skunks show up? How will Mitch get rid of the smell?

The Savvy Reader will be looking closely to see that your act breaks are compelling. Now, you may notice that series on the air occasionally have a lame act break. That doesn't give you the freedom to have a mediocre act break in your script. Those writers already have the gig, but you're trying to get a gig. The writers probably had a good act break but had to cut it for time or because it didn't drive the story. You're trying to prove you can do the job at a high level, so you don't have the luxury of an act break that sighs instead of sings.

Endings Matter

Do you have a solid ending to each scene, preferably a joke ending? Writers call the last line of a scene the *blow,* or the *blackout,* or the *button.* Your scenes should not trail off without a joke or end abruptly without a joke. You may not need a joke to end absolutely every scene, but you should end every scene with some kind of clever and driving finish. And, most of the time, that should be a joke.

You Have to Earn Your Resolutions

Do you resolve things too easily? The characters need to have goals, obstacles to those goals, and unanticipated complications as a result of dealing with those obstacles. It is not satisfying storytelling if the characters solve their problems with ease. If a mom has to pick up two kids in two different locations at the same time, and she simply calls her sister and asks her to pick up one of the kids, then you have a small obstacle that's easily overcome, with no complications. That's boring. If the sister says she'll do it but misunderstands which kid she's supposed to pick up, and she and the mom wind up picking up the same kid, then you have what looked like an easy solution get complicated.

Rationing the Information

Have you overexplained or underexplained things? Sometimes, as a writer, you want to lay something in so clearly that you overdo it. And sometimes, you have something so deep in your own head that you think it must be clear on the page, but it isn't really. So, as you work through your script again, check to make sure that the information that needs to be out there is clear but that you haven't gone overboard in explaining things.

One of the most common ways of overexplaining is to repeat information the audience already knows. If someone tells John that Mary is coming over this afternoon in one scene, don't have someone else tell him again in the next scene (unless, of course, you're doing it for comic effect, to heighten John's anxiety, annoyance, or whatever emotion you're milking for comedy with John's attitude toward Mary). Telling the audience something they already know is not only boring but also a waste of precious screen time, and you have less than twenty-two minutes to tell your story. Even if you're writing a sitcom that's on a pay cable channel like HBO, in which case you have twenty-seven to twenty-eight minutes, you still don't want to tell the audience things they already know.

Now It's About the Jokes

Now you need to start to think funny. The Brits call this "tickling the script," and it's the most fun part of the process. How do you do this? The most important thing is simple—think like the characters. The best laughs always come out of character.

Situation is important, but the character who's terribly cheap and is in a situation where he has to spend money is much funnier than the generous guy in the same spot. So, lean on the character's attitude. If a character is sarcastic, instead of her saying, "I don't know," maybe she says, "I don't know why you think I care." If a character isn't too smart, let him be as dumb as he can believably be. Think about each character on the series, since each has his or her own comic flaws—she's pompous, he's oversensitive, she's naïve, he's bitter, she's a pushover, he's a glutton, and on and on. You know the characters on your show, so use their weaknesses to strengthen your comedy. Exaggerate their character traits, and remember that it's not always about overplaying a reaction; sometimes the exaggeration is in underplaying, which can work surprisingly well, depending on character and situation.

A secret every comedy writer knows is that the setup is more important than the punch line. If you have a good setup, either in a situation or in a verbal joke, the punch line is easy. So pay close attention to your setups, and know that the jokes will readily follow.

Look for comic turns. If a character says he'd never interfere in someone's business (the setup), then show him turning around and interfering in that business (the punch). The audience expects that and is gratified to see it.

Another trick is to look for *callbacks*, something you have established earlier in the script, perhaps something that wasn't even a joke, that can be mined later for humor. If a character in the first act says her unlucky number is three (the setup), in the second act have three IRS inspectors show up to her audit (the punch). An example from a series is in the "Andy's Play" episode of *The Office*. It's established that Michael auditioned for a community theater production but wasn't cast. When he goes to see Andy in the play, an usher asks Michael, "Are you the guy that did an entire *Law and Order* episode for his audition?" Michael denies it, but in the Tag, which is the very short segment prior to the end of the show and after the last commercial, Michael is onstage at the community theater auditioning and he starts reciting, by heart, the boilerplate opening lines of *Law and Order*.

As for verbal jokes, they come in a wide variety of forms, often dependent on some sort of surprise. They can be twists on common phrases or reversals of common sentiments. ("I should have the courage of my lack of convictions," said Tom Stoppard.) They can exploit varying meanings of words or phrases (as in the vaudeville classic: "Call me a taxi." "Okay, you're a taxi"). Jokes can employ double entendres (simple words like *it, in,* and *thing* do a lot of work here, as in the bumper sticker "Math teachers do it with unknowns"). Malaprops, or unintentional misstatements, work for some characters. (Yogi Berra supposedly said, "No one goes to that restaurant anymore. It's too crowded.")

And never forget the "rule of three." Establish a pattern with the first two elements of the joke, and then twist up the pattern in the third. ("If peanut oil comes from peanuts, and olive oil comes from olives, what does baby oil come from?" asked Lily Tomlin.)

Comic devices come in many forms—alliteration, repetition, incongruity, misunderstandings, absurdity, stereotypes, physical gags (though be careful of these in a spec since, as we said, the stage directions are not always read carefully). Use any of these devices to amp up the comedy in your script. But always remember that the best jokes come out of character and from milking each character's comic flaws.

The yin and yang of comedy are surprise and predictability. We laugh because something is surprising, and we also laugh because something is predictable. Aristotle wrote that the most satisfying ending of a tragedy is both surprising and inevitable; the same thing is true of jokes.

Once More unto the Breach

You've heard that writing is rewriting. To a writer, that's like saying tomorrow the sun is going to come up in the east. The truth is that writing happens by accretion. Yes, of course there's inspiration, the occasional visit from the muses, but plowing through your work again and again, gradually building it up and making it better through revision, is what every writer does. If you're determined to join our merry band, the writers of the world, you must put your shoulder to the plow and forge ahead. So now—rewrite!

The Chambers "After You've Written Your First Draft . . . Write the Second" Checklist

 What to look for as you rewrite? Problems and opportunities.

 What's your page count?

 Do you get off to a fast start? Do you have a good joke or two on page 1?

✓ Is your exposition laid in naturally?

✓ Have you serviced all the regular characters and do they sound like themselves?

✓ Are your act breaks spaced evenly, and do those act breaks pop?

✓ Do you have a solid ending for each scene?

✓ Do you resolve things too easily?

✓ Have you overexplained or underexplained things?

✓ Ready to put in the jokes and "tickle the script"?

✓ Rev it up to rewrite!

Writing Is Rewriting, Rewriting, and Did We Mention Rewriting, Again?

Again with the congratulations, this time on your first rewrite! We say "first rewrite" because, well, you'll need to do more.

Put It in a Drawer

The best thing you can do now is to "put the script in a drawer." That's a writerly way of saying you're too close to the script to look at it objectively. So, if you can, try not to look at it for a few days or a couple weeks. Of course, if you have some inspiration that you think will make it better, you can make a note of that, maybe even insert it in the script. But if you don't, give yourself a little time away from the script. Otherwise, you're never going to have the fresh eyes you need to see its weaknesses and know how to bolster its strengths.

When you go back to writing, keep in mind the items on the "After You've Written Your First Draft" checklist. Those are the issues you need to continue to think about and work on as you move forward.

Hear It Out Loud

Once you've taken some time away from your script and then gone back through it a few times, you will eventually come to the point where you think that your script is in pretty good shape. Now we recommend you stage a reading. There's nothing like hearing your words acted out loud to know if they play in the world and not just in your head.

So, have a reading of your script, with friends. Your script is not fully polished and finished yet, so do *not* invite anyone who means something in show business to this reading—not agents, producers, studio or network executives, managers, directors, writers you know casually. (The single possible exception to this is writers who are close friends and whom you trust, and we mean that you trust them a lot.) Don't read anything aloud yourself; just listen. Get someone else to read the slug lines (those headings that are always capitalized and that indicate a change of scene, location, and time) and stage directions, and assign parts to your actor/readers. If all involved agree, you may want to record the reading. Once it starts, your job is to listen and take notes for yourself. You will hear which jokes fall flat, what scenes don't play, which sequences and speeches feel too long, what transitions are clumsy, which characters' voices are out of rhythm, and lots of other things that just don't sit quite right.

Listen, Don't Defend

After the reading, ask all the people involved what they thought of the script. Again, your job is to listen. *Do not*—repeat—*do not defend your work*. You may have good reasons why you did something, but you're not going to get true and unvarnished opinions if people feel you don't really want to hear what they think. And you want true and unvarnished opinions. Someone who tells you, "That was really great," is more likely feeding your ego and being nice, but as pleasant as they feel, compliments do not help your script get any better. Defending your work is a sure way *not* to get much good, solid feedback.

So, simply listen and take notes on what people say, whether you agree with them or not. In the privacy of your next rewrite, you can decide which of the notes you got are worth considering, and sometimes a note you were ready to dismiss will have, as you reflect further, more value than you initially thought. The same holds true for people you ask to read the script at their leisure and then give you their thoughts. Do not defend, but listen, learn, and perhaps, if appropriate, discuss it with them in an unchallenging way. Then, in the privacy of your study, make your own judgments.

Finally, you should genuinely thank anyone who came to your reading or is willing to read your script and give you feedback. They've gone out of their way and taken their time to try to help you.

Maximize the Funny

Now that you've heard your words aloud, as you go through your script again look carefully at your jokes. Is each one fresh? Which ones could be sharper? Don't be a pioneer (comedy icon Garry Marshall's term for an "early settler"), meaning don't settle for those mediocre placeholder jokes you first came up with. But also, don't throw out your gold nuggets just because you're tired of them!

Classes and Writers' Groups

Since you're now starting to take your script out into the world, you should consider taking a class in comedy writing like those we teach at UCLA Extension Writers' Program. Another very helpful thing is to join or start a writers' group. Writing television comedy in the real world is, by and large, done around a table by a group of writers.

When you get an assignment or a job on a show, you will not come up with the story idea all by yourself, go off and write it, then turn it in and see it produced just as you wrote it. No, the story will be worked out "in the room" or "at the table" with other writers. You may write the first draft yourself, but after that, it's another group effort to rewrite your draft multiple times before it's finally shot. That system works; the script benefits from the creative input of a variety of comedic minds.

To be in a writers' group is to mimic, to a degree, the atmosphere of a professional writers' room. It's extremely helpful to hear how your stuff works, or doesn't work, for others who are interested in writing television comedy. You also get another benefit, which is the opportunity to carefully read and think about the work of others. Believe us, when you do get a chance to work on a television writing staff, you are not just thinking about your own writing but constantly reading and thinking about the work of others. A writers' group provides you with great mental exercise in framing stories and thinking of jokes.

The Importance of Appearance

Before you send your script out to anyone who can really help your career, make sure it looks flawlessly professional. Proofread it carefully. It's helpful to read it from back to front so you're not in the story flow. Have someone else proofread it for you too. You may even want to pay a professional proofreader. Why is this so important? Well, some Savvy Readers are sticklers for grammar, spelling, and punctuation. You don't want your funny script to be put in the reject pile because it has easily correctable errors, like writing *their* when you mean *they're* or *there*.

As we suggested earlier, copy precisely the way the scripts are written for the show you're writing (but without making it look like a production script). Start with a title page that has these three items centered: the name of the series in caps, the title of your episode in quotes, and "Written by" you (if you're writing with a partner, use an ampersand [&] between your names, not *and,* which in Hollywood indicates separate writers doing separate drafts). Then write your contact information in a lower corner. Do not date the title page, and do not indicate it's copyrighted or registered with the Writers Guild. That makes you look like an amateur. (By the way, if you're too worried about being ripped off, you may want to rethink aiming for a career in show business. We've been ripped off before, and so have most writers we know; it comes with the territory.)

Use the same standard font on the title page and throughout the script. That font is Courier 12 or Times New Roman 12. PDFs are increasingly common; for hard copies, regular white paper only, three-hole punched, and bound with two brads, in the top and bottom holes. No other binding is professional—not spiral, not spring-bound, not stapled or paper-clipped. Paginate in the upper right-hand corner, starting with the first page of the script (not the title page).

If you're writing on a screenwriting program (Final Draft and Movie Magic are the ones most commonly used by professionals), the formatting of your script will conform to industry standards. But if you're writing your script on a regular word processing program, you'll need to use the tab key a lot to make your script look professional. Don't worry. It's not that hard to do. In fact, before screenwriting programs, that's how it was done by everyone.

If you're writing an episode of a single-camera show, you don't need to use the editorial transition CUT TO in your script. It's a bit passé these days and interrupts the read. If, however, a joke is dependent on a particular transition, or a passage of time needs to be indicated, you should probably use a transition like SMASH CUT TO for a visual joke or DISSOLVE TO for a time transition.

If you're writing an episode of a multiple-camera series, make sure you're following the very particular format of that species of show. If you haven't been able to get a script for the show you're writing, find a script from another multiple-camera show and mimic that. These scripts are different from those of single-camera shows (and film scripts, too). The dialogue must be double-spaced, and the stage directions are fully capped. Most multiple-camera shows will use editorial transitions between scenes, like CUT TO and DISSOLVE TO, and you should, too. You want to be sure your script looks like a multicamera script and not a single-camera one. That's a dead giveaway to the Savvy Reader that you don't really get it.

Finally, use standard margins—don't fool with them to squeeze in more material, expand a script that's too short, or make your page count look reasonable. The Savvy Reader knows just how the margins should look and will instantly see you're cheating.

You're Looking Good!

Congratulations one last time! You wrote to "The End," then rewrote multiple times, polished, and refined. Now send your script out into the world and start working on your next one. Why? Because writers write, not just one script but many scripts. And any Savvy Reader who you're fortunate enough to get your script to and who likes it is 99.99 percent sure not to say, "I want to buy this." No, the Savvy Reader will tell you it's good and ask the question every writer knows so well—"What else have you got?" If you have more work, if you can prove you're not a one-trick pony but can write consistently good material, you may be on your way to making it as a television comedy writer.

The Chambers "Writing Is Rewriting, Rewriting, and Did We Mention Rewriting, Again?" Checklist

✓ Put the script in a drawer for a bit before you rewrite it again.

✓ Hold a reading and listen to your script being read aloud.

✓ Listen to what people say about your script, without defending your choices.

✓ Maximize the funny.

✓ Think about taking a class and/or joining or starting a writers' group.

✓ Make sure the physical presentation of your script is flawless.

✓ What else have you got?

Postscript

As we recommend in this chapter, you should try to find a sample of a produced script for the show you want to write and then mimic the format it uses. (One caveat when you copy a particular show's format: Avoid notations that only apply to production scripts, like numbering the scenes, having "Continued" at the top or bottom of the page, listing the characters in each scene immediately under the slug line, and any other information that's unnecessary until the script is being readied for production by the director and crew.)

If you can't find a script for the show you're writing, you can follow one of the formatting samples below.

Example of a Single-Camera Format from a Pilot Written by Julie Chambers & David Chambers, "Too Mean to Die":

"TOO MEAN TO DIE"

<u>TEASER</u>

EXT. TOWN SQUARE — DAY

This is London...Missouri. It's a typical weekday noontime.

<u>CAMERA FOLLOWS</u> CARSON POPE, 29, handsome, walking down the street. He looks more metro than the townsfolk he passes.

INSIDE the ROOM

                    CARSON
          (to camera)
     Otis Cribble? Everyone here in London,
     Missouri, knows Otis Cribble. He owns the
     newspaper, two banks, all three liquor
     stores....

A LITTLE KID runs by. Not breaking stride, Carson
grabs him just before he runs into traffic. His
MOTHER hurries over.

                    MOTHER
     Thank you, Carson.

Carson nods and smiles, hands her the kid, and
walks on.

                    CARSON
     Cribble owns over half the farmland here in
     Schuyler County.

He comes upon a little OLD LADY using a walker.

                    CARSON (CONT'D)
     Turning a little blue there, Miss Grimm. Maybe
     a tad more oxygen?

Carson adjusts the valve on her oxygen tank. She
takes a deep breath, smiles and nods at him. Carson walks on.

                    CARSON (CONT'D)
     Otis owns the radio station, the Internet café,
     four Laundromats . . .

Carson picks up a piece of litter, puts it in a trash can, and goes by MR. RANDLE, a store owner, sweeping the sidewalk.

> CARSON (CONT'D)
> Morning, Mr. Randle.

> MR. RANDLE
> Morning, Mr. Pope.

Carson continues walking down the street.

> CARSON
> Otis Cribble owns nearly everything in this town...but he doesn't own me.

Carson walks into the biggest building on the square.

CLOSE ON: A sign over the door reads, "THE CRIBBLE COMPANY," with a tile mosaic of a man who looks a lot like Dick Cheney.

> JUMP CUT TO:

INT. EXECUTIVE SUITE — A MINUTE LATER

The man in the tile mosaic, OTIS CRIBBLE, 65, aggression oozing from every pore, swivels to face Carson. The dark wood walls are lined with trophy heads of elk, bear, and moose.

> OTIS
> Pope! How the hell did you get in?!

INSIDE the ROOM

                    CARSON
I told your secretary I was hand-delivering
these legal documents.

Carson touches Otis with the documents. Otis lets
them fall to the floor.

                    CARSON (CONT'D)
Consider yourself served.

                    OTIS
    (into intercom)
Dolores, you're fired!

                    DOLORES (O.C.)
    (over intercom)
Again?

                    OTIS
Pope, why don't you take that fancy law degree
to St. Louis and make some real money?

                    CARSON
Then who would keep Cribble Construction from
overcharging the county for roadwork? See you
in court.

Carson walks out.

**Example of a multiple-camera format from a pilot written
by Julie Chambers, "The Management":**

                    "THE MANAGEMENT"
                    COLD OPENING

EXTREME CLOSE UP: DOMINICK, AN ATTRACTIVE
TWENTY-EIGHT-YEAR-OLD GUY, TALKS STRAIGHT TO
CAMERA.

                    DOMINICK
     After six years of working at one of the
     largest, most prestigious talent agencies in the
     world, I finally quit. Walked away from all the
     stress and pressure, all the glamour and money...
     (STARTS CRYING) My god! What have I done?

INT. BANK — DAY
PULL BACK: TO REVEAL HE'S CONFESSING TO A BANK
TELLER WHO LOOKS A LITTLE WEIRDED OUT BY THIS,
BUT OFFERS HIM A TISSUE.

                    TELLER
     Would you like that in twenties, sir?

THE TELLER DOLES OUT THE CASH.

                    DOMINICK
     (BUCKING HIMSELF UP) But it's good, right? Now I
     can spend more time with my family. Family is
     the most important thing.

THE TELLER GIVES HIM AN OPTIMISTIC SMILE.

                                        CUT TO:
     INT. DOMINICK'S KITCHEN — AN HOUR LATER
     DOMINICK'S WIFE, RACHEL, 27, IS CLEARLY A
     TRANSPLANT FROM LONG ISLAND TO L.A.

                    RACHEL

You quit your job?! What are you, flipping
crazy?!

DOMINICK TURNS TO HIS ONE-YEAR-OLD, BABY ZOEY,
WHO SITS IN A CHAIR ATTACHED TO THE KITCHEN
TABLE.

> DOMINICK
> Daddy isn't flipping crazy. Daddy needs to
> spend more time with the family. Like Mommy has
> been nagging him to do!

> RACHEL
> Omigod! I meant come home for dinner once in a
> while. Not quit your job!

> DOMINICK
> Honestly, it was quit my job or lose my mind,
> sweetheart.

BABY ZOEY THROWS CEREAL AT HIM.

> RACHEL
> If you were working at the agency and lost
> your mind at least we would have health
> insurance. You could have gotten on heavy meds
> or taken shock treatment, or something.

> DOMINICK
> Well, I thought I could try something else,
> before going the lobotomy route!

CHAPTER 7

Writing the Half-Hour Comedy Pilot

by Phil Kellard

The most important question you need to ask yourself when thinking about writing a pilot is . . . why should a network put this show on the air, and is there an endless number of stories to tell? By *endless,* I mean one hundred episodes' worth of stories—stories that can captivate a bunch of strangers out there in TV land for at least five seasons.

Successful sitcoms can make the network, studio, and creators more money than anything else on television. It's wine-and-art-collection money. Buying-castles-in-France money. Owning-private-jet money. Mrs. Tiger Woods money. FU money. Yes, *Law and Order* and all its one-hour drama cousins are on television every minute of the day in every country on the planet and maybe in outer space. But that's an anomaly. Half-hour comedy syndicates better than all other genres. At its height, *Seinfeld* made the network $200 million profit every year, and then sold into syndication for $1.7 billion. It made its cocreators, Jerry Seinfeld and Larry David, about $250 million each over and above their eight years' worth of series salaries. Warner Bros. sold *The Big Bang Theory* for a record $2 million per episode to Time Warner's TBS and Fox. We're talking billions of dollars. In the words of writer-director Garry Marshall, "Funny is money."

I can't promise to give you the secret to coming up with the next *Seinfeld* or *The Big Bang Theory,* but I can share tips and strategies for creating an original half-hour comedy pilot script that shows your talent and originality. In my thirty-plus years in this business, I've pitched and written pilots for ABC, CBS, NBC, the WB (when that was still around), Showtime, Syfy, the Disney Channel, Spike, Comedy Central, Nickelodeon, and more. I've also taught students in dozens of UCLA Extension Writers' Program courses on sitcom writing, and I can tell you what you need to know to create a solid script that can last a hundred episodes and beyond.

Specifically, you need to know what a pilot is, why it's important to have in your portfolio, and how to generate its Big Idea—the innovative premise that can spawn a wealth of original and entertaining stories. You need to know how to create fresh and interesting characters that viewers will remember, relate to, and want to watch each week. You need to develop these characters' relationships and mine the humor in them. You need to know the difference between premise-based and typical-episode pilots and what kind of pilot fits your material. And finally, you need to know how to pitch your pilot.

"Hold on!" you might say. "How about giving me a step-by-step guide to outlining and writing my pilot?" That's a fair question, and the answer is that the process for writing the beat sheet, outline, and script of a pilot is exactly the same as for an on-air show, whether it's a single-camera or a multicamera script. The *big* difference is the subject matter. When you write a spec of a current show, you have the distinct advantage of working with an established world and characters; you are following a template. This is where aspiring sitcom writers need to start their education—you're Picasso copying the great masters of figurative art; after that, you can invent Cubism or write a sitcom pilot.

Once you have a couple of spec scripts under your belt, you will know exactly how to outline and write your pilot and be prepared for the creative challenge of conjuring up a brand-new world and its inhabitants. If you need to learn the basics of building a spec story, outline, and script, work your way through chapters 5 and 6 of this book. If you're ready to tackle pilot writing, here we go.

Daunting? Yes. Can this chapter help you do it? Until somebody changes the rules . . . definitely.

Know the Who, What, When, Where, and Why of a Pilot

A pilot script is the intended first episode of a potential television series. It's the "who, what, when, where, and why" of the series and one of the earliest stages of the development process. It's kind of like a concept car for the automobile industry. It tells the network and you as a writer whether it's going to be an Edsel (*The Paul Reiser Show*) or a Mustang (*2 Broke Girls*). The pilot script has some very specific functions. It establishes the premise, characters, tone and look, setting, style of dialogue, and pacing, and tells where the series is headed, all the while making the story interesting and funny. And remember, these characters are new, unfamiliar, never seen before—or for our purposes, never read before. The pilot must achieve all of this in twenty-eight to thirty-three pages.

That's the "who, what, when, and where" of a pilot. What's the "why"?

Agents and producers (people who read material who can actually do something with it) want both new *and* established TV writers to have original material ready to show. Of course, you must have a couple of writing samples of on-air shows to demonstrate that you can replicate a series. But in addition, you have to have something different and unique to sell your writing talent. As a new writer, think of an original comedy pilot as your calling card. It shows *your* voice, *your* brand of humor, and *your* sensibility. It demonstrates that you can create characters and generate ideas for series, and can go from being "just a writer" to being a "writer-creator."

In addition to being a must-have writing sample, your pilot might even have a chance of getting sold, because today's TV comedy marketplace is *huge*. Along with the big five networks, buyers for half-hour sitcoms have expanded to FX, USA, ABC Family, TV Land, Hulu, the

Disney Channel, Cartoon Network, Nickelodeon, E!, Comedy Central, TBS, Logo, BET, IFC, and yes, Country Music Television. There are also many nonwriting producers (producers who don't write but find and develop television shows) with deals at studios who need material to sell to the networks. Add to the mix online series, satellite, even cell phones that need to buy content. There's far less money here but more opportunities. Becoming a creator gives you ownership of your intellectual property.

Okay, for now, put selling your pilot out of your mind. We'll come back to that topic at the end of the chapter. Relax and get ready to tackle the hardest part of the process: creating a new, fresh half-hour comedy that's worth reading and grabs the attention of your readers.

Learn from the Best

Watch, read, and study as many pilot episodes of great shows as you can get your eyes and hands on—the classics as well as the current hit shows. You can find them on numerous Internet script sites, on Hulu and Netflix, or you can buy the box sets in book and video stores. Watch iconic pilots for series like *Mary Tyler Moore, All in the Family,* and *Seinfeld.* They still hold up as pilots and as series, and every serious student of television should know them and learn from them.

Watch pilots for current shows like *Modern Family, How I Met Your Mother, New Girl,* and *The Big Bang Theory.* Study how they introduce characters, what makes these characters tick, and what kind of stories they tell in their subsequent episodes. By watching and reading pilot episodes by good writers, writers you admire, you absorb their styles and their storytelling techniques, just as you did when you wrote your spec *30 Rock* or *How I Met Your Mother.* This is how your talent will grow.

Create "the Big Idea" (aka a Strong Premise)

When my writing partner Tom Moore and I first went onto the writing staff of *Doogie Howser, M.D.,* we loved working with Steven Bochco (having just finished two seasons on *Hooperman* with him and John Ritter), but we didn't know if a series about a sixteen-year-old licensed physician had "legs." By that I mean we weren't sure this idea could generate an endless amount of emotional stories with a strong beginning, middle, and end. The network didn't much like the pilot and really didn't like the casting of Neil Patrick Harris as the teenage wunderkind.

It turned out the network, Tom, and I were all wrong. *Doogie Howser, M.D.* was based on a powerful Big Idea: a sixteen-year-old doctor in a major hospital who is also dealing with the everyday problems of growing up. This concept generated tons of stories in both worlds, from AIDS and racism to adolescent friendship and loss of virginity. The show lasted for four seasons and launched the unstoppable career of Neil Patrick Harris.

Give Your Big Idea Legs

The first thing you need to do is come up with a strong premise—to figure out what your show is going to be about and make sure your concept is rich enough to hook the audience and keep them watching.

Think about *The Office*. Based on the British series *The Office* (2001–2003), the American version premiered in 2005 and, for nine seasons, chronicled the everyday lives of a bunch of going-nowhere, idiosyncratic office workers set in a midsize company selling paper, a dying industry, located in Scranton, Pennsylvania, a dying industrial town. On the other hand, *Up All Night* is a show about a couple trying to adjust to life with their newborn baby. Okay, I know what episodes one, two, three, and maybe four would be, but what happens when the baby finally starts sleeping through the night? I think the producers also realized this shortly into the first season, and the show became more about the workplace, and from that came more stories.

Make Your Big Idea as Unique as Possible

While I've known all through my television career that characters are what sell television shows, I also know that your pilot must be built on a strong premise. Even though every premise has been done or pitched in one form or another, it's your job as a pilot's creator to try to come up with a unique take. Do some diligent research. Is there something like your concept already on the air? Is your approach to a familiar idea fresh and innovative enough to distinguish it from the pack of current shows? If the answer is no, then—you guessed it—dump that idea and move on.

Next, and this is very important, is your concept something you would like to watch, something you've been dying to see on television? If the answer to that question is yes, then congratulations, you've got, as far as you know, a breakthrough project, which you're passionate about and can't wait to write.

Put Your Own Interests and Passions into Your Big Idea

Write what interests you. It doesn't have to be your life story, but I happen to think the best stories and concepts come from personal experience. Once again, it's your voice, your vision. Come from your sensibilities. How do you see the world? What individual voice can you bring to a show? Chuck Lorre and Bill Prady weren't science nerds, but they brought their sensibilities, point of view, and sense of humor to *The Big Bang Theory*.

Open your senses as a writer. This is where you let the right side of your brain take over and let it flow. Observe and absorb everything that goes on around you. Stories and ideas often come out of everyday life. While sitting at a Starbucks and observing a bickering couple, I noticed a small article on the last page of a discarded newspaper. It was about a husband and wife who were both police officers and had recently received a commendation from their chief.

I took that piece of information, combined it with the bickering couple, and turned them into married, decorated police chiefs who worked in two cities divided by a main highway. One oversaw the public welfare in an affluent, clean suburb, the other in a crime-ridden, badass town. The couple faced the same kind of division in home and family that they did at work. I called it *Divided We Stand* and pitched it to a network the following week. You never know what you can come up with while goofing on people over a nonfat grande latte.

Figure out what kind of show works for your sensibilities. In network meetings, a common question is, "What is your passion project?" What is the show you really want to write? Who are you as a writer? You may be an edgy, cable-network kind of writer. You may be an eight o'clock, family kind of writer. Play to your strengths. What is the tone of your show? Warm and fuzzy or dark and cynical? *Californication* funny or *Mike & Molly* funny?

Put Your Big Idea into a Logline

Don't confuse a Big Idea with a Complex Idea. In fact, try to keep your premise simple. You should be able to reduce your series concept to a few sentences, something that you or an agent or producer could rattle off in a "short pitch." Put it into a clear and concise logline (one or two sentences that crystallize the concept) that exhibits the show's potential and elicits interest.

Pilot Logline #1:

"It's about a large Chinese/Irish/Italian family that runs a small restaurant. We see the series through the eyes of the eldest daughter, who helps out as a waitress during the day and is a pro bono street lawyer at night, where she meets and falls for an ex-convict graffiti artist that she's defending. Her life is further complicated by her four adopted children and . . . she's a witch." WRONG!

Pilot Logline #2:

"Two men, estranged from their wives, become roommates and end up undergoing the same domestic trials and quarrels each had with his former spouse." RIGHT!

The second is the logline for the classic series *The Odd Couple*. Clear and concise—you get it all right away. It describes a show that is much easier to get a handle on, and much easier to write, than the first. You've got enough to deal with in your pilot's first five pages—setting up the premise, establishing your characters and their attitudes, capturing the tone and pacing, plus trying to be hilarious right out of the gate. Don't make the process more difficult than it already is by introducing too many characters and a concept that you need a flow chart to understand.

Give Your Big Idea a Twist

There are different things that you can incorporate into your show's template that can tell stories in a fresh way. Play with the narrative. The confessional or interview (talking directly to the camera) has become a popular device. Flashbacks and voice-overs help set a show apart and enhance the way scenes transition. *How I Met Your Mother* is a mystery played in reverse. *Weeds* and *United States of Tara* deal with darkly comic drama. *Glee* mixes it all up with a generous dose of awesome music. The sitcom has opened up over time. It's linear, nonlinear, dark, musical, time traveling, and you had better be aware of all the possible options when trying to come up with your Big Idea.

Test Your Big Idea

A good way to test your idea for legs is to think of one episode. Make up a funny story line. Nothing elaborate, not a lot of detail, just broad strokes. Beginning, middle, and end. It should be just enough to grasp how the problem starts, escalates, and resolves. Think of another one. Now think of two more. Don't stop until you come up with ten stories. Good. Write them down; we'll use them later.

While it's not necessary to have all the episodes for a season prepared, it is valuable to have designed the big beats for at least ten episodes.

The details can be filled out if the pilot gets picked up for series, but it's the best way to demonstrate that the concept can sustain itself beyond the first episodes and that there is plenty of growth and surprises ahead for the characters.

It's essential to know the arc of at least the first two seasons before a writer goes to a buyer. For example, if the concept is about a young couple who got married in a fever after a very short courtship, the first season is probably about the husband and wife getting to know each other—something they skipped over during their passionate, impulsive, monthlong relationship. The second season might be about whether to have a baby or not . . . or trying to have a baby. For now, you should just start getting a sense of where the series is going as you move forward in creating the pilot.

Create Relatable and Funny Characters

More Character, Less Plot

With an original concept, your most intense work, the "heavy lifting," is going to be done on your characters. In my UCLA Extension course "Master Class in Half-Hour Comedy Pilot Writing," I spend the first four weeks just dealing with character. You only have to turn on the television and look at any show, especially the savior of the sitcom, *Modern Family,* to see how crucially important character is. The viewing audience wants to identify with characters they feel good about, who are more outrageous and funnier than they are but identifiable nonetheless. These are the kind of characters that we want to visit with every week. *Modern Family* is a hit because Phil, Claire, Jay, Gloria, Cam, and Mitchell all have a little bit of us in them.

So before you write a word of the script, generate reams of information on each main character. Your secondary characters won't require as much. Then hone it all down to a paragraph or two on each character. Use adjectives.

Know Your Characters Inside and Out

I spend weeks building out my characters and start seeing them as living, breathing human beings before I go into the networks with a show. My goal is to know my characters so completely that if there's a sale, I'll have an endless resource to rely on as I, hopefully, spend years writing them.

My brother, Rick Kellard; Tom Moore; and I sold a pilot entitled *Big Weekend* to Fox a few years back. We created a character by the name of Julian. When we first meet him in the script he walks into the men's room at a popular Chicago bar. Julian notices someone in the stall. From his jacket pocket he takes out a clip-on tie and puts it on. From his other pockets he produces a small dish with candies, gum, small hotel bottles of cologne, face cream, mouthwash, and a comb. He places all these items near the sink and puts some change and a dollar bill in the dish. When he hears the flush he turns the water on and takes a paper towel from the dispenser. The man exits the stall and washes his hands. Julian hands him the paper towel and watches the man put on some cologne, then place a few bills in the dish before he leaves.

In the next scene, we find Julian paying for a drink at the bar with the cash he just earned. Not a word of dialogue is spoken, but you understand who Julian is pretty quickly. We thought this character was unique and we introduced him in a unique way.

When we pitched Julian and all the other characters in *Big Weekend* to the network, we knew them inside and out. We knew what TV shows they liked to watch, their eating habits, their quirks, their first sexual experiences, their politics, ad infinitum. If you know what a character's favorite TV show is, it gives you a way to start a scene. It gives you jokes. It gives you dialogue from character. It gives you and the audience an insight into the character. If your character enjoys a pickup basketball game every once in a while, you have a locale to play out scenes.

Create Your Characters' Past and Present

In preparation for the actual writing of the pilot, you have to know every-thing about your characters and everything that makes them funny in future episodes. I mean *everything*. What we see on the page or on the screen is only the tip of the iceberg. You, as the writer, have to create the whole iceberg before you write FADE IN. Create a backstory for your characters. What was their childhood like? Who were their parents? Who were their friends? Did they have money? What did they study? What social class were they in? Were they popular in school? Did they date? What was their sex life like?

On *Friends,* Monica had a backstory of being extremely overweight as a child. This detail informed dialogue and jokes for the five other main characters, especially her brother, Ross, and gave the writers a flashback episode. When creating *Modern Family,* Steve Levitan and Christopher Lloyd made Phil Dunphy a former college cheerleader at Fresno State, which gave a story line to Phil and his daughter Haley when they visited his alma mater in "Go Bullfrogs!" Look deep.

Describe your characters' lives in the present. What kind of relation-ships do they have now with family, friends, and lovers? Where do they work? How do they relate to the other characters at work? Do they have children? How do they parent? What do they look like from head to toe? Where do they live? What are their hobbies? How do they like to spend their leisure time?

Draw on Characters from Your Own Life

Who makes you laugh? Is it your cousin with the wild laugh and the catchphrase "Yeah, so what?" Is it your ego-driven best friend who talks fast to hide the fact that he thinks slowly? Is it your cuttingly sarcastic ex-girlfriend who gives herself a pep talk every morning? Think about the people in your life, bend them, tweak them, change their names, and put them in your pilot. All of this is still only the tip of the iceberg. Keep looking deeper. Keep asking your own questions until you have a full character history, past and present.

Explore Your Characters' Psyche and Behavior

Dig deeply into your characters' psyches: their flaws, attitudes, idiosyncrasies, complexes, and dreams that drive them through a story. Jessica "Jess" Day (Zooey Deschanel) on *New Girl* was created with an aversion to confrontation. Also among her personality traits is her tendency to burst into song, sometimes making up lyrics reflecting her situation. These are compelling characteristics that play out throughout the series.

What characters do, what decisions they make, what complications they bring into their lives because of who they are, is funnier than what they say. Audiences remember behavior long after they've forgotten the funny lines. When people talk about the show the next day, most everyone will say, "Did you see what so-and-so did last night?" "Did" . . . not "said." Behavior drives story. Behavior creates the context for the jokes.

Take a character (and a real person, in this case) like Larry David on *Curb Your Enthusiasm*. All the stories on that show, all the funny situations, are generated by who Larry is. He's a man who can't go a full day without getting himself into an awkward or stressful situation. We look forward each week to seeing what ridiculous and often surreal problem he's going to have to get himself out of and, in doing so, get himself into further hilarious trouble. None of his problems would occur if he weren't someone who couldn't keep his mouth shut, who couldn't keep his nose out of everyone's business, who couldn't let things be. The whole show emanates from his character flaws.

Establish Your Characters' Relationships

Once you've got your main characters fleshed out, the next most important thing is to set up how they relate to each other. While these relationships will evolve as the series continues, your script won't become a series unless there is a firm foundation for the characters' interactions with each other from the get-go. On *Seinfeld,* nobody ever liked Newman. The cast's attitude toward his character charged all the scenes with him. Eventually, all Newman had to do was show up at Jerry's door or run into the gang on the street, and the audience would already be laughing, waiting for how they were going to avoid him or bite their tongues because they really needed him.

Since your pilot's regulars are going to be in all the scenes in various groupings, sometimes all together for a couple of scenes, you have to know what drives the relationships intimately. Is one character always eager to please and annoyingly upbeat? Can another always find the positive side to anything? If her apartment building were burning down, would she say, "At least now there's an unobstructed view of the Hudson River"?

A word of advice: Six characters is a good number. Stop there. All your characters have to be involved in the script, moving and talking and pushing the story forward. Remember, you have to service all of them and the reader has to follow them. Anything over six lessens your chances of keeping all the balls in the air.

Develop the Humor in Your Characters' Relationships

How these characters will be funny together is key to your series' success. Look for opposites, conflicting lifestyles, rivalries, and past disastrous relationships. Love/hate is always good. Two guys in love with the same girl: One guy is brash and self-centered; the other is shy, way too sensitive, and tongue-tied around her. It's familiar, yes, but introducing another character, a third guy—someone she's hopelessly and confoundingly in love with—can make it fresh.

For instance, her new boyfriend is seriously overweight but kind and caring, not like all the jerks she's used to dating. He's going through the *Biggest Loser* phase of his life and hopes to lose beaucoup pounds by

Christmas. She's committed to helping him through the first hundred pounds. We now know what everybody wants and what everybody is afraid of. The first two guys can't believe they might lose this girl to a needy guy with a weight problem. The needy guy just won the lottery by landing this beautiful girl, and is going to take walks with her and listen to her and make her his special lasagna, provided she eats it in another location. And he'll even put up with her two guy friends. When he calls out for a group hug, she's amazed by his openness and acceptance of her friends. The brash guy's response is, "Dude, you're already a group hug." The shy guy hugs him, hoping to impress the girl. End scene.

Put It All Together: The Opening Scene

Establish the tone and your characters for the reader as fast as you can. Look for simple, efficient ways to tell the reader who they are in the first few pages. If you can do it on the first page, even better. Here's an example of how to do it.

Let's say your show is about two guys sharing an apartment. One guy, let's call him Ralph, is an obsessive type A with a big heart. The other, Jerry, is easygoing, very likeable, but is drifting through life at the moment without purpose. Scene one can start with Ralph, focused on cleaning up the place, rearranging furniture, changing his mind, obsessing. On the page, his behavior fits his character description. He's being the guy you want the reader to know and like from the first beat on page 1. He's a compulsive multitasker, so he's on the phone giving directions to his place to someone who's lost but close by. He's talking about how badly he feels having to kick his pal Jerry out. He's trying to be strong, because he knows he has to do it. There's the big heart. We're still on page 1. From the bedroom comes Jerry in boxer shorts and with bed head. That paints a picture, but it has to be filled in with some character description. Jerry is a person who was born with a Xanax gene that helps him sleep peacefully through the night and forget that he hasn't worked in over a year.

                    JERRY
    Another awesome morning!

He's obviously a positive guy.

                    RALPH
    It's two in the afternoon.

                    JERRY
Brilliant. So I can crack a beer without looking like
a guy with a problem.

                    RALPH
    Tell me you're going on some interviews today.

Big-hearted Ralph is still hopeful.

                    JERRY
I'll be surfing the Web for employment opportunities, interspersed with a conservative amount of
virtual 3-D porn. You should check that out.
First-class.

Clearly, Jerry is deep in denial. So now the reader knows what the
problem is. These friends have a confrontation ahead of them, one that
could change their friendship forever. We meet them as the problem is
getting out of hand. From the conversation on the phone, we learn that
Ralph can't financially carry his friend anymore. Maybe the person on
the other end is his cousin and she is looking for a new place because her
building went condo or burned down. When she arrives, Jerry is still in
his shorts and has cracked a beer. Cousin Nicky needs a description, a
quick snapshot of who she is—maybe she's a driven, outspoken career

woman who wonders why she can't maintain a relationship. When she walks in she could show us why, by burning Jerry.

                    NICKY
        I don't know how else to say this, but...
            (indicates underwear)
        Your doggie door is open.

                    JERRY
        Sorry. For very long?

                    NICKY
        I'm guessing since you were twelve.

She's outspoken. She can continue telling us about
herself by getting right down to business with
Ralph.

                    NICKY
        I'm on my lunch hour. Show me my room.

Whoa! That's news to Jerry. Ralph hasn't broken the news to him yet. We're probably on page 2 now. Nicky's move shows us that she's a little insensitive too and sets the story off in motion.

By taking time and getting the character descriptions onto the page as sharply as possible, backing them up with behavior and dialogue, the people in your script can come to life quickly and get your pilot rolling right away.

Don't Forget the Jokes

A few things about the jokes: Bottom line . . . you can either write jokes or you can't. One can't be taught to be funny. Writing a joke is a very special art—maybe *knack* is a better word. You can learn how to make a joke better, but the DNA of a good joke is elusive, and as far as I know, nobody has broken down the genome.

When writing a pilot, test all the jokes regularly. If the script is still making you laugh after a few months of perfecting it, that's a good sign. A pilot should contain as many "home runs" as possible, which doesn't mean overloading it with jokes. It means pushing the writing to a higher level, so you wind up with solid funny moments. If you find yourself writing a line that makes you think, *Yeah, that'll be funny,* you've failed, because you're thinking . . . not laughing. Scrap it, and write another one.

Choose Your Format: Premise Pilot or Typical Episode

A strong pilot is a sample of everything that will happen in the series. It sets the template, tone, and style. You have to introduce the world and your characters and hint at the series arc. You have to describe the series and what you can do with action and dialogue. There's a whole lot of stuff to accomplish in the pilot, and there are two ways to write it: as a premise pilot or as a typical episode. You have to decide, based on all the work you have done so far, which is better suited to your material.

The Premise Pilot

A premise pilot spends a lot of time fleshing out the Big Idea, providing information about the world, placing each character in it, and explaining his/her current situation. Sometimes the premise pilot shows some kind of big change to an already-existing world; the starting point is at the moment the main character's world is turned upside down or changes.

The premise pilot can be challenging to write because it often includes many things about the world, including people, that may never be seen or dealt with again. However, the fact of the matter is that more than half of the pilots ordered every year are premise pilots. A premise-based pilot launched the multi–Emmy Award–winning *30 Rock,* which kicks off when Liz Lemon, head writer for a *Saturday Night Live* type of sketch comedy series called *The Girlie Show,* is called upstairs to meet the new vice president of East Coast television and microwave oven programming for NBC GE Universal Kmart, Jack Donaghy. This opening episode focuses on Jack trying to convince Liz to hire loose-cannon movie star Tracy Jordan to draw in young male viewers to *The Girlie Show* and the crew reacting to this news.

In *Mike & Molly*'s pilot, Molly hears Mike share at an Overeaters Anonymous meeting, falls for him right away, and asks him to speak to her fourth-grade class. The overweight teacher and police officer then become a couple. Again, this marks the beginning of how the main characters meet. Premise pilot.

The classic series *Mary Tyler Moore* dealt with the life and trials of a young single career woman and her friends, both at work and at home. In the pilot episode, Mary Richards, on the rebound from a busted relationship, relocates to Minneapolis, where she quickly finds a new apartment, an associate producer's job at WJM-TV, and new friends. Premise pilot.

The best thing to do for your pilot if it's a premise pilot is to choose the most obvious starting point, yet try not to be too obvious about it.

The Typical-Episode Pilot

Writing a typical episode for a pilot is just that. You're writing an episode that could fall anywhere in the first three or four airings of the show. This form of pilot introduces your characters but also gives us a sense of what future episodes will be like, how your characters interact every week. My personal preference is to write a typical-episode pilot, because I think that to get a feel for the universe, everything should be in place and everybody should already be rockin' and rollin'. It demonstrates how your show's story engine runs and that it can keep running for a long time.

The pilot for *The Office* (US and British) is a typical episode. In the US version, Michael Scott gives a tour for the documentary camera crew and first-day temp Ryan Howard. We find out about Jim and Pam's relationship and meet the rest of the characters. Along the way, the pilot becomes a typical episode because it deals with a problem that the series regulars could face anywhere along the history of the show: the news that corporate headquarters is planning to downsize an entire branch.

The *South Park* pilot has Cartman telling the boys about the nightmare he had where aliens abducted him from his bed. Kyle and Stan try to convince Cartman that the dream was real. This could have easily been episode six or twenty-six. Typical episode.

The Middle is a show about the daily mishaps of Frankie, a married woman, and her semidysfunctional family and their attempts to tackle life in the city of Orson, Indiana. In the pilot, Frankie desperately tries to close a sale with disastrous results; her daughter, Sue, tries out for show choir with calamitous results; and her son Brick has trouble relating to his teacher with odd results. Typical episode.

"What If?" Scenario: A Nonpremise Pilot Turned into a Typical Episode

I'm going to share with you a scenario I've written that has absolutely no connection to any *New Girl* pilot, either living or dead, and it's designed to show you that there are many ways to turn a story on its head. If you've got a premise pilot in your head, but you think it might be better for the marketplace to deliver it as a typical episode, keep thinking. Keep twisting it. Then decide which pilot format is best to tell your story.

The pilot for *New Girl* is a premise pilot. Jess Day, an offbeat and quirky teacher, leaves her cheating longtime boyfriend and moves into an apartment with three single males she's never met before: prickly bartender Nick, womanizer Schmidt, and intense personal trainer and former athlete Coach. The guys try to help "adorable" Jess reenter the dating world.

With a few adjustments—actually, some radical changes in story—it might have been a typical (nonpremise) first episode. Suppose Jess has been living with the guys for a while now. She's also been dating a guy for a few months, and he asks her to move in with him. She's totally smitten. Maybe he's one of those guys that she thought she'd never get. Her roommates don't like him and question his motives. They have to deal with her leaving, and she has become such a big part of their lives. They could reminisce about how she first came to look at the apartment and they weren't sure about letting her live there. Flashbacks.

But the story is basically about how she learns that she's not ready to move in with another guy yet, given her last relationship. This is a deal breaker for the guy she's going with, because he's one of those serial live-together guys. So she ends up staying, and through this story, the audience sees how Jess came to live with her roommates, why she feels safe, and that there might even be a potential romantic interest in store with one of the roommates.

Simple and Emotional

Successful series tap into what the audience wants to see again and again—something they can care about. How do you achieve this in your own pilot? Keep it simple; keep it emotional.

All in the Family was a classic sitcom that ran from 1971 to 1979, topped the Nielsen ratings for five years straight, and is on most everyone's top ten list. In the pilot episode, Mike and Gloria Stivic plan a surprise party to celebrate the twenty-second wedding anniversary of Gloria's parents, Archie and Edith Bunker. Simple. The entire episode takes place in the Bunkers' living room in the working-class neighborhood of Queens, New York, with the four main characters and next-door neighbor, Lionel. Simple. A heated argument quickly erupts between Archie (a World War II veteran and, as he came to be widely known, "a lovable bigot"), and Mike, a self-important liberal college student, thus kicking off the first of many conflicts that captured the generational, social, cultural, and political divisions in America in the 1970s while keeping its viewers cracking up. Emotional.

Pitching the Pilot

The Bible

For yourself, the reader, your agent, and maybe someday the network, the next thing you should write is a series bible that lays out your creation in a couple of pages. The bible is yet another selling tool for your show and for you.

Start with a short synopsis. The first sentence should be your logline; remember to make it compelling and simple. Next, write a condensed version of your overall series—just a few paragraphs, up to one page. Now add your character bios; describe your main characters in three or four sentences each and secondary characters in one or two lines. Follow the bios with short summaries of the first ten episodes, keeping them funny and interesting. Don't add an episode just to make your number. If the story doesn't grab you, it won't grab anyone else either. Finish the bible with a half-page wrap-up of how you'll tell the stories and how the series works.

You can put the synopsis and the bios up front, the episodes and the last page in the back. Now you're ready to sell your script.

The Pitch

For the TV writer in Hollywood, it's all about pitching your ideas, whether you're an experienced staff writer on a specific show, a freelance writer trying to sell an idea and script to a showrunner, or—as you might well be—a newly minted writer of a pilot who needs to practice the skill of selling his script and himself and learn to be a writer and salesperson that producers want to hire. Most TV shows are sold on the basis of a pitch.

Envision that you've caught the attention of some Important Comedy Execs and they've invited you to a meeting. Practice the steps below with your friends, family, and classmates if you have them; practice in front of the mirror, in the car, in your head.

Prepare and Practice

If you've gone through all the steps in this chapter, you know your series idea inside and out. Now make sure you get passionate about it! You've done your character work, so practice describing your characters' comedic idiosyncrasies and flaws, what drives them through the series. You've outlined ten episodes in your bible, so choose a couple of the best ones to show how your series will unfold and that it has legs.

Design the pitch so you take all this material and turn it into a story, and then practice the pitch on people who can give you some feedback. Train like an athlete for the big day. I pitch the whole thing to myself just before I go to sleep, in the shower the next morning, and in the car on the way to the meeting.

In the Room with the Execs

Sitting in an outer office waiting to go into a room filled with execs can be intimidating and nerve-wracking. Sometimes you don't know who or how many people are going to be behind that door or how their day has gone so far. The only thing you can manage once that door opens is your pitch. Make sure you can answer any question about the series—before it starts, while it's on the air, and for the reunion show long after. Everything else is out of your control. Breathe.

When the small talk stops, the spotlight is on you. Start off with the Big Idea, the premise. Hook them fast. Draw them into your intriguing concept with your compelling logline. Make them see the show and understand why it stands apart from all the others.

Next hit on the characters, one at a time. Here comes the payoff for all your hard work. Describe the people who will populate your new, exciting world—their attitudes, unique voices and outlooks on life, the behavior that makes them funny. Explain the conflicts. Show how your secondary characters contribute more conflict. Hit them with some dialogue, and give them some jokes. Keep the pitch clear, concise, and funny.

The Home Stretch

It's almost over. Now you can breeze through those three or four examples of typical stories you'd put these great characters in where conflict and hilarity will ensue for countless episodes. If you're counting, it's one hundred. If you've hit the ten-minute mark, you're bordering on too long. Oh, yeah, and deliver all this without referring to any notes or pages. This is all happening extemporaneously. My brother, Rick, rips up all his notes before he walks into the room. It's a great statement of confidence.

Now it's their turn. If they have a lot of questions, that's a good thing. If you are pitching a television show at a network, it's because they've read your work and feel you could bring them a good idea, or you've been picked by a producer or studio who is excited about your writing. Yes, there are a few jerks who sit there silently, smugly, with a look that says, "Impress me," but most development executives are welcoming and convey the feeling, "I'm impressed. Tell me your story."

A Final Word

Your half-hour comedy pilot is your voice, your vision. The TV industry is changing—it always is. At this writing, blogs, Twitter feeds, YouTube, and even self-published books through outlets like Author Solutions are being trolled by executives for potential pilots. Having a digital presence is a great way to attract attention, and a pilot based on a digital presence has a chance of selling because execs are way more comfortable buying something based on established material, even if it's just a Twitter feed. But remember that, as the writer-creator, you have to bring the goods. Commit to doing the deep work of developing your Big Idea, of creating characters and stories, of studying the masters, and of honing your craft. I'll see you on the other side of your hundred episodes.

CHAPTER 8

Sitcom Master Class:
Creating Comedy Through Character

by David Isaacs

Plot springs from character. . . . I've always sort of believed that these people inside me—these characters—know who they are and what they're about and what happens, and they need me to help get it down on paper because they don't type.—Anne Lamott

The Sitcom Mantra: Character Rules

For the past thirty-five years, I've had the good fortune to make my living as both a television and a feature film writer. Writing for the big and small screen is what I set out to do, so it's safe to assume that I've been blessed. I've had a part in writing some prestigious TV series, including *M*A*S*H, Cheers, Frasier,* and *Mad Men*. In short, a sweet, fulfilling ride, although there has been one drawback, albeit a small one, that to this day I don't relish facing.

When you become a professional writer—and believe me, with Kardashians running amok we need you more than ever—you will be approached almost weekly with a bit of a professional dilemma. Family and friends, acquaintances, and even strangers will barrage you with ideas for TV series. Most folks know a good show when they see one, but obviously, few know how to begin to execute one. Unfortunately, that does not stop them from believing they've got a hit on their hands. All they need is for you, the pro, to confirm that. Or better still, take it the rest of the way to Emmy glory. Trust me, the minute you sell your first script you'll run into people who want you to affirm their knockout idea.

I'm by subspecies a comedy writer, or sitcom writer to be even more specific, so I get a version of the following quite often.

                    DISTANT COUSIN PETE
         (confidentially)
Dave, I work in a hardware store. You wouldn't think
that a hardware store is funny, but you can't believe
the crazy stuff that goes on there. The people who have
no idea what they're looking for, traveling salesmen
that'll offer you all kinds of things, even women, to
get you to stock their caulking product. I always think
it'd make a great sitcom. You've never seen one take
place in a hardware store before.

You get the picture. Hardware store, supermarket, dentist's office, particle acceleration lab—they're all potential settings for a funny new series, chock-full of franchise-specific high jinks. You know what? In the hands of a skilled comedy writer, any of them could be, even the one dealing with a potential thermonuclear antimatter disaster!

My polite response to these well-intentioned creators is three questions that usually end the fantasy of quick riches right on the spot. I simply ask:

1. Who are the characters we'll follow in this setting?

2. How do we relate to them?

3. What do they want and how do they go about getting it?

Mr. Buzzkill strikes again.

It's not that I'm afraid of competition. (Instructor's note: That will be my only lie, I swear.) However, I feel it's incumbent upon me to use my hard-earned pulpit to spread the message that no comedic series, however unique in setting or concept, resonates without strong characters that make the trip worthwhile. *Cheers, Taxi, 30 Rock,* and *The Office* are all wonderful shows set in varying workplaces, some more familiar—we might even say clichéd—but the characters and their relationships and conflicts are fresh, original, and above all relatable to a varied audience.

I learned early in my writing career that character rules. It's the two-word mantra I repeat to myself, and to anyone who asks me how to become a Successful TV Writer. My mantra trumps even the most novel concept. Let me give you a recent example of what I mean.

From the moment it premiered, one of my favorite on-air comedy series has been *Modern Family.* It's funny and it's fresh, which is saying something considering the family comedy has been mined more than any other genre. There is no more recognizable setting on TV, in both live action and animation, than the overstuffed living room and the stairway leading to nowhere. We've all seen our share of multigenerational shows and experienced a lifetime of comedies with precocious kids and confused parents. We've witnessed TV families in all kinds of second-marriage configurations and contrived circumstances.

Modern Family, while certainly "modern," still had to win over a jaded viewing public. How did creator/writers Christopher Lloyd and Steven Levitan earn their audience? Not with just a novel gimmick, but with well-rounded, identifiable characters like Claire (Julie Bowen), trying her best to wrangle three children and a husband who would rather be his kids' "homey" than just their father. Claire's father Jay (Ed O'Neill) is an equally deft creation: the family patriarch trying for a second go-round at youth with a hot-blooded Latina wife who comes equipped with a young son who is anything but the kind of kid he can relate to.

However, the writers knocked it out of the park with Mitchell (Jesse Tyler Ferguson) and Cameron (Eric Stonestreet), a gay couple who've adopted an Asian baby and are obsessed with proving that they are perfect parents. The adult members of this extended modern family deal with real issues, fears, and hang-ups that create the fuel that powers memorable series: conflict.

Setting, concept, and circumstances can be inspirational in their own way, but I believe that creating comedy through character informs all the important elements of good filmic storytelling—point of view, scene structure, and emotional arc—and does it naturally. From the inside out, if you will.

Character Is Story

On the first night of my UCLA Extension class "Creating Through Character: Utilizing Character to Develop an Original Comedy Series or Screenplay," I write on the board, in very large letters, the word *plot*. Then I give a warning: "I do not want to hear this word used in our class." There is always murmuring in the ranks. How can you possibly avoid using the word *plot* in a narrative writing course? The answer is, "It's hard, but it's worth a try." Another loose definition of *plot* is a section of ground where bodies are buried. It's my little pointed joke, but there is a method to my madness.

New writers tend to worry themselves sick over plotting. How will they ever figure out all the setups and roadblocks and twists and turns that will lead to a satisfying resolution? Here's a complaint I hear from students all the time: "I come up with good ideas and have no trouble writing dialogue but I can't plot to save my life." Well, two out of three isn't bad, but if you fear actually telling the story then you struck out on the big one. It's like saying, "I have a stylish car body and great tires but no engine."

When I started out as a screenwriter, I was just as intimidated by *plot* as anyone, and the truth is a cleverly told episode of *The Office* still feels like black magic to me. So how do you learn to plan out a story and still sleep at night? One way is to avoid the word, the concept, the devil in the details of plot. I ask you to turn to your new friend, *character*. Your buddy will do a lot of the heavy lifting for you.

After I've banned the word *plot* from class, it's obviously up to me to explain how character is our salvation. Let me start by giving you a set of basic ingredients for creating a strong character, one that will generate conflict and its by-product, story.

Strong Character = Strong Story

Very simply, the keys to a strong character are: attitude, desire, and flaw.

Attitude can be defined as worldview, or the manner in which a character approaches life in general. How does an individual carry him/herself in society? Is he/she inherently optimistic or pessimistic? Self-assured or lacking self-esteem? True believer or skeptic? Laid-back or ever-cautious? Rational or superstitious? Every one of us has a particular mind-set that defines us. For narrative purposes, the more defined the better.

Desire is, of course, a deep longing for something. It might be love or companionship, might be money, might be a great job, might be freedom, might be a car, might be status, might be a child, might be revenge. We've all had the feeling of wanting something badly. It's not always what we need, but that doesn't stop us from wanting it, sometimes desperately.

Flaw is that part of a character's nature that prevents him/her from functioning in his/her own best interest. For example, acute jealousy, extreme ambition, fear of failure, and fear of death are all practical flaws. For our purposes we could also rename the classic Seven Deadly Sins—wrath, greed, sloth, pride, lust, envy, and gluttony—as the Seven Deadly Flaws and add those to our list. After all, good old Will Shakespeare kept himself busy for years exploiting the flaws in his characters; *Othello* would just be a play set in Venice about Iago the annoying gossip if Othello had been a loyal, trusting husband.

Case Study #1: George Costanza from *Seinfeld*

Let's use a familiar character in the world of half-hour comedies to demonstrate the formula of "character is story." Since it's my class I get to choose, and who better than one of my favorite personalities of all time: none other than the hapless George Costanza from *Seinfeld*. As played by Jason Alexander, he is the embodiment of utter frustration, the frustration that makes him a symbol for all of us who choose the wrong path on a daily basis. Let's deconstruct George using our three key elements.

Attitude: George is a self-described loser in life. Distilling that title down to one word, he's a pessimist. George is dead certain that the world is against him and so is rarely surprised when things go badly for him. He may decide that he's found the answer to his troubles, but deep down he knows that he's destined to crash in flames.

In one quite clever episode, "The Opposite," George has the idea that the smart way to live his life is just to do the opposite of what he would usually do in any particular circumstance. He becomes the anti-George. It actually works for a while, but when you believe deep down you're a loser, well . . . I don't know nature- or nurture-wise how George developed his attitude, but after watching him interact with his parents, Estelle and Frank, I've got to lean toward nurture. For example, when George tells his parents that Jerry and he are going to write a pilot for NBC, his mother's first reaction is to blurt out, "What do you know about writing?"

Desire: George is after something in almost every episode—a hot woman, a front-office job with the Yankees, an opportunity to make some fast money (a sitcom staple), a TV writing career, winning a dubious bet—whatever it is, he's relentless in his pursuit. His desperation alone makes him a wonderful character. However, I think that all of George's longings add up to one all-encompassing desire: The man wants respect. He needs to be looked up to, well thought of, loved, and in command. It's what makes him feel right, it's what he craves, and if you're as big a fan of *Seinfeld* as I am, you love to watch him chase after it and more often than not fail.

Flaw: George has a number of flaws, but the one that stands out to me is his inability to tell the truth. Lacking self-esteem, he has little or no faith in his own abilities. He feels more comfortable lying about himself than letting folks know who he really is, and the fantasies he concocts inevitably make a character that creates conflict and thus narrative by his very nature.

In a very funny episode titled "The Marine Biologist," George tells an attractive woman he meets that he's a noted marine biologist. We know that his fabrication will complicate the situation and eventually come back to haunt him—which it does when he must stride into the ocean to save a beached whale just to cover his lie. With little or no positive rein-forcement from friends, George further embellishes his lie to Jerry and company: "The sea was angry that day, my friends."

In another episode, "The Conversion," George literally changes his religion to Latvian Orthodox to hold on to his current girlfriend, who insists that she must break off with him because he's not a member of the church. He is willing to make a commitment he has no intention of keeping just to avoid rejection. George Costanza is a guy with some big personal issues. Another way of putting it is that he's a comedic story-generating machine.

Case Study #2: My Own Cocreated Show, *Almost Perfect*

Let me give you an example of how character is story from my own career, straight out of my handy-dandy "creating comedy from character" toolbox.

In the mid-1990s, my longtime writing/producing partner Ken Levine and I were under contract to Paramount Television, where we were devel-oping new series ideas. As part of our deal, the studio assigned us to assist another writer, Robin Schiff, who was developing for them as well.

We were immediately intrigued by an idea that Robin had about a thirtyish professional woman like herself who is juggling a high-pressure job and a brand-new romance with the "man of her dreams." This char-acter, whom we named Kim, is a determined, full-speed-ahead type (at-titude) who's worked hard to win her "dream job." However, on the day she gets that very position, she meets Mike, the smart, ruggedly hand-some guy she believes she's been waiting for. She desperately wants both work and romance to succeed (desire) but her inability to compromise (flaw) works against her.

That inner conflict spoke volumes and promised all kinds of stories that would flow from Kim's predicament. For example, Kim has a nicer home than Mike, makes more money than he does, chooses work over a needed night alone with Mike, hates sleeping over at his smaller place. All relatable situations complicated by one of Kim's flaws, her need to be in control. Long story short, the three of us pitched the idea to CBS, got a pilot commitment, and the series, called *Almost Perfect*, was on the air the next season. The show never hit the big time (I'll give you a moment to Google it), but we could never blame that on the ease of storytelling that came directly from elements of the main character.

I learned a great deal from guiding a network series, and in an indirect way the experience led me to teaching in the UCLA Extension Writers' Program. After we had completed twenty-four episodes for the first season of *Almost Perfect,* we met with the CBS execs to determine if we were coming back for a second go-round. The network's audience research had concluded that Mike, the boyfriend in our series, was "not strong enough." Our writing team formulated a scenario to create more conflict between Kim and Mike in order to bolster his character. We presented it to the CBS execs in our next meeting.

But despite our fix, we were told in no uncertain terms that the character of Mike needed to be eliminated. That presented us with a particularly cruel dilemma. Without Kim's boyfriend we had no inherent conflict for stories. In short, what was our series? We were given a second season (your first instinct is to stay alive), but we had no premise to guide us. We concocted stories based on Kim and her coworkers on the job, but those episodes had no focus or theme. Even our title, *Almost Perfect,* made no sense. We were without a pivotal character and limped along until CBS mercifully finished us off five episodes into the next season.

The moral: There is no compelling story, and certainly no series, without the framework of character. That's the lesson I felt compelled to pass along when I created my "Creating from Character" course.

Character Is Conflict

As I noted in my discussion of *Modern Family,* conflict is the element that fuels story. While we tend to think of conflict in more dramatic terms, it's essential as well in building comedy, unless of course your goal is to create the next *Jackass.* Then all you really need is a willing main character and fire.

The best comedies are constructed around a core relationship. There may be one per series or there may be more, but the physics are the same: The irresistible force meets the immovable object. Diane Chambers vs. Sam Malone (*Cheers*), Mike "Meathead" Stivic vs. Archie Bunker (*All in the Family*), Felix Ungar vs. Oscar Madison (*The Odd Couple*), Ray Barone vs. Debra Barone (*Everybody Loves Raymond*), even Lucy vs. Desi. Someone wants something, someone is an obstacle to their getting it, and if the conditions are right, meaning the two characters have strong contradictory attitudes, desires, and flaws, then sweet conflict ensues. The difference between a memorable comedy and a forgettable one is right in those conditions. (Instructor's note: Great casting makes a difference as well, a big one. When you've figured out the secret of casting, please let me know.)

Diane Chambers (Shelley Long) and Sam Malone (Ted Danson), in particular, are the alpha and omega of romantic comedy. Diane, the intellectual and controlling romantic, meets Sam, the slow-to-mature, bed-hopping ex-jock. They are incompatible; what's more, they know it; and yet, there is a sexual tension between them that they can't resist. They are built to conflict. Even when Diane, in an early episode, "Let Me Count the Ways," grieves over the death of her beloved cat and is finally comforted by Sam in his office, he can't resist exploiting her vulnerability to turn the moment to sex. Sam's attitude toward romance compels him to take advantage of the situation. Diane's attitude compels her to question Sam's real motives. A tender moment quickly turns awkward and funny.

Another great pairing is Liz Lemon (Tina Fey) and Jack Donaghy (Alec Baldwin) in *30 Rock,* which is set behind the scenes of a fictional live sketch comedy series based loosely on *Saturday Night Live*. Liz, the smart but highly insecure writer, must answer to Jack, the ends-justify-the-means company man, who just oozes entitlement. Despite her outward dislike for Jack's methods, Liz knows she has a lot to learn from him, and Jack in turn knows how to push her buttons and loves doing it. Their relationship is strictly professional but the way they spar plays like a great romantic comedy.

That dynamic is on display in a wonderful early episode called "Jack Meets Dennis." Dennis is Liz's sometime boyfriend, an immature lout if there ever was one. She puts up with him because her romantic expectations, like all her expectations outside of the job, are low. As Jack says to her, "Lemon, what tragedy happened in your life that you insist on punishing yourself with all this mediocrity?" Jack offers to mentor Liz, show her the finer points of life and make her into a well-rounded person. Her pride won't let her accept, but Jack will not take no for an answer. Liz eventually realizes that Jack is right, she shouldn't settle for mediocrity, and in a very funny scene, she agrees that Dennis must be dumped: "He's not a sandwich I want to eat for the rest of my life."

Alas, Dennis preys on Liz's softer side and in the end she reports back to Jack that Dennis has moved in. Liz is not so easily changed. There is inspired madness in the halls of *30 Rock,* but the stories are beautifully anchored in the battle of wills between Liz and Jack.

Here are a few more examples of hit comedy series that possess an array of comic styles and points of view but are all built on inherently conflicting relationships:

- *Mad About You* (Jamie vs. Paul)

- *Frasier* (Frasier vs. Martin, Frasier vs. Niles)

- *Two and a Half Men* (the original—Charlie vs. Alan)

- *Roseanne* (Roseanne vs. Dan)

- *Home Improvement* (Tim vs. Jill)

- *The Simpsons* (Homer vs. Bart)

- *Modern Family* (Claire vs. Phil, Mitchell vs. Cameron, Jay vs. Gloria, Jay vs. Mitchell, Jay vs. Phil, etc.)

You'll notice that most of my choices are marriage/family-based series. By its very nature, marriage is conflict-defined by the personal agenda (attitude, desire, flaw) of its two participants. Most folks back away from a tense situation before things get out of hand, but that's much harder to do when you live in the same house. Needless to say, family is a wellspring of disagreement.

Modern Family feasts on it. The three couples have their marriage battles, but Mitchell also struggles with Jay, who has yet to fully accept his son's sexual orientation. Phil feels less than respected by Jay, his father-in-law. Claire harbors resentment toward her stepmother, Gloria, who is Claire's age and damn sexy to boot. All these issues on the table and we haven't even gotten to the kids. The creators of *Modern Family* have a treasure trove of story lines from which to choose.

Character Is Theme

As I mentioned at the outset, I've had the good luck and timing to work on some great series. The one thing the various creators had in common was a firm understanding of their characters' motivations. On the other hand, I've been on series with a complete lack of same (sorry, no names), and we continually struggled with story and ultimately the direction of the series. I've learned, many times over, that grasp of character leads to control of theme. When a writer knows his/her protagonist, the protagonist's worldview (attitude), what that individual most wants (desire), and what is holding him/her back from achieving it (flaw), then he knows what he is writing about.

A great series and a contemporary example of how character drives theme is on display in NBC's *The Office*. (Instructor's note: Like a lot of viewers, I'm a big fan of the British version starring Ricky Gervais and was skeptical of any knockoff, but the writer/adapter Greg Daniels won me over with his distinctly American take on the original concept.)

Michael Scott (Steve Carell), the office manager of the Scranton branch of Dunder Mifflin Paper Company, is a man with no discernible leadership skills, unless you count his desperate need to be liked. His cheery demeanor is in direct contrast to his staff, most of whom reflect the soul-sucking tedium of their work right in their expressions. There is little esprit de corps among the troops but that never stops Michael from trying to live up to the slogan on his coffee mug, "World's Greatest Boss." Michael, as ill-informed and dense as they come, is always proactive. No matter the problem, work-related or personal, Michael will throw himself into the fray under the guise of benevolent dictator and find a way to make matters worse.

One of my favorite episodes is "Conflict Resolution," and it's a great example of how *The Office* melds character with theme. Michael overhears an argument between coworkers Angela (Angela Kinsey) and Oscar (Oscar Nuñez) that is being mediated by Toby (Paul Lieberstein), the human resources coordinator. Michael insists on taking command and resolving the conflict himself. Imbued with his newfound mediation skills, Michael then launches into resolving all the personnel conflicts in Toby's HR files. His meddling opens wounds all over the office, but somehow those wounds are healed despite Michael's bungling. In the end, his good intentions indirectly save the day.

The brilliance of *The Office* is its subtle ability to have all the employees of Dunder Mifflin, despite their negativity, show their better nature when it counts. That theme flows through Michael.

Another series I've enjoyed, unfortunately short-lived but recently relaunched, is *Arrested Development*. The need for family is the series' theme and it flows through Michael Bluth (Jason Bateman), a pragmatic soul who seems to be the only lucid member of his highly dysfunctional family. The Bluths are a selfish, greedy, and pretty unbearable lot, but Michael is determined to hold them together, not just for their sake, but for his son, George-Michael (Michael Cera), who has no one other than his dad. A great exchange between father and son in the pilot episode sums up the heart of the series. Michael: "What have we said is the most important thing?" George-Michael: "Breakfast!" Michael: "No . . . Family." George-Michael: "Oh right! I thought you meant in the things you eat." Michael is fighting an uphill battle in every episode.

For sheer brilliance in melding character and theme I have to refer you to *All in the Family*. For those of you not old enough to remember the series, it was nothing less than a cultural phenomenon. For most of the early 1970s (in that dark age before viewers could record and download), *All in the Family* was the very definition of appointment television. It kicked off the CBS Saturday-night lineup at eight P.M. and restaurants and movie theaters stood empty.

The pain of change was the theme at the heart of *All in the Family* and it was personified in the character of Archie Bunker, played by the late great Carroll O'Connor. Archie was popularly referred to as a bigot, and on the surface he certainly is, railing against African Americans, Latinos, gays, and any other group he feels is encroaching on his neighborhood, his job, and, in his words, "the good ole US of A." Still, he's a decent man, certainly loved by his adoring, hilariously innocent wife, Edith (Jean Stapleton).

Beneath it all, though, Archie is frightened. He is scared of change. He is losing his daughter, Gloria (Sally Struthers), who is his only child, to Mike Stivic (Rob Reiner), an angry young man who has little or no respect for Archie's opinions. The neighborhood he grew up and raised his daughter in is changing economically and ethnically. A world he doesn't recognize is closing in around him and down deep he's scared and holds this new world responsible. Needless to say, America at the time was going through the same struggle with social change, and *All in the Family* reflected that in its theme and in Archie Bunker.

Creating Through Character

Students come to the first class meeting of my UCLA Extension Writers' Program course with all sorts of TV ideas in every stage of development.

Some have the germ of an idea, some arrive with that notion of the funny workplace, and some have sketched a rough outline of their story. A few have already completed a script and hope to prepare for a rewrite by further exploring their characters. Regardless of the concept they bring in, or the stage of development they're at, we start from scratch and ask, "Who are your main characters and how are they built emotionally?"

So how do the students go about getting to know their characters? We start with a simple exercise. I ask for ten words that describe the main character, or protagonist. In the case of a screenplay, it would be the person we will follow on a journey of sharp emotional change as he/she is confronted with challenges and obstacles to a specific goal. For a television series, we are dealing with a more incremental open-ended journey, but the main character grows nonetheless.

Here's an example of how this exercise works. I'll use a character fairly well known to common television-watching culture: Dr. Frasier Crane.

Frasier is:

Caring

Proud

Witty

Intuitive

Honorable

Hedonistic

Competitive

Analytical

Sophisticated

Dedicated

Those are just ten descriptors, and given what a complex character Dr. Crane is, I'm sure anyone familiar with Frasier could come up with several more without too much trouble. Nevertheless, these ten words describe Frasier pretty concisely. He's a dedicated, intuitive psychiatrist, a caring son and brother, a man of sophisticated tastes. He overanalyzes just about everything, but his intentions are honorable. All in all, this is a good guy.

Be aware, though, that for any character to generate story, we need contradictions. A couple of words on the list help there. Frasier is a prideful man, competitive, quick to take exception and offense. In many ways, Frasier's pride is his flaw. And while he isn't a hedonist in the extreme sense, Frasier is certainly a man who enjoys his pleasures, including good food, wine, and women. It wouldn't be out of the ordinary for him, even with his sophisticated knowledge of human behavior, to be compromised over a beautiful woman.

An early episode in the series, "Call Me Irresponsible," played on that very dilemma. Frasier advises a caller to drop his "on again–off again" girlfriend. When the girlfriend arrives at the radio station to confront Frasier, they end up hitting it off and start dating. When her ex-boyfriend calls back the show and says he's had a change of heart and wants her back, Frasier tells him that he's making a mistake. His brother and fellow psychiatrist, Niles, hears this exchange on the radio and lets Frasier know that he is committing a huge breach of professional ethics. Frasier refuses to acknowledge the fact; he wants this woman and he will sleep with her, no matter what.

However, he is hardwired ethically, and when the chips are down, in a very funny final scene, Frasier cannot touch this sexy woman without getting sick to his stomach. That's generating story through the emotional makeup of a character.

Our second exercise is to generate ten words that describe the antagonist, the person(s) who functions to contrast and conflict with the protagonist through various means, including questioning the protagonist's motives and blocking the protagonist's agenda with his own. We tend to think of the antagonist as simply the villain, but in any story, there has to be someone serving as devil's advocate.

Let's use Frasier's father, Martin Crane, as an example. The creators of *Frasier* (David Angell, David Lee, and Peter Casey) wisely built the series on the cornerstone of the Frasier/Martin relationship. The parent and child have little but family ties in common, and yet the son has to suck it up and take care of the father who is no longer able to live independently. In fact, the title of the pilot episode is "The Good Son," so the show's primary relationship and theme are made clear right from the outset.

Martin Crane is:

Proud

Sentimental

Loyal

Pragmatic

Unpretentious

Sports junkie

Old-fashioned

Fair-minded

Taciturn

Blunt

It's easy to see that Martin is built to contrast with Frasier and Niles. The sons are both psychiatrists, trained to scrutinize every bit of human behavior. Martin is a cop, trained to survey a situation and act quickly and decisively. He has little tolerance for his sons' approach to life, let alone their highbrow interests. Nevertheless, Martin's a bit of a contradiction in his own right. He's certainly a no-nonsense fellow with blue-collar sensibilities, but he has a sentimental attachment to friends and family, which he does his best to conceal. His pragmatism, though, provides him with a wisdom that his highly educated sons don't often display.

Frasier and Martin are the yin and yang of the series down to Martin's beat-up recliner, which clashes with Frasier's designer furnishings. Their struggle to connect created a story dynamic that evolved throughout *Frasier*'s eleven seasons. In "Breaking the Ice," an episode that deftly combines humor and heart, Frasier and Niles go ice-fishing with Martin, each hoping to get closer to their dad. Frasier, stuck in a fishing shack on a frozen lake, has never been more out of his element, asking at one point, "Couldn't we just see a performance of *The Iceman Cometh*?"

However, Frasier sticks it out because he hopes that his father will say "I love you" to him—words he's heard Martin say to everyone but him. Martin, of course, has a hard time ever expressing emotion to his sons; as he says, "Every year in this country thousands of guys go fishing and love never enters into it." But in his heart, he appreciates what his sons have done for him and he does express the thought. He has to take a stiff drink to do it, but finally says, "I love you."

In "Out with Dad," we might say turnabout is fair play. This time Martin is on Frasier's turf when he is forced to go to the opera. Frasier is actually hoping to meet Emily, a girl he has his eye on. They do meet, but Emily's mother is with her and takes an immediate liking to Martin. He's not interested but doesn't want to spoil Frasier's chances with Emily, so he tells the mother he's gay. His chancy move backfires when Emily and her mother decide to fix Martin up with Emily's gay uncle Edward. Martin discourages Edward by forcing Niles to pose as his gay boyfriend. All of this discomfort and deception is motivated by Martin's loyalty to Frasier. They share little common ground, but they are father and son and will struggle to do right by each other.

In class, I ask that the ten-word exercise be done for all the main characters students are considering in their project. It's the quickest and most efficient method for exploring connections and conflicts among all the characters in a film story or TV series. It's a great help to head into your outline with a strong sense of how your main characters relate to one another.

Character Is Command

A writer beginning a screenplay or teleplay, staring at a blank computer screen and paralyzed with doubt, is a familiar cliché. Anyone who writes fears the tyranny of that open-ended monster called plot. My experience has taught me that to know your hero is to control his or her story. It is where authorship begins, and that is first and foremost what you as a writer want to develop.

Many of us believe that finding the "hot idea" will lead us to success. It's certainly true that the industry is always looking for something different, but an audience will reject any new comedy series that feels inauthentic. All of the series I've referenced owe their success and renown to recognizable characters and the conflict between them. In every case the "authors" brought something of their own lives and relationships to the work, and I assure you that's half the battle in achieving such success. (The other half is some serious casting luck.)

There is one last bit of advice I like to give my writing students as our time together ends. All writers subscribe to the axiom of "write what you know." It's a cliché, as the cliché goes, because it's true. But I like to take that idea one step farther. My advice is, "Don't write what you think will sell; write what you want to see." Start with characters interacting in a world that you know better than anyone. You may not crack the ceiling right away, but I guarantee that you will be working toward perfecting your craft and command as a writer.

SECTION III

Being a Professional in
the Television Business

CHAPTER 9

Launching and Sustaining a Television Writing Career
by Alison Lea Bingeman

Writing for television requires an undying optimism and a genius ability to suspend disbelief. There's high stress and long hours, and no job security. You live constantly with the nagging feeling that your show's going to get canceled or you'll get canned and never work again. It's hard! But if you think you've got some writing talent, a love of the art and craft of television, and enough drive and desire to pursue it, then read on. This chapter is for you.

There is no magic pill to take when learning to work in television. No doubt about it, a career in TV takes talent, dedication, hard work, and some say luck (we'll get into that later). I can't give you a formula that, if followed exactly, will guarantee success. What I can offer are a few pointers I've drawn from my own experience and those of other writers, executives, and agents I know about how to get into the business and stay there. For my part, I've spent more than twenty years working in the television industry. My career has spanned both film (*Hurt*) and one-hour television in most genres (*CSI: Miami, The Outer Limits, Bomb Girls, Flash Gordon, Relic Hunter*). I've written for cable and syndication as well as network shows. My career has been long and strong, and I'm happy to pass along some of the things I've picked up on the journey.

Though launching a career in television and sustaining it are very different processes, both have common threads, which I will elaborate upon in this chapter. The first is knowing your marketplace. The TV market is a many-headed hydra and more heads are growing every day. Staying up-to-date with the current trends is important. Creating relationships with decision makers is another key element, while the third is all about—you guessed it—writing. The beauty of being a writer in our world is that no one can stop you from creating your own stories and scripts. An actor needs a stage and a role. The director needs a set and a script. All you need as a writer is a laptop and a great idea. The possibilities for invention and reinvention are endless. We'll get into that. First, let's talk about taking those initial steps.

Launching a Career in Television

Every writer has her own account of how she got started in the business. In 2007, when I walked the picket line with other striking writers for the Writers Guild of America, we swapped stories about how we all got our first break. No two stories were alike. One guy studied film at a prestigious college and had written a few scripts in school. He looked up one of his college buddies, then working on a TV show, and bingo—he got his first staff job. Another was a produced playwright. She wrote a few samples, got an LA agent, and was offered a job on a top cable show. Then there was the guy who began as a writers' assistant on a show and eventually got his foot in the door with a freelance script. He parlayed his freelance episode into a staff writer job.

Every story is different. Some say that luck has a lot to do with it. I believe we create our own luck. So let's talk about how to position yourself so when that lucky break appears, you'll be ready for it.

Where Do You Start?

If you are planning to enter the American television industry, the best place to begin is where the majority of television is made in the United States: Los Angeles. The reality of the business today is that most writers' rooms are run out of Los Angeles. LA is where the deals are made, the meetings are taken, and the writing gets done. To launch a career in television, you will need to ask yourself if you are willing to shift your command center to Southern California. If you are serious about becoming a successful television writer, Los Angeles is the best place to get started. Okay, then, you say you are willing to do this. What next?

Know Your Market

If you were a budding clothing designer, you would need to know the latest trends in fashion before attempting to sell your new line to Macy's or Saks Fifth Avenue. The same goes for the TV industry. It's large and complex and your job is to know as much about it as you possibly can before you enter it. How do you find out about it?

Watch a Lot of Television

Now you've got a perfect excuse when your significant other wants to drag you away to do something annoying: "Sorry, honey—can't. I'm doing research." Yes, now you have free license to watch television, and a lot of it. If you are interested in writing half-hour comedies, your job now is to be current with the sitcoms on the air. Watch as many as you can, and often. There is a catch, however. You can't mindlessly zone out in front of the TV screen anymore. Not only do you need to know the shows, you need to know the players. That means knowing what networks broadcast what kind of shows, what studios produce them, and who makes the decisions to green-light the shows you are coming to love so much.

In a nutshell, the major networks attempt to capture a broader, more diversified audience, so their shows, while mindful of demographics, aren't totally driven by them. Cable networks are the opposite: Their goal is to appeal to a very specific audience. Spike, for example, offers programs for teenage boys; Lifetime is for soccer moms. Your job is to pay attention to what shows are on which networks. Identify common trends on each network. Are you seeing mostly female leads on the shows? Do the shows have a primarily urban or small-town setting? Which networks create the hard-edged, gritty shows and which ones air the lighter fare? Identify each network's demographic. Ask yourself why *Louie* isn't airing on ABC. And why isn't *Happy Endings* on FX? Be smart. The more you know about each network, the better you will be able to position yourself in the marketplace. And, when you finally get your chance to pitch new shows, you won't look ridiculous by pitching a half-hour comedy about two middle-aged women to Syfy.

Find out what genres interest you. Are you drawn to CBS police procedurals like *CSI,* lighter cop shows like *Castle* on ABC, or grittier fare on Showtime like *Homeland*? Pick your favorites. Look them up online, research the creators of the show, the showrunners, the writers on staff, and the actors too—see what they've done in the past and begin to follow their careers. The Internet Movie Database (IMDb.com) is a terrific resource. A writer friend of mine tells me when he watches TV and finds a new show he likes, he immediately logs on to IMDb and looks up all the writers and cast on the show. He's extreme, of course, but if you ask him who is working on what show, he'll know. Get to know the players in the business. And the best way to start is by researching the shows you love.

Later, as your journey into television continues, you will begin to know the television executives at both the networks and the studios. Executives are hired to oversee current and developing programs and are constantly on the lookout for that new, fresh voice. If they read your material and like your work, they will recommend you for staff on shows they cover. There is a distinction between executives who work on current shows (on the air) and those in development (pilots). Track them all. And if that isn't enough to do, you will also need to get to know the nonwriting executive producers, like Ron Howard at Imagine and Jerry

Bruckheimer, who are both currently producing some of the hit shows on television.

In order to get staffed on a show, you will need to get approval from the studio involved, the network, and the nonwriting executive producer (if any). Usually, the showrunner makes the ultimate decision on your hire; however, these other players also have a say. Get to know who these people are and cultivate relationships with them. They can be great allies.

Read Pilots

How do you get ahold of pilot scripts, you ask? This is where connections come in. Most agencies have pilot scripts on hand or have access to a website where they can be downloaded. Assuming you don't have agent representation at this point, you'll want to have friends who do, so they can share the bounty with you. Actors especially will be keeping up-to-date with the pilots, because pilot season is their best opportunity to secure a series role. They will most likely be up to speed on finding the most current pilot scripts. Another option is to troll the Internet for pilot scripts. Check out SimplyScripts.com, where you can download teleplays on current shows.

Read the Trades

It used to be that reading the trades meant buying subscriptions to *Daily Variety* and *The Hollywood Reporter*—the two most well-known trade papers in the business. This was an expensive proposition. In today's market, you are in luck. *Deadline Hollywood* at Deadline.com is your best bet for learning all about the entertainment business. And it's free! You can also keep up with *Variety*, which has ceased its daily print version, and *The Hollywood Reporter* on their websites. Again, it's all about staying current with what is going on in the television industry.

At first, reading the trades is a bit like reading Greek, but keep up the work and soon you'll be tossing around names over lunch with the best of them. Also check out writers' blogs on the Internet. *No Meaner Place*

(NoMeanerPlace.com) is a terrific place to read interviews with writers and showrunners. Jane Espenson and John August both have popular writing blogs about the life of a working Hollywood writer. Read them and find others. Knowledge is power.

Branding Yourself

So now that you've got a firm grasp on the workings of the television industry, start envisioning where you see yourself in it. This might sound ridiculous to some of you, but it's important. Be intentional in the launch of your own career. Are you going to be an animation writer who will create the next *South Park* or the next *Smurfs*? Do you want to be the new writer on *Boardwalk Empire* or *Fringe*?

When you set goals for yourself, you'll start a conversation about where you want to go. This conversation is important. What you are doing is creating a brand for yourself. With so many voices out there, consider how you want yours to be heard. Are you the bad-boy writer who creates hard-edged action? Or the political animal deft at satire? Think about Lena Dunham (*Girls*). She is known for her emotionally raw yet comedic portrayals of young, sophisticated women. That's her brand. What's yours? Put some thought into this. It's crucial for a long and strong career writing in television.

I came to Los Angeles with a passion for movies and a desire to write. I worked with an established writer for a few years developing projects before I struck out on my own. I got a couple of gigs writing low-budget features shot overseas. The films never got made, but they served as samples for oddball cable shows starting up at the time. I took those jobs and the ones after that. Five years into the business, I realized I wanted to be writing and developing one-hour dramas and began to set my sights more keenly on my goal. I fell in love with the shows I wanted to write for, wrote sample scripts for them, and eventually found myself working on them.

Save yourself some time. Be bold now. Set your sights on where you want to be in five years and work on writing samples that will get you there. Be single-minded. Start the conversation about where you want to be and share it with others. Remember what I said about creating your own luck? This is key. When people you meet understand what you want to do in this business, they will begin to share that dream with you and even help create opportunities for you.

Be specific. One-hour drama or half-hour comedy? Teen soaps or hard-edged police procedurals? Now that you know the commercial market, find where your tastes, talents, and abilities can fit in. I'm not saying don't be flexible. If your first break into writing for TV is on the Cartoon Network, take it even if writing animation is not your dream job. You'll gain invaluable experience and might just find you love it and want to keep working in that world. If that's not where you ultimately want to be, don't lose sight of your goal. Keep the conversation going.

I suggest writing a pitch paragraph for yourself. For example, "I'm a lawyer with five years of experience in the Chicago district attorney's office. I have several produced plays to my name and my goal is to write one-hour crime drama on a major network show." There's power in those words. That said, the most powerful tool you have as an aspiring writer is your pen. To get to where you want to go, your ultimate ticket is your own writing.

Write—a Lot

And when you think you've written enough, write some more. Writing scripts is the best advice I can give you in this chapter. You always have the opportunity to write—full-time, part-time, or in your spare time. That's what you want to be doing to launch this career. I worked with an executive producer who was deputy chief of the LAPD. He got up in the wee hours and wrote spec television scripts. Eventually, he was producing a hit network show. This kind of a schedule could work for you. Others might find it too challenging.

One young writer I spoke with started her career as a television executive. As she worked with writers, she quickly realized that she wanted to be a writer herself. At first, she tried writing in her spare time but found she didn't have the focus she needed to build a body of work. She quit her executive post and picked up a job waiting tables. Every day, from nine A.M. to five P.M., she wrote scripts; at night, she worked. In two years, she built up a core of sample work. She's now on staff on a cable show. Whether you are able to manage that other career and write on the side or find a job that allows you to write as your primary occupation, you want to dedicate yourself to your craft.

This brings up an important point. Are you willing to make the commitment to become a television writer? Many wannabe writers neglect to ask themselves that question. Talking about writing can be more fun than doing the work. I know that from experience, because I come from the Dorothy Parker school of writing: "I hate writing. I love having written." Before you quit your job, move to Los Angeles, and spend endless solitary hours in airless rooms writing, make sure you can commit to the discipline. Know that the scripts you labor over may or may not sell. Realize that you will get many nos before you get a yes. Can you handle rejection? Are you able to make an honest assessment of your abilities and learn how to work on your weaknesses? Writing for TV takes perseverance and dedication. Know before you start if this kind of work is for you.

I've known directors who began as writers and couldn't stand sitting in that room facing the blank page. For them, their creativity sparked with a script in hand. Know who you are and if the writer's life is for you. I repeat: Before you quit your day job, make sure you can devote the time and energy it takes to launch this career.

Building a Portfolio

By now, you know what a spec script is and the difference between writing a spec for an on-air show and writing an original pilot. Which should you write? The answer is both. Spec scripts for existing shows work to showcase your talent. You want to demonstrate you know the show and understand its structure, can capture the voice of the show both tonally and through its characters, can track character arcs throughout the season, and can come up with an original, engaging story. If you are a good mimic, this is the place for you. That said, I've worked with writers whose voices are so unique, they can't adapt their style. Unless you are David Milch, you need to prove you can.

The downside to writing specs for existing shows is that they are difficult, if not impossible, to sell. You could write a *Modern Family* script that knocks it out of the park, but chances are if the writing staff were to read it, they would think, *That's not our show.* . . . Think of specs for shows as calling cards. If you've done a terrific job, there will be writers, agents, and executives out there who are fans of the show and will recognize your talent. Write specs for the shows you love and want to work for. Pay particular attention to first- and second-season breaking hits, as network executives get bored with reading older shows. And again, write a lot of them.

Writing original pilots, in my opinion, is your ticket into writing for episodic television. Why? It's your voice on that page—your characters, your franchise, your world. A spec pilot is the perfect place to showcase your talent. And if the script is good and the timing right, you could have a chance at selling it. Make no mistake, writing an original pilot is a big challenge, but there is no better way to show other writers as well as producers and networks what you can do. I interviewed a young staff writer who told me when he is not on staff, his goal is to write a new pilot every three months. A showrunner I know said the same thing: When you are not working on a show, write three pilots a year.

In my own experience, I write about one new pilot a year, but I also develop three or four ideas to pitch. This allows me to build an up-to-date portfolio of my work so that when the networks call, I will have a script for that cool show they are looking for. Remember what I said about creating your own luck? Again, you are positioning yourself so that when the lucky phone call comes, you will be ready for it.

Networking

Networking: Start it now and continue with it throughout your career. Relationships are key for getting jobs and keeping them. Have you ever seen a position for writer/story editor for a TV show advertised on Craigslist? No, you haven't, and there's a reason for that. People hire who they know or people who come with strong recommendations from other people they know. Though networking seems counterintuitive to the writer's life—after all, we sit in rooms all day, interacting more with the characters in our stories than real people—it's a skill you must develop. As a television writer, you must be not only a talented, creative, knowledgeable writer but also a good salesperson. A TV writer once gave me the formula of 60/40 for success in the business. You need to spend 60 percent of your time writing, the other 40 on sales. This means creating and maintaining relationships, taking meetings, and pitching.

I always tell my UCLA Extension students that the place to begin creating relationships is in the classroom—where everyone's goal is to write for television. That's a start. I encourage them to find the other class members they feel simpatico with and read each other's work. When a feature film I wrote went into production, it was no accident the director and two producers were all graduates of the American Film Institute. They had worked together on student projects, trusted each other, and were excited to re-create the same relationships in the real world. By taking a class with like-minded peers, you have instantly increased your number of contacts by fourteen to twenty. Exchange ideas; share strategies and contacts. Be generous.

Another way to find your posse, as you wend your way into the TV industry, is to join a writers' group. Scriptwriters Network offers seminars and a working writers' group that meets regularly. Or you could start one of your own with the writers you know. I have belonged to several in the past and found them useful. Like the UCLA Extension courses, a writers' group holds you to deadlines. Above all, writing is a discipline. No matter what your job is during the day, you will want to spend time each day writing. A writers' group can help you develop that discipline and will put you in contact with other writers working to launch their careers too. If they are as generous as you are with your experience and knowledge, the group can also be a useful source of information.

Obviously, you need to be discerning when you pick your members. You want them to be as talented and motivated as you are. In my groups, writers had to send in an audition script and the group had to agree on granting them membership. Now I have a small circle of writer friends to whom I send my material. They read it before it goes out to agents and networks. They are writers I know and trust. I also know their strengths and weaknesses as readers and can filter their comments accordingly.

Writing is a solitary process. Attending events and seminars about writing is another way of getting out and networking. Check the Writers Guild of America website and find speakers and seminars that interest you. Attend. Take notes. Introduce yourself. You don't want to become that strange writer who never leaves her house and has too many cats. Enough said.

Teleplay Competitions and Workshops

Now that you have that smokin' pilot under your arm and know a few people, your main goal will be to get noticed. Entering teleplay contests and workshops is a good way of attaining recognition. Teleplay competitions are not as prevalent as screenplay contests, though there are a few worthy of note. Slamdance has an annual TV script competition. UCLA Extension has the Television Writing Competitions, which are unusual in that they recognize excellence in both specs and pilots, and the odds of winning are much higher because only Writers' Program students who have taken two TV writing classes are eligible. Check out Scriptapalooza and Final Draft's Big Break competition as well. Whichever ones you enter, research them well before you send your script and entry fee. You want to make sure they are respected, are well connected, and can deliver on the promises they offer.

Participating in workshops or internship programs offered by studios and networks is another excellent way to gain recognition as an emerging talent. The programs are designed to find promising writers and initiate them into the business; some focus on training racially or socially diverse writers. The Warner Bros. Television Writers' Workshop is one of the most well known and the competition to get in is fierce. It meets for three consecutive months, one evening a week, on the Warner Bros. lot, and is free to those accepted. A friend of mine went through the workshop four years ago and said it was the best thing she had ever done to launch her career. She was taken through the steps of creating a spec pilot and was mentored by executives, who then put her forward for Warner Bros. shows. It's a win for the studio as well because it builds a farm team of writers.

NBC Universal's Writers on the Verge is a similar program. Disney/ABC has an internship program where the participants are actually paid. Research them all. When your spec scripts are in the best possible shape and you think you know a thing or two about the business, go ahead and apply.

The Writers' Assistant

Perhaps the most celebrated and straightest route to a staff job on a television show is working as a writers' assistant. Working side by side on a show with writers can be a terrific way to learn what a television writer's life is actually like. (The glamour will be stripped away fast—trust me.) Working on a show will clue you in to how a writers' room works, which is another skill set you will need to develop as a TV writer. Learning to work with other writers will be critical to your success. The experience could also give you a boost to a freelance episode on the show and even a staff position. It's been done. I have worked on several shows where the assistant was promoted to staff writer. Before we go there, let's take a look at what the job entails.

Most staffs on shows have an assistant to the writers, and the job can have various aspects to it. Essentially, the job is to care for the writers.

That could mean supporting the entire writing staff or just the head writer/showrunner. Your task is to make life easier for the writers and ensure the script department runs smoothly, which could entail getting coffee, ordering lunch, replenishing office supplies, doing research for a story, and setting meetings with the network. The job could include taking detailed notes in the room when writers are "breaking story" (which means creating the story). You could also be script coordinator, which means proofing drafts of outlines and episodes, locking scripts for production, and generating revisions. The duties are primarily administrative, so if your organizational skills are top-notch, this could be the entry-level job for you.

The advantage of working as a writers' assistant is that you will get practical experience and see for yourself what a television writer's job is all about. The pros' creativity in a writers' room, their ability to brainstorm concepts and structure story, to write drafts and submit them on time, and to address notes from both the story room and the network will all be played out before your eyes. These are aspects of the job you will need to master as a TV writer, and to observe experienced writers doing this can be the best education you will receive in the business. If you do succeed in securing this job, consider it a paid learning opportunity.

Working as an assistant might also afford you the opportunity to write a freelance script for the show. Showrunners often allow their assistants to collaborate with a staff writer and write an episode, though don't come to the job expecting it. Some showrunners don't ever give their assistants scripts. Find this out before you take the job—ask around. Does the person you are going to work for promote from within?

I spoke with one former writers' assistant (now a staff writer) who said he worked on four seasons of three different shows before he was offered a freelance script. His advice? Do your job well. Learn as much as you can, but above all, take care of the writers for whom you are working. That way, they will become invested in your success as a fledgling writer. Happy writers are helpful writers.

There can also be disadvantages to taking this career route.

Currently, the writers' assistant is a tough job to get. You will need to employ the same strategies to land this job as the ones you will be using to get hired as a writer. Attend events, enter competitions, network with fellow writers, get to know executives, have great material and get it read, and create a circle of professionals who are invested in your success. These are all the steps you will take to get someone to make a phone call on your behalf for a job on a show as a writers' assistant. All that for what?

Depending on the show and its budget, assistants are paid at or around minimum wage. Is it worth it? If you are single, with few financial commitments, I would say yes. Pursue it. If you are married with three kids and a mortgage, you might reconsider. Only you can decide. Before you start applying for the job, however, make sure you can do it. Otherwise, don't waste your time.

In addition, a possible drawback of working as an assistant is that, for some, it becomes a ghetto. Ten years working as an assistant and still no freelance script? It happens. Perhaps your writing isn't strong enough to prompt your boss to give you that chance. Perhaps the drive for you to take that step is not in you.

Another important aspect to a successful career in television is a willingness to engage in honest self-assessment. Is it really everyone else's fault you didn't get that promotion? Or is there something within you that's holding you back? Go to your executive producer and ask what it is you need to do differently. The answer might surprise you and activate a new course of action. Constructive criticism is useful, so don't argue back. If you need to scream, find a pillow.

Establishing Yourself in Another Domain

You think you aren't cut out for the writers'-assistant route. You never were a gofer ("go for this, go for that") and don't plan to be one in the future. Are there any other ways into the TV writing business? Lucky for you, Hollywood loves both entrepreneurs and writers who have managed to establish themselves successfully in other mediums. If you are a playwright, your produced work could open doors for you in the television world. Showrunners often seek that unique voice to complete a writers' room. Looking toward playwrights has become a frequent practice. If you are a playwright wanting to break in, you will need to find an agent right away to represent your work (more on that later). This doesn't mean you don't have to build your portfolio of TV spec scripts. You do.

With the recent downtick in feature film production, there has been an influx of feature writers developing material for television. An executive producer who runs the company of an Oscar-winning director recently confided in me that the best writing in the industry right now is in television. And it's no wonder. The work can be steady, lucrative, and immediate. A TV script can be written in April, shot in July, and air in September. For a feature writer, who can spend up to five years developing a script for production, this is music to the ears. So if you have several feature credits under your belt—yes, even low-budget, self-financed films that went straight to DVD—you will have some street cred in television. Again, you will need to have an agent and develop a firm strategy to launch yourself in the TV world.

For those of you who haven't established yourself in other mediums, you can go the entrepreneurial route. As you know, film and digital media have progressed today to the point where it has become economically feasible to write and produce your own material on a microbudget. You guessed it—I'm talking webisodes.

A lot of creative people have tossed their hat into that ring and have produced their own material for the Internet. Anyone can shoot a three-minute minicomedy episode and post it on YouTube. Granted, the cyber universe has gotten pretty crowded and it's more of a challenge to go viral than ever before. Nonetheless, creating webisodes and posting them online is a viable, creative enterprise for someone who wants to break into television. *Sanctuary,* a science fiction one-hour show, started as a six-part webisode series. Its popularity on the Internet drew Syfy's attention. The show ran four seasons. Need I say more?

Sustaining Your Career in Television

You've sold your first script to television or gotten your first job on staff on a hot TV show. Now what? How do you keep the magic going? Not only that, but how do you keep it going for the next twenty-five years? A lot of what I covered in the "Launching a Career in Television" section of this chapter applies to managing a television writing career: keeping current on the market, always writing new material, and nurturing your relationships. But now they work on another level. Let's take a look.

Representation

You may be surprised that I saved the discussion about agents, managers, and attorneys until now. In my conversations with various writers and agents working in the business, the opinion was unanimous: Find your first job and the agent will come. This doesn't necessarily hold true for managers, but more on that later.

Agents and Managers: What's the Difference?

An agent represents you in the television marketplace by submitting work to production companies and networks on your behalf, as well as solicits work for you. All reputable agencies in Los Angeles are signatories to the Writers Guild of America and are regulated by guild guidelines. For their work, agents take 10 percent of your gross income on all your television commissions, not including residuals. An agent can have up to twenty-five clients, though at the bigger firms, an agent can represent hundreds of writers as part of an agency team. The bigger writers/clients at these firms can have up to four agents representing them. Agents often represent writers who will be competing for the same jobs you are.

At best, an agent is your business partner who knows and likes your work and will develop strategies with you to sell your material and staff you on television shows. Your agent also is licensed to negotiate deals for you. You must have an agent in order to work. Most producers and networks will not read work that hasn't been submitted by an agency.

A manager is like an agent in that he advises and opens doors for his clients; however, technically a manager is not allowed to solicit work on your behalf. Most of them do anyway, and honestly, you will want a manager who will look for work for you. The advantage of having a manager is that his client list is much smaller than an agent's; therefore, he can devote more time to developing your career. Managers also commission 10 percent of your gross writing income and are not signatories to the Writers Guild of America. They cannot negotiate contracts on your behalf.

Often managers are working as producers, especially if you are developing original material. Managers can attach themselves to your projects as producers, and this can work to your advantage or not. On the plus side, numerous management firms have successfully launched television franchises as well as writing careers. Producing managers might also be able to attach talent (actors) to your project, which can sometimes increase your chances for a sale.

That said, having a manager attached to your pilot could also hinder a sale. Television studios often do not want a manager on board as a non-writing executive producer to a pilot. You could also find it difficult to attract top producers with a manager/producer attached. The producers' fee is often set and they may not want to share it with someone else. When managers are attached as producers, they don't commission 10 percent but negotiate their own credit and fee. Clearly, you will need to firmly establish the parameters of your business relationship with your manager before your television project hits the market.

For you, the fledgling writer, a manager can also work to find you an agent. Many managers are former agents themselves, so their contacts can run deep within the industry. At their best, managers can bring another set of relationships to the table, increasing your access in the industry. They can also advocate for you when you are up for a job. After the agent, they can make that second phone call on your behalf to the network or showrunner. This can work to your advantage, especially if your agent has submitted multiple clients for the same job. The disadvantage of managers is that they are not regulated and anyone with a modicum of experience in the industry can hang a shingle and call himself a manager. Bottom line: Verify your manager's bona fides.

The Attorney

Television writers who have attorneys are usually working above scale and have projects that require complex negotiations when they sell. When you are selling your original material (a pilot), you will need an attorney to structure your deal. These are great problems to have. Attorneys commission at 5 percent. It's not to your advantage, while still working for scale, to have an attorney. However, if you find yourself in need of legal advice, you can secure an attorney who can negotiate for you on your specific project or deal only. Though the best scenario could be to hire an entertainment lawyer on an hourly rate, those attorneys can be hard to find. Recommendations from your agent and other writers will point you in the right direction.

Managing Your Team

Now that you have your team in place, do you sit and wait for the phone to ring? Unfortunately, there are many writers who have done just that. The key word in this equation is *partnership*. Your agent and/or your manager are your partners and your job is to be as proactive as they are. The brand they are selling is you, and it's your job to work on that brand as hard as they do.

When you meet, talk strategy. Find out how they plan to position you in the market and be clear about the efforts you are going to be making. Before you write a spec, for example, check in with your team. The network submission desks might be flooded with *Glee* scripts right now, so it might be in your best interest to write a *Revenge* episode instead. Take their advice and their notes on your material. They have a vested interest in your career.

And be respectful of their time. I usually touch base with my team once or twice a week. If I'm working, I let them know how it's going. If I am looking for work, I e-mail them updates on my writing and the people I have met. Keep your interactions brief and to the point. If they aren't returning your phone calls or e-mails, then it's up to you to fix it. Address the issue directly with them. If you find you are not satisfied with the results, then consider finding other representation. Remember, this is your career, and it's up to you to manage it.

Doing Your Job Well

Let's assume you've secured that staff writing job on a show and you've got a great management team in place. What next? The first thing: Do your job well. Writing a series is a complex process and you will gain so much experience by working in the writers' room. There's a lot to be learned there about story construction, launching ideas in collaboration, and finding creativity in the room. You will have already done this on your own when writing your specs. Now you get the chance to be creative within a group. Take the time to learn from the more experienced writers. Discover how to be collaborative. If your idea doesn't fly, don't defend it like the Alamo. Learn to move on to the next idea and watch how bad ideas can sometimes generate good ones. Knowing how to be an effective member of a writing staff is critical to your success as a writer in television.

Writers' rooms are like boyfriends—no two are the same. I have worked in rooms that are toxic and ego-driven, and some where creative generosity abounds. You will need to do your job well in both. Social skills are crucial. Brush up on them. Be collaborative. To write on staff requires being a team player. As one television writer put it, personality is the key to longevity. Mediocre writers sometimes have great careers, and great writers have lousy ones if they have difficult personalities. Showrunners would rather staff the room with solid writers who get along with others than with prima donnas who disrupt the flow. Big heads and petty egos abound in the entertainment business—don't be one. No one will want to work with you.

On a related note, a piece of advice from a junior writer I interviewed: Don't think every silence in the room means it's time for you to speak up and shine. He's right. If it's a great idea, by all means say it out loud, but don't forget one of your primary jobs is to support your showrunner and the other writers. I've watched several writers' careers go south because they always had to be the smartest kid in the room. Working in the writers' room for months at a time is a lot like going to summer camp. You want to be the person people want to spend time with.

Another important aspect of sustaining a career in television is to meet your deadlines. Schedules can get very tight once the series goes into production. You actually can't take that extra day to polish up your dialogue. Thousands of dollars can ride on whether or not you hand in your script on time. If you want to keep your job, don't be late. Writing for series television often means writing fast. Take this time to hone the skill. It will serve you later.

Know What You Are Good At

Are you the guy who always has a good fix to a failing story? Do ideas come to you in the room and they're actually good? Or are you a rewrite gal who can polish up a script like nobody's business? Does your dialogue jump off the page? Are you funny? Or do you make your readers cry? As you continue your career in television, you will quickly discover your strengths. Be aware of them and put them into play whenever you can, because your skills are very much needed in a writers' room, whose primary purpose is to produce scripts on time, on budget, and in a way that both satisfies the demands of the show and gives the audience something new and exciting.

Writing on staff is a team effort, and the more you can do to support your staff, the more you will be appreciated and respected. Your goal is to be asked back on the show, and if you are seen as a collaborative, talented writer with strengths that enhance the writers' room, you will be a writer in demand.

As we all know, no one is perfect, and for all the strengths we bring to the table as writers, we also have weaknesses. It behooves you as a professional to be aware of your shortcomings and work to improve them. Does story structure challenge you? Then read and reread the scripts already produced. Most writers' rooms keep detailed story notes on a daily basis. Review them each day before you go into that room. Make notes on new ideas when you aren't in session with other writers.

A lot of the magic happens outside of the room. Is your structure impeccable but your dialogue stiff as a board? Tape conversations. Write them up and work on the lines until they flow. It's important for you to be able to do an honest assessment of your skills and be constantly working to improve them. Yes, some of your writing talent is God-given; the rest comes through hard work and discipline. I have seen many writers hone and improve their skills over the course of their careers. And those who don't? Well, they now have day jobs.

Live Within Your Means

Okay, you've been hired back for a second season. You've maybe even had a bump-up to story editor. The promise of making big bucks in television is very real. When TV writers are working, we make good money. The Writers Guild works hard to ensure that even writers working for scale make good coin. When we work, we thrive. You might work for two solid years to get staffed on a show, and when you do, your first impulse could be to splurge. Go ahead, vacation in Hawaii—after you've paid off your credit cards, that is. But don't get carried away and buy a house in Maui. Even though you might suddenly be making more money than you're used to, save it. This year could be a great year. Next year may not.

If you want to stay viable for years to come, you'll need to manage your money well. If you live beyond your means while you are working, then what happens when you're not? Be prudent and average your income over a three-to-five-year span, and you'll see more realistically how much you are earning over time. If you can, have money tucked away to support yourself for at least a year. When you are not on staff, you need to be spending time writing new specs and managing your relationships with meetings and lunches. You don't want to be spending your precious creative time looking for a day job to pay for a mortgage you can't afford. Get the drift?

In Conclusion

I hope this chapter has given you a deeper understanding of what a career in television looks like. If you were to put this book down and never pick it up again, there is one thought I would like to leave with you: Above all else, love what you do. A career as a television writer requires hard work and sacrifice. After six months on the job, trust me, the glamour will be stripped away. Know what you love. Is it the endorphin rush that occurs when you're writing that action sequence? Do you find you secretly love your characters more than even your significant other? Do you live for the thrill of the chase when a deal is in negotiation? Make sure you know what you love about working as a television writer and stay close to that, always.

CHAPTER 10

The TV Year

by Richard Hatem

Week Fifty: The Answer, Wednesday, May 17, 1:21 P.M.

Your cell phone rings. You check the screen. It's the network. *Okay. It's the network. Okay.* Deep breath. Calm down. After all, you're not surprised, right? You've been expecting this call. After fifty weeks, and *thousands* of phone calls (no joke), and hundreds of pages of rewrites (also no joke), and dozens of meetings with studios and networks and directors and actors and writers, and a handful of really bad nights, it all comes down to this one phone call.

This has been the longest, hardest, scariest year of your life. Also the best. You've done things you'd never done before, faced new challenges, and survived. You've met people who will be your friends for the rest of your life. In a lot of ways, you're a totally different person than you were a year ago, and they can't take that away from you.

Your phone is still ringing. Your fate has been decided. You want to answer it. You do not want to answer it. And in the split second before you press the little button and learn your fate, you ask yourself—*How in the name of God did I get here?*

Week One: The POD Pitch, Thursday, June 2, 10:36 A.M.

It's the first week of June. The TV year has officially begun. While the studio and network executives recover from upfronts (the annual meeting of advertisers in New York, where they gather to see what shows each network is offering up), producers and writers all over town are meeting to prepare pitches that they'll try to set up—somewhere.

You have an idea for a show, but you have no produced credits yet. You managed to get a junior agent at a midsize agency to "back pocket" you, based on an original pilot spec you wrote last fall. *Back pocket* means it's an unofficial relationship, a handshake deal. They'll set a couple meetings and if something happens, great. And if nothing happens, everyone goes their separate ways.

Today is the first of those meetings. You have an eleven o'clock with Ethan M— of Drumbeat Entertainment. He's put a couple reality series on the air, and this season, he wants to branch out into scripted drama development. He's open to hearing anything, which means he's open to hearing you. True, you've never done a pitch, much less sold one, but in TV, it doesn't matter. A good idea can come from anywhere. And companies like Drumbeat—and about five hundred others just like it—survive by scrounging ideas, wherever they can find them. Drumbeat is a POD.

"What the hell is a POD?" Your friend Paula, who works at another POD, 100th Monkey, explained it to you: *POD* is an acronym for "Producer with Overall Deal." An overall deal means a producer (like Ethan M—) strikes a deal with a studio (like ABC Studios) that basically pays him to bring ideas for TV shows. According to the deal, the studio has first shot at any of the material Ethan M— brings in. In return, the studio provides Ethan M— with office space and a yearly "salary"— usually just enough to cover one employee (like Paula) and some random office supplies. For this, Ethan M— is expected to bring in quality pitches and scripts. If he doesn't, after a year, maybe two, said deal can end.

The TV business is starting to make sense. In your mind, you picture it like a giant orange tree. The PODs are the roots, stretching far and wide underground, searching for ideas anywhere they can find them and then channeling them upward, like water and nutrients, to the studios—the trunk of the tree—where they are then fed ever upward to the branches: the networks. A select few of those many, many ideas will ultimately blossom, having successfully gone through all the stages of growth, from pitch to script to pilot. These are the oranges. But even then, only a few will be picked to become television shows. The rest will die on the vine.

Last year, over four hundred one-hour drama pitches to the five major broadcast networks (ABC, NBC, CBS, Fox, and the CW) turned into two hundred fifty pilot scripts, which turned into forty pilots, which turned into fifteen new shows. The odds are stacked against you.

But none of that matters right now. You walk into the small offices of Drumbeat Entertainment, tucked away in the old Animation Building on the Disney lot in Burbank. Ethan M—'s assistant (bizarrely also named Ethan) offers you water. You know, by now, that being offered water by an assistant is the one constant in this completely unpredictable business. It's the one thing you can hang on to. You accept the small plastic bottle of water. But you are careful to drink it in tiny sips. You don't want to struggle through your pitch, desperate to use the bathroom.

Ten minutes later, at exactly 11:08 A.M., Ethan M— swings his door open, smiling. "Sorry to keep you waiting. Did you get some water?" You did. "Come on in."

Something strange happens while you're pitching. Or maybe not so strange, because it *always* happens: *You start getting into it.* Every time you do it, through all the fear and nerves and worry, you find yourself slowly beginning to *enjoy* the telling. You're scared to death, but you're also having a blast. It's like skiing—one wrong move and you're face-down in the snow, but if you just stay in the flow and don't overthink it, you're gonna be just fine. . . .

Later that afternoon, your agent calls. "Are you sitting down? Ethan loves it." This is amazing. You figured you'd have to pitch this idea a dozen times to a dozen PODs. But here you are, first pitch of the year, and *boom*. Maybe this TV game isn't so tough after all. . . .

Week Five: The Studio Pitch, Friday, July 8, 4:16 P.M. (ABC Studios—Frank G. Wells Building—Disney Lot)

You've spent the last four weeks working with Ethan, refining your pitch, filling in details, focusing the conflict, honing the main character's motivation. . . . Turns out, Ethan is a very smart guy. (Plus he always pays for lunch.) And just what is this idea, anyway?

> Ellie Jamison (30s) has just been promoted to homicide detective at the NYPD. But when her father suddenly dies, she goes back home to Dark Springs, Oregon, where she unexpectedly finds herself stepping into his job as sheriff, investigating not only his death—which may not have been just a simple boating accident— but other, darker mysteries in this strange small town. . . .

Your show is called, obviously enough, *Dark Springs*. It's a good title, mysterious yet hopeful. And yes, it sounds like bits and pieces of a dozen other shows. But you've been at this just long enough to know that familiarity is the lifeblood of television. There's a *reason* that lawyer, doctor, and cop shows keep cropping up on the network schedules, year after year after year. Television is about comfort first and novelty second. There are a hundred *Law and Orders* for every *Lost*. A pitch for a crime show with a female lead is something every network will take seriously. You have that in your favor, and you know it.

Your meeting today is with Kevin F— and Tamara S—, VPs of drama development at ABC Studios. And you know that they have been listening to pitches from writers like yourself all day, all week, all month— and will continue to listen to them all summer and into the fall. Their decision to partner with you—or not—will be based on many factors, the top two being: 1) *Will our network [in this case, ABC] be interested in developing this show?* and 2) *Are there other networks who will be interested in developing this show?* Their first responsibility is to ABC.

And if Kevin and Tamara are any good at their job—and they are—they know *exactly* the sort of thing ABC is interested in developing. They know because every year, every network develops internal memos detailing in broad strokes the network's development goals for the new TV year. Some of the things ABC is looking for this year include "sexy medical franchises featuring 'five minutes from now' technology; must have unique character hook" and "serialized family dramas (not New York or Los Angeles), with either legal or crime franchise" and "supernatural dramas of any kind." These memos aren't publicly distributed, but they get out, and you've seen it, and you know your story might fit their "serialized family drama" needs quite well. Plus, it's a cop show. You're in good shape.

The assistant leads you and Ethan down the hall and into a large, comfortable office. Kevin and Tamara are there; handshakes all around. "Did you guys get water?" Yes, you got water. Everyone settles into soft chairs and couches surrounding a cluttered coffee table. Ethan M— gives you a glowing introduction, talks about your brilliant spec script that first brought you to his attention, and explains how this new idea you're about to pitch is the perfect project—not just for you as a writer, the ultimate marriage of material and artist, but perfect for the network. But you're barely listening. You're looking out the window through gray haze at the hills of Griffith Park across the 134 freeway, trying to center yourself and remember why you ever thought this idea was so great. And now, as eyes turn to you, you begin to speak. . . .

Week Nine: The Network Pitch, Thursday, August 4, 3:30 P.M. (ABC Administrative Offices—Burbank, California)

This is the one that matters. You nail this, you have a deal. You will be paid the Writers Guild minimum (at the very least), around $85,000, to write a network pilot script. True, if the network doesn't like it, ABC

Studios—your new partners as of that last meeting two weeks ago—has the option of bringing it to other networks. But then the odds of a deal drop significantly. Besides, this is an ABC idea, developed for ABC by ABC Studios. This is the place. This is the day. This is the meeting. It all comes down to this. . . .

6:26 P.M.—"Are you sitting down?" Ethan asks when you pick up the phone. Why is everyone always asking you if you're sitting down? "ABC passed. They didn't think the idea was right for their network." *What?! The bastards! The idiots!* This is what you say, but what you feel is, *Of course they passed, the idea is garbage. The true depth of my nontalent has finally been revealed for all to see. I have been exposed as a fraud by the top drama-development executives at a major television network. My career nosedive has begun. . . .*

"We have a meeting at CBS on Monday." Ethan sounds hopeful, stoic, unbowed. But that's his job. He's a producer. You're a writer. Your job is to be fragile, injured, and neurotic. There is nothing in the world you want to do less than repeat this embarrassing exercise on Monday in front of another group of network executives, who, by the way, will know, as they watch you pitch, that you've already been rejected by ABC. You're damaged goods. And worse than that, you're baldly trying to peddle your substandard "idea" to them. What do you take them for, fools? If ABC doesn't want your terrible idea, why would CBS?

Because of a little show called *CSI,* that's why.

CSI was developed by ABC Studios, rejected by the ABC network, and subsequently sold to CBS. Several billion dollars later, everyone learned a stark lesson: One network's garbage is another network's gold.

Week Eleven: Tuesday, August 16, 12:21 P.M.

Congratulations are in order—CBS bought your pitch. Turns out they are looking for "crime procedurals with female leads." So far, so good. You are now officially employed for the remainder of the year. That's the good news.

Here's the bad news. You've spent the last two weeks going back and forth with Ethan and ABC Studios attempting to create an odd document called a "story area." This is not an official step in your contract; you will never receive a check marked "Delivery of Story Area." No one can quite explain what this document is, or what it should look like, or what exactly it should include, or how long it should be. But more and more, every network requires one as a precursor to the outline. And you have learned to despise it.

The closest anyone has come to explaining it has been this: The network needs to know the general plot of the pilot episode of your show as early as possible so they don't, for instance, end up with nine pilot scripts all involving a kidnapped child as a major plot point. Okay, fair enough. But why does the studio keep asking for more "character arc" information? And why do they keep asking you to "imply tone"? What's really going on here?

Here's what's going on: *The network wants to begin guiding the development of the script immediately.* Not when you turn in the script. Not when you turn in the outline. *Now.* Even at this early stage, Beverly, Gabe, and Hannah (the CBS VPs of drama development you're working with) want to be in control of what's happening. They don't want anyone wandering off the development trail—not now, not ever. They have very clear marching orders from their bosses: Bring in scripts that reflect our development agenda. *Don't surprise us.* And so, in turn, they do not want *you* to surprise *them.* They are, as the kids say, up in your grill. Get used to it.

It's at this point that you begin to intuit a fact very crucial to your success: *The executives at the studio and the network are your partners, and your fates are intertwined.* They are depending on you to create a great script. You are depending on them to guide that process so that the end product is something that the network, realistically, will want to produce, based on its development agenda for that season. This interdependence will require trust and patience from all parties. But in television, the most collaborative of all mediums, it is the very nature of the beast. And the sooner you internalize this truth, the better.

Week Sixteen: Wednesday, September 21, 10:44 A.M.

You get a scary call from Ethan: The network suddenly has a problem with your pilot. It's "the father thing." While they initially loved the idea of Ellie going home to attend her father's funeral and then investigating his death as a possible murder, they've started having second thoughts. Does it have to be her father? Could it be someone else maybe? Like . . . her old boyfriend?

You start to panic. No real reason; changes are changes. But panic is your first reaction to almost anything when it comes to work, and by now you've learned to just let it wash over you like an ocean wave, knowing it will eventually recede on its own.

The network wants to discuss its concerns; there's a conference call scheduled for this afternoon at five P.M. So you and Ethan schedule a lunch-hour "work session" at Nate 'n Al to plot out some ways to address concerns in advance. When Ethan arrives, he tells you some interesting things about where this note is coming from. Apparently, one of CBS's new shows, *Shadow of Doubt,* just premiered on Monday night to surprisingly low ratings. The numbers were so bad that some people, taking their cue from Nikki Finke and *Deadline Hollywood,* are speculating that its second episode won't even air. "Did you see it?" Ethan asks. No, like the rest of America, you didn't watch. Well, Ethan did. And guess what the pilot episode was about? "A young Boston lawyer goes back home to Rock Ridge, Maine, for Christmas—and finds himself joining his aging father's law firm." Okay—so what does that have to do with *Dark Springs?* Only everything.

According to Ethan, there is a network-wide pox on any show involving someone going "back home" to work with a parent. You remind Ethan that in *Dark Springs,* Ellie doesn't go to work *with* her father—her father's dead. She goes to work *in his place.* Doesn't matter, he says. The very act of "going home" is probably enough to make the network sour on the entire idea. You do *not* want to spend nine months of your life developing an idea that makes the network execs wince every time they think about it because it reminds them of a recent stinging failure. CBS was being kind in only suggesting that perhaps the father could in fact be an old boyfriend. Ethan knew halfway through the other show's disastrous premiere that they were in big trouble. Ethan suggests the two of you reexamine *the entire concept.*

Panic. Ocean wave. *Tidal wave.* How can some horrible show no one even watched suddenly have such an impact on *your* idea? It doesn't make sense. *It's not fair.*

But inside your panic, there is a rock of calm. Because way deep down . . . *you don't absolutely hate the idea of the old boyfriend.* In fact, it could work. So you and Ethan order, and talk, and eat, and talk, and talk, and talk. At a certain point, you realize you're writing down notes on the paper place mat. And in the course of a lunch, here's the new version of *Dark Springs* (now titled *Turquoise Bay*):

In a darkly comic new one-hour drama, Ellie Jamison (30s) has just been promoted to homicide detective at the NYPD. Feeling like she has finally accomplished something worthwhile, she decides it's safe to go to her fifteenth high school reunion in her hometown of Turquoise Bay, California, a picturesque yet still comfortably funky beach town. She unexpectedly hooks up with her old (hot) boyfriend, Jason Phelps (30s). But things take a strange and chilling turn when she wakes up the next morning to find him murdered. She's the prime suspect. And she is shocked to learn that Corey Axelrod (30s), her best friend's little brother (who always had a crush on her back in the day), is now the town's one homicide cop. In an effort to clear her name, they team up to find out who killed Jason. And in the process, Ellie finds out that this idyllic seaside town has more than its share of intrigue and crime. Maybe Ellie won't be going back to New York City so soon after all. . . .

You're excited. You love it. It's sexy, it's fun—and it's still a police procedural with a female lead. And now it's *nothing* like *Shadow of Doubt.*

Except for the "going home" part. Which you have to have. But still: no parents, tons of love interest, sunlit beach setting . . . It's different. *But is it different enough?*

Following procedure, you call the studio first. Everything must go through the studio before going to the network. You and Ethan manage to get Kevin and Tamara on the phone around three P.M. You pitch the new version. They love it. And in their enthusiasm for telling you how much they love it, they tell you all the things they never really thought worked about your original idea. Fantastic. Whatever.

At five P.M., you pitch CBS. Ethan has given a heads-up call to Gabe, warning him that you already have a new version of the show that addresses "the father thing." You pitch the new version. The network loves it. And just like that, in the course of a day, you're writing a different pilot.

Week Twenty-one: Friday, October 28, 4:33 P.M.

The past five weeks have been a bit of a blur. A quiet blur. You've been working on your outline and everyone has been pretty much leaving you alone. Ethan calls more than you'd like, just to "say hi," check on how things are going, and see if you need any help. But for the most part, you're into your "writer space," and it feels great.

You finally sent the completed outline to Ethan last week, and he loved it. His notes were minimal, and some were even helpful. And then, just about ten minutes ago, you sent it off to the studio for a weekend read. You plan to enjoy your first weekend off in over a month—a weekend without any work hanging over your head. A weekend of well-deserved good feelings. But something is creeping up on you. The familiar, vulnerable, worrisome feeling you get when you turn something in. It's a "waiting" feeling. And just like the man says, the waiting is the hardest part. Better get used to it. You're going to spend a lot of time waiting over the next six months. And it's not going to get easier.

Week Twenty-two: Tuesday, November 1, 11:20 A.M.

They have notes. They want to set a call for tomorrow at five P.M. (great, more waiting). Ethan has a heads-up: Their biggest note is tone. The thing the studio loved most about your "new version" was the fun, sexy vibe between Ellie and Corey. But they're just not sure it's coming through. Right now it's feeling a little flat and unclear. They're just not getting the relationship.

Of course they're not getting the tone, you think. *It's an outline. There's barely any dialogue. The timing of the scenes is wonky. Wait until they read the pages,* then *tell me they have tone problems.*

Doesn't matter; you'll have to do at least one more pass for the studio, trying to somehow imply "sexy" and "fun"—which are, ironically, two of the very last things you're feeling right now. . . .

Week Twenty-four: Friday, November 18, 10:00 A.M.

You're on hold, waiting for the network notes conference call to begin. After what feels like hours of small talk with Ethan and the studio, Gabe and Hannah from CBS hop on the line. And let's face it: You're scared to death. You feel sure that what you're about to hear will tell you everything you need to know about your pilot's future. A weak reaction and a lot of general "overall" notes means your project is already off track—*and you haven't even written a single page of the script yet.* On the other hand, an enthusiastic reaction means your outline is better than the other ones they've been reading, and maybe you're already pulling ahead of the pack.

The network reaction is surprising: They love the outline, but they want big changes. They say the plot works fine, and they love the characters—they just want *more.* More scenes between the two leads, Ellie and Corey; more scenes with Ellie's funny, sassy friend Lauren; more scenes with Ellie's mom, who—in Ellie's absence, and since the death of her husband years ago—has become a sexually liberated übercougar. They even want Ellie and Corey to sleep together—in the pilot! (Personally, you were thinking they *might* sleep together toward the end of the first season. . . .)

So congratulations—they love it. But now you have a ton of work to do to keep up the pace.

Week Twenty-nine: Wednesday, December 21, 3:45 P.M.

You did everything they wanted. And they're thrilled. Just a couple of tiny notes, but otherwise, this pilot is just exactly where they want it to be. You'll make the changes next week and have an official "first draft" for them the first week of January. After all the worry and all the surprises, you've ended the year on a legitimate high note. God bless us, everyone!

Week Thirty-two: Monday, January 9, 1:15 P.M.

Trouble. Gut-sinking trouble. Turbulence-on-takeoff kind of trouble. It's all over *Deadline Hollywood* this morning. CBS has just picked up a pilot about a female cop who teams with her ex-husband, a lawyer turned reality TV star, to solve crimes.

So basically, your show is dead.

Sure, it's not *exactly* your pilot. In your show, Ellie teams with a friend/crush, not her ex-husband. And while the pilot they picked up takes place in Chicago, yours takes place in a beach town. But, man, the big problem is *tone*. They're both relationship dramas with overtones of sex and comedy. Both could be considered *Castle*-esque. Clearly, this is something that the network wants. Clearly, they ordered two versions to see which one they prefer. And clearly, they have made their choice. And it ain't yours.

Ethan tells you not to worry. The network has not officially passed, and until they do, there's no reason to panic. But he sounds weird when he says it. His voice sounds different than it usually does. You identify the change: He sounds distant. As if there's already a process of emotional detachment taking place. He's already lowering this project on his mental to-do list. It's the most demoralizing sound you've ever heard.

Twenty minutes later, the studio calls. They have you and Ethan on conference. They explain what's happening: According to their conversations with the network, your show is not dead at all. In fact, it's still "very much in the mix," whatever that means. This particular competing project was ordered early to show respect and loyalty to the producer—a huge movie director who has made a handful of $100 million–plus movies and is now branching out into TV. This is the network's way of indicating their enthusiasm for him. It's political. Your fear and misery makes you candid. You ask the obvious question: If the network's so eager to be in business with this guy, then—even if they do green-light both pilots—won't they just pick up his series? Is this whole thing just turning into an exercise in futility? The studio says no. Once the pilots are in, the prize really will go to whichever show they think is best. In fact, at that point, the odds may switch back in your favor: Since the deal with the famous director is so huge, your show will ultimately be cheaper to produce on a weekly basis.

You try to wrap your head around all this. You're in uncharted territory, and it's going to take you a while to get your bearings. Everyone tells you to sit tight for a few more days. Fine. You can sit tight for a few more days.

How hard can that be?

Week Thirty-four: Tuesday, January 24, 4:15 P.M.

It's been two weeks. Every day you expect to hear something. You compulsively check *Deadline Hollywood* and read about other people having their pilots picked up. You keep thinking you'll somehow read about your own pilot, but of course, that makes no sense. You know that Ethan will call you with any news. He's following this like a crazed bloodhound in a way that almost makes you feel sorry for him. There are days when his concern is so strong, it actually lets you off the hook. He's worrying enough for two. But in unguarded moments, you realize that you are entirely unprepared for news of either the good *or* bad variety. You know that you will feel bad if your pilot is not produced. You will instantly put on "the failure coat," that heavy, wet garment you've spent so many years schlepping around in, feeling embarrassed and ashamed and angry and self-loathing in varying degrees. It's a horrible feeling, but it is familiar. It's a part of your life, and there's not much you can do about it. Like rain in Portland, it's just the cost of doing business.

But what if the answer is yes? What if they say *yes, we'll shoot your pilot*? You haven't allowed yourself to really go too far down that road because of the old "don't jinx it" thing. Only think about failure. Brace yourself for failure. That has always been your way, and it has always seemed safest, but—what if you do not fail? Then what? Well, that's tougher. Because you really don't know what that would entail. You imagine a moment of pure ecstasy. You win and everyone else in the world loses. So that's nice. But then what? What exactly happens next?

This question fills you with an odd sense of vertigo, like you're somehow suddenly whooshed to a great height, but you're unclear of the mechanism by which it's happened—or its reliability. There is no road map. You do not know the landscape. You feel slightly disoriented and scared, as if the pilot of your transcontinental flight has suddenly dropped dead of an aneurism, and for some reason, you are suddenly required to land the plane. It's like that nightmare where you're onstage and it's opening night, but you have neglected to memorize your lines—or even read the play. Failure is familiar. Success? It's something you have never seriously considered beyond knowing deep in your soul that it's something you want more than anything.

At four fifteen the phone rings. It's Ethan. "Are you sitting down? . . ."

Week Thirty-six: Thursday, February 9, 2:22 P.M.

After a lifetime of waiting in line, you're finally on the ride. For once, the conversation isn't about rewrites. (That'll come later.) The conversations you're having now feel very important and grown-up. Sure, you're no kid, but still—these are conversations you've never been a part of. Conversations about directors—and of even more immediate import, *casting* directors. Since your project was picked up so late in the season, you're already behind schedule. You've got barely a month to hire your entire above-the-line crew: director, line producer, director of photography, production designer, costume designer. Plus, you have to cast all the roles, figure out where you're going to shoot the thing, and when, and for exactly how much. In this case, *you* means you—and Ethan, and Kevin and Tamara from the studio.

Thankfully, Ethan has some experience with this stuff, so you've elected to listen more than talk and only speak up when: (a) someone asks you a question; or (b) you have a halfway decent idea. You're trying to find your place in this postscript-centric world. And all the questions you have can be boiled down to one basic question: When should I *insist* on something?

You've always had this vision in your head of the powerful, artistically driven writer/producer. In your imagination, this person knows everything he wants ahead of time, is never in doubt, and most importantly, *must constantly wage war with everyone to maintain the creative integrity of the piece.* This philosophy presumes that everyone you work with is actually a covert adversary. The network, studio, director—and every other person involved in the production of your pilot—is secretly plotting against you to undermine your creative vision *and to defeat you personally.* There is a handy showbiz term for this kind of thinking: *paranoia.* Okay, so maybe they're not consciously trying to destroy you and your career. Maybe they are all just so incompetent and obtuse that they will destroy you and your career *by accident.* There's a handy showbiz term for this sort of thinking, too: *narcissistic perfectionism.* You don't want to be a jerk, but you don't want to be a pushover either. Someone has even told you that the first thing you should do when you walk onto the set is fire someone. That will let everyone know who's boss.

Ethan has some advice, and it's brilliant in its simplicity: "State all your concerns in the form of a question." For instance: Let's say you got a bad feeling from the line producer you've all just interviewed. To you, he seems brusque and a little arrogant, and uses pragmatism as a bludgeon to shut down interesting ideas. First, wait and see if anyone else brings this up. If no one does, you can broach the subject by saying, "I wonder, is this the most collaborative guy we can find?" Usually this is all it takes to get a conversation started. The outcome of that conversation is always up for grabs. But really, a conversation is all you can reasonably ask for.

You've always prided yourself on your ability to be collaborative and open-minded. The next three months are going to put that to the test. . . .

Week Thirty-seven: Wednesday, February 15, 10:01 A.M.

There is nothing—*nothing*—like the first day of auditions. It's a day you will remember for the rest of your life. Real live actors, several of whom you recognize from other shows you love and hate, are walking into this small, poorly lit room. And they nervously introduce themselves to you, and they compliment you and tell you how much they love your script, and they begin speaking the lines that you wrote. It is infatuating and intoxicating. You have never felt more honored. Or important. And when they leave the room, Ethan and the director (more on him later) and Barbara L—, the casting director, look at you like an equal and the four of you share a few words about what you think of the actors and their performances. That first day of auditions will never be matched.

Because by the third day, the fun is over. You have heard your lines read one hundred times, and by now, they all sound terrible and dull and unfunny. And every single actor mispronounces the name of the street where the character lives, and if they *all* mispronounce it, that makes it your fault—not theirs. And people you would have loved on day one you hate on day three. And the worst part is that you realize that no matter how difficult you used to think the life of a writer was, there is no more hellish existence than that of an actor. You thought sitting in judgment of others would finally allow you the opportunity to assess others fairly and generously, in the way you always wished others would assess you and your work. And now, you realize what a fool you were, because *there is no way to judge these actors fairly.* It is physically impossible for you to hear your lines with the same degree of enthusiasm and bigheartedness on day three as you did on day one.

And guess what? You've got four more weeks of this. With each passing hour, you trust your instincts less. You find yourself dismissing people *the very first second you see them.* They walk in the room and you wish you could say, "Just walk back out. You're simply not right for the role." But you can't say that. So you try to keep the door in your brain and your heart open just enough to actually hear magic if it happens. You owe it to these people, who are walking in with nothing other than their bodies and their voices to work with. There is something shameful in the process, something that shames *you.* You're judging people for all the things you've always been told not to judge people by: their looks, their voices, and the most superficial aspects of their surface attributes.

But what choice do you have? You can't "get to know" these people. There are too many and there's not enough time. They're all reading your terrible lines in more or less the exact same way. And the ones who try "novel" interpretations are invariably the worst of all. And besides, will the average TV viewer be any more forgiving? Won't they instantly respond to—or reject—the person on their TV screen based on some instantaneous assessment that they are not even fully aware of? Won't they be just as unconsciously harsh—even more so? So maybe you should just go with it. Trust your demoralized soul to react to whatever makes it happy without thinking about it too much. Pretend you're watching TV and simply wait for someone—anyone—to pop.

And while you're at it? Forgive everyone you have ever hated for dismissing you based on a first impression.

Week Thirty-nine: Tuesday, February 28, 3:58 P.M.

Your show no longer takes place in a beach town. It takes place in a small town in the Pacific Northwest. Turns out it's more "cost efficient" to film your show in Vancouver.

Money has become an everyday concern. It seems like from the moment your pilot was green-lit, your relationship with the studio has turned oddly adversarial as far as money is concerned. They've told you and Ethan how much money is available and that's that. The budget they've given you has nothing to do with the actual needs of the show. It's just a pile of money. And according to the way everyone figures it, including Kevin and Tamara, your studio partners, it's about 20 percent less than you need. Kevin and Tamara are "lobbying" their bosses for a budget increase, but with every passing day, it's becoming clear: *There will be no more money.*

Other pilots have more money. Other pilots *at the very same studio* have more money. But for reasons you don't know (and will *never* know), yours has been budgeted with less. And what this means is that, for the first time, you will be doing a rewrite based on monetary concerns.

First, the script is too long. At least that's what the director keeps telling you. You have eleven days to shoot your pilot, and the assistant director has it boarded at fourteen. (You learn that each scene has been allotted a certain amount of time to film. For every scene you cut or reduce, you save time. And money.) So you've already changed some night scenes to day scenes, cut certain locations to save time on crew moves, and cut the overall page count by 10 percent. A new board is released. Now it's down to thirteen days. You still have to cut two entire days of shooting. At six pages a day, that means cutting twelve more pages. That's 20 percent of your script.

It's impossible. You have until Thursday.

Week Thirty-nine: Thursday, March 2, 12:12 P.M.

You have cut ten pages from your pilot. It still works, but barely. It's injured. You send the script to the studio and the network. The studio has approved the cuts. (Of course they have; they're the ones demanding them.) You have a phone call with the network. And get this: They *do not approve the cuts.* They know full well how much money you *don't* have.

They know *exactly* what the studio is putting you through. They know the impossible situation you are in. But are they kicking in any money? Are you joking? They are simply telling you that these cuts are not acceptable and that this is not what they asked for when they selected your pilot. And the problem is handed back to you. Find some other way to make the money work without making these changes.

It is impossible. You have until Monday.

Week Forty: Friday, March 10, 1:29 P.M.

Welcome to Vancouver! You flew first class—*first class*—and you're staying at the greatest hotel *ever*! (Not that *other* Vancouver hotel where everyone always stays. This one is right on the water, and it has an aromatherapied lobby, and everyone here is beautiful.) You feel like a big deal, maybe for the first time ever. And it's a great feeling.

There is an actual production office set up north of the city where people you have never met are employed in various capacities to produce your written work. They treat you with respect and behave as if you are their boss. And you kind of are. You have never felt luckier in your life.

But you have trouble getting to sleep at night. With each passing day, the scope of the pilot and the number of people involved grows. There are too many factors, too many variables to be actively in control of all of them. And you try to remind yourself that you don't *have* to control them. All you can do is try to be aware of them and step in when necessary. At this early stage in your pilot-making career, you know that the less you speak, the more you will be heard. That doesn't mean be silent. It *does* mean don't talk just to be saying something. Pick your battles.

Week Forty-one: The First Day of Shooting, Tuesday, March 14, 11:23 A.M.

And here it is, your first battle. A crew of a hundred people stand in the rain on the streets of Vancouver. You've been shooting one scene for just over three hours. Which puts you one hour behind schedule. One of your lead actors is having trouble with his lines. You and the director have shared worried looks for the past hour. Finally, your director says he thinks he has enough to work with and decides it's time to move on. And you suddenly feel dread rise in your chest. Because you *don't* think there's enough to work with. What can you do? You have to speak up now or forever hold your peace. So you approach the director on the set and express that you are a little worried about having enough usable coverage of the lead. And you ask, in your most diplomatic tone, if he thinks it's maybe a good idea to do one more take, just to be sure.

And your director says no, he does not think it is a good idea. He quietly points out that the takes have been getting progressively worse. The actor is freaking out. He knows he's blowing the lines, and he's becoming more stressed with every take. It's getting to a point of diminishing returns. Going for one more take isn't likely to do anything other than push your actor farther into his own head, magnifying his self-consciousness. Your director has a different idea: Move to the next location (indoors, where everyone will be happier), and change the order of coverage in subsequent scenes so that the lead is filmed last, giving him time to get comfortable with the scene, the set, the other actors—and his lines.

You feel weird. Heard—but chastened at the same time. It takes a while to figure it out, but it finally dawns on you: Now that production has begun, the director is in the driver's seat. Sure, you (or the studio, or the network) can step in and insist on pretty much anything you want. But on a set, the director is still looked at as king, and to undermine that authority is to take a huge—and unnecessary—risk. If the cast or crew loses confidence in the director as the "boss" during production, things can get out of hand very quickly. You've hired this director for a reason. If you just intended to use him as a proxy for each and every one of your ideas, you're cheating yourself out of his artistic contributions and the benefit of his experience. Once again, you'll have to walk a tightrope balancing between overaccommodation and micromanagement. The best piece of advice comes from Tamara at the studio: Discuss all your ideas, concerns, and suggestions with the director *in private,* come to a decision, and then let the director implement the changes on set.

Week Forty-four: The Director's Cut, Wednesday, April 5, 3:55 P.M.

This is a very difficult day for everyone. It's difficult for the director because he is turning in his "first draft" of the pilot to you, the writer/producer. And he wants you to love it as much as you wanted the studio and network to love the first draft of your script, all those months ago. And it's difficult for you because you just finished watching it, and you think it's awful.

Somehow every performance feels false, the timing is off, and the weaknesses in the script have been highlighted to a point of embarrassment. Worst of all, it's boring. Every plot twist just kind of lies there like a beached whale in the hot summer sun, drawing flies and generally stinking the place up.

Ethan sees the look on your face. He suggests you both take a walk around the studio lot, get some air, and have a frank discussion about your reactions. So you do. You take a walk, and you spill your guts. You freak out. It's not the first time, and Ethan is used to it. And he surprises you by not disagreeing. Wait a second: Isn't he *supposed* to disagree? Isn't he supposed to tell you that you're wrong and the pilot is fantastic? Well, he doesn't. Instead, he tells you something unexpected: "First cuts always suck. Not because they're bad, but because you are finally seeing what the pilot *is* instead of what you always hoped it would be." He explains that the feeling of being simultaneously underwhelmed and panicked is very common. He tells you it will never look this bad again. From here on out it will only get better. You pray to God he's right. . . .

Week Forty-six: Thursday, April 20, 4:58 P.M.

As far as the TV year is concerned, April truly is the cruellest month. You have moved into a new phase of intense paranoia, because all around you, all you hear are rumors. Rumors about *the other pilots*. Which ones are fantastic and which ones are terrible, which ones are "a lock" and which ones are "dead." And every time you hear a rumor, you know that somewhere in town the same conversations are going on, but in those, *your* pilot is being discussed. You haven't felt like this since high school, when people talked about who liked who and who was dating who and who was going to prom with who. It all seemed so important, so exciting, so scary—and so out of your control. The studio has assured you that the network loves everything they've seen of your pilot. And the network has actually been very forthcoming about how much they like it. But one thing becomes very clear: Liking your pilot and *picking up* your pilot are two very different things.

Everyone has a story. The director, the studio executives, the actors, the editor, the post-production supervisor; they all have a story of the "golden pilot" that was an absolute favorite until the middle of May, just before upfronts, when it suddenly died. You also hear stories of long-shot pilots declared dead way back in February that suddenly surge to the forefront out of nowhere and win the day with a series order. So, it's both a warning and a reassurance when everyone reminds you, "Nothing means anything until you hear from the network in May."

You have been told more than once that you will not hear a definitive answer until May 17, because that's the day CBS announces its fall schedule at upfronts. That's where the networks get the advertisers excited about spending their money buying commercial time on these wonderful new shows. It's a party for the advertisers, who get treated to big shows and private dinners and meetings with celebrities. But for you and the other writers and directors and producers, it's the final phase of a grueling, ten-month worry-fest that only ends when you know for sure your pilot's fate.

So, for now, you spend your days in the editing room, cutting and recutting and selecting music and adjusting the few special-effects shots you have, and basically trying not to think about the fact that all this might be for nothing.

Week Forty-seven (Part One): The Series Document, Monday, April 24, 9:53 A.M.

You knew this was coming. Everybody's been talking about it for months. The "series document." And frankly, you could have started working on it weeks ago, but you didn't. Hey, you were busy watching actors audition, and having dinner with your director so you could discuss how he would bring your brilliant script to life, and enjoying first-class flights to Vancouver, and hanging out with the actors you finally cast, and watching dailies, and . . . doing anything but writing. Because let's be honest: Writing is hard, but producing is pretty fun. Sure, it has its challenging moments, but mostly you've had a blast. Well, the producing part of your job is winding down and now the writing part is coming back. And guess what? If they pick your show, there will be so many writing chores dropping down on your head, it just might kill you. So you might as well get back into the swing of things.

The series document is an informal, nonpaid, yet absolutely essential part of your responsibilities as pilot writer. In this document, you will recap the concept of your show—but now you will also map out what the first season might look like. How will the characters develop? How will their relationships grow? What will happen to them over the course of the season? You don't have to go into tremendous detail, but you do have to give a general sense as to the direction the series and the characters are heading. You are also expected to provide anywhere from four to eight "sample story lines." In other words, what will be the main story line of, say, episode five?

The series document is a vexing task this late in the game. You can't help but feel that, rather than increasing your odds, this document will kill your chances of a series order completely. The network will love your pilot, but then they'll read what you have in mind for the rest of the season and hate it. You picture them tossing down the document and breathing a sigh of relief: "My God, can you believe we almost *ordered* this piece of crap?"

Then, Hannah at CBS tells you something weird: The document will never be read by the top guys—*nor was it ever intended to be*. It's really just a set of talking points for Hannah, Gabe, and Beverly to reference if their bosses ask them questions during the decision-making process. They want to be totally prepared for anything. And if it comes down to it, they will use the series document as ammunition in the fight to get your (read: *their*) show picked up.

That changes everything. For the millionth time, you have to remind yourself of the one simple fact you keep forgetting: *The network is your ally.* It doesn't feel like it, but it is true. They want to pick up your show. They want to pick them *all* up. But they can't, so some of the children they have raised will have to be killed. This knowledge doesn't make you feel a lot better, but it does make you feel slightly less paranoid.

Week Forty-seven (Part Two): The Final Network Cut, Friday, April 28, 7:22 P.M.

You're done. You have just turned in the final cut to the network. *For the next three weeks, you have nothing to do but wait.*

Why, oh *why*, do you have to turn in your final cut so early? What in the name of God are they going to do with it for *three weeks*? This is the question you ask Tamara from ABC Studios over drinks at Tam O'Shanter, a cool old Scottish-themed restaurant in Atwater Village near her house. She tells you the network still has a lot of work to do figuring out what they're going to pick up. They'll do some testing. This means they will screen your pilot for a hundred randomly selected people wandering through the lobby of the MGM Grand Hotel in Las Vegas. (Why Las

Vegas? Because people from all over the country vacation in Las Vegas, making it a great cross-section of the American viewing public.)

After the screening, they'll sit down with these people and ask them specific questions about your pilot: Did you like the main character? How did you feel about the music? The pace? Was it confusing? Was it boring? How likely are you to watch future episodes? Would you definitely recommend this show to your friends? Would you definitely *not* recommend this show to your friends? These reactions are taken very seriously by the network.

The network executives will also show your pilot, along with all the other pilots the network has developed, to all the other creative executives at the network. This will generate a sort of in-house reaction where people can feel more or less free to offer up any opinion at all. Oddly enough, this is also a big factor in which shows get picked up. After all, who knows what a good CBS show looks like more than the people at CBS?

Finally, they will give the pilot to their sales and marketing department for the most important evaluation of all: Can they sell it? If the answer is yes, even a poor-quality pilot has a chance. If the answer is no, even the most beautifully rendered pilot is in danger.

And all of this is just the beginning. How many spots does any given network have to fill? If it looks like a large number of their existing shows are about to be canceled, maybe that means they will pick up more pilots than originally planned. Or vice versa. How expensive will these shows be to produce? How many pilots will they pick up from their in-house studio and how many from outside? When it comes right down to it, the biggest question is: What are the network's specific needs at this exact moment in time? Maybe the premise of your show fit into their grand scheme nine months ago. But nine months is a very long time in television and a lot can change.

After a third margarita, Tamara (who has become a good friend of yours since way back in August) lays it out: "The pilot is fantastic. It's everything we want it to be and it's everything *the network* wants it to be.

I think it will be a great series. In a sane world, there is no way they don't pick this up." And she leaves it at that, not bothering to articulate what you both already know: *The world of TV is not sane.*

Week Fifty: Tuesday, May 16, 7:25 P.M.

The last three weeks have been difficult. You have not been an easy person to be around. You know it, and you're sorry, but can anyone blame you? Now it is "Pilot Eve," as your friends have started calling it, and they've come up with a totally goofy idea: drinks on the patio at the Castaway in Burbank. This restaurant is way up in the hills, and from the deck, you can watch the sunset across the valley and see the lights come on in Burbank, Studio City, and Toluca Lake. The Castaway is not a showbiz hangout. It is not hot or hip or trendy. But the drinks are great and they are typically served with umbrellas and those little plastic monkeys you love so much. And the view *is* truly amazing. It is not only amazing, you realize, but also oddly appropriate. Because you are looking out across the true center of the television and movie industry—the studios along the 134 freeway: Disney/ABC, NBC, Warner Bros., Universal. If only the out-of-towners knew: Hollywood Boulevard is about souvenir T-shirts. If you want the real Hollywood, go to Burbank.

Your friends know you're nervous. Beyond nervous. They know you've more or less been waiting for this your entire life. And your friend Hugh has put this little outing together. Your instinct is to say, "We should wait until after I've heard the news. Then either I'll want to celebrate, or I'll desperately need to get drunk." But Hugh sees it differently. As far as he's concerned, *this* is the Golden Moment, when hope is still alive, dancing out there over the lights of Burbank. Don't wait on "them" to tell you when and how to celebrate—you've got plenty to celebrate already. They made your pilot. You like your pilot. Even more, you like the people you met along the way—and they like you. You've had a good year of ever-rising hopes and fortunes. Tomorrow it all may end. But that doesn't change the fact that *this year happened*. So celebrate that.

Besides, what are you really gonna do if it all comes crashing down tomorrow? Well, you'll be devastated. But take comfort in the fact that you will not be alone. There will be plenty of devastation in the television business this week. There already has been. People you know have seen their pilots die. But—seriously—what will *you* do if your pilot dies?

Easy. You'll try again. You might need a few weeks to sleep and recover. But that's the nice thing about the TV business. It's like Vegas. There's always another game in town, always another seat at the table. In a few short weeks, the TV year starts all over again. And there will be plenty of people willing and eager to hear your pitches. Yes, you'll be starting back at the bottom of the hill. But so what? You're at the top of the hill now, if only for this moment, and the view is truly breathtaking. You worked hard to get here. And after all, isn't this exactly what you hoped your life in LA would be when that plane from Ohio landed six years ago? Now here you are, surrounded by friends who will still be your friends tomorrow no matter what. You have a drink in your hand and a dream in your heart.

But what about tomorrow? It'll get here soon enough. For now, just look at the lights and keep on dreaming.

Tomorrow . . .

Your phone is still ringing. You finally pick up. It's Gabe and Hannah and Beverly from the network. Kevin and Tamara from the studio are conferenced in. Ethan is on the line, too.

"Are you sitting down . . . ?"

ABOUT THE EDITOR AND CONTRIBUTORS

Editor

Linda Venis, PhD, is the director of the Department of the Arts at UCLA Extension, where for more than two decades she has guided the growth of the Writers' Program into the nation's largest screenwriting and creative writing program. Dr. Venis has taught at UCLA and USC and is the recipient of the UCLA Distinguished Teaching Award. She lives in Los Angeles, California, with her husband, Gary Berg, and daughter, Laura.

Editorial Board

Ellen Byron
Cindy Davis
Peter Dunne
Tom Lazarus
Steve Mazur
Billy Mernit
Linda Palmer

Ellen Sandler
Steve Sohmer
Victoria Wisdom

Contributing Authors

Alison Lea Bingeman, WGA member; credits include the independent feature film thriller *Hurt; Bomb Girls; CSI: Miami; NCIS; Relic Hunter;* and *The Outer Limits.* Her work has appeared on CBS, HBO, Lifetime, USA, Nickelodeon, and Showtime.

David Chambers, WGA member; credits include more than a dozen prime-time network shows; Emmy Award nominee for *The Wonder Years* and *Frank's Place;* Humanitas Prize recipient. His episode of *The Simpsons* was nominated for a Writers Guild Award.

Julie Chambers, WGA member; credits include a Writers Guild Award–nominated episode of *The Simpsons* and episodes of *Becker, The Buzz on Maggie,* and the Showtime movie *The Princess and the Barrio Boy.*

Charlie Craig, WGA member; currently consulting producer on *Pretty Little Liars;* writer–executive producer–showrunner on Syfy's *Eureka.* He was writer and supervising producer for *The X-Files* and *Invasion* and has run six prime-time and cable shows on ABC, Fox, USA, and Syfy.

Richard Hatem, WGA member; created the ABC/Touchstone television series *Miracles* and has written and produced episodes of *Tru Calling, The Inside, Supernatural,* and *The Dead Zone.* Feature film credits include *The Mothman Prophecies,* which he coproduced.

David Isaacs, WGA member; former producer on *Mad Men;* a story editor on *M*A*S*H;* writer/consultant on *Wings* and *Frasier;* cocreator of *Almost Perfect.* He won an Emmy Award for coproducing *Cheers* and two Writers Guild Awards for Best TV Comedy Script.

Phil Kellard, WGA member; Emmy Award–winning writer-director who executive produced *The Wayans Brothers* and *Martin;* produced *Doogie Howser, M.D.; Hooperman;* and *My Two Dads;* and wrote pilots for the Disney Channel, Showtime, and Syfy.

Richard Manning, WGA member; writer-producer whose credits include *Farscape, Star Trek: The Next Generation, TekWar, Beyond Reality* (which he cocreated), *Sliders,* and *Fame;* created and produced *Fusion,* a Web series pilot.

Joel Anderson Thompson, WGA member; credits include *House M.D., Boomtown, Battlestar Galactica,* and *Falling Skies.*

Matt Witten, WGA member; Emmy- and Edgar-nominated writer and supervising producer of the drama series *House M.D., Medium,* and *The Glades.* He has written for *CSI: Miami, Judging Amy, Law and Order,* and *Homicide: Life on the Street.*

INDEX

Index

Index

Index

Index

Index